Community Resilience under the Impact of Urbanisation and Climate Change:
Cases and Experiences from Zimbabwe

Edited by
Innocent Chirisa
&
Christopher Mabeza

Langaa Research & Publishing CIG
Mankon, Bamenda

Publisher
Langaa RPCIG
Langaa Research & Publishing Common Initiative Group
P.O. Box 902 Mankon
Bamenda
North West Region
Cameroon
Langaagrp@gmail.com
www.langaa-rpcig.net

Distributed in and outside N. America by African Books Collective
orders@africanbookscollective.com
www.africanbookscollective.com

ISBN-10: 9956-550-05-1

ISBN-13: 978-9956-550-05-0

Note on Contributors

Archimedes Muzenda is a senior research associate at the African Urban Institute and a Machel-Mandela Fellow at the Brenthurst Foundation. His research interests are land use planning, urban environmentalism, place-making and urban governance. He holds a BSc Honours in Rural and Urban Planning from University of Zimbabwe and an MPA from Central European University.

Audrey Kwangwama is currently engaged as a Lecturer at the University of Zimbabwe. Prior to that, she was engaged by Renaissance Partners as a Property Specialist responsible for supporting Renaissance Partners Property Division. She joined Renaissance Partners on 1 November 2008 until its relocation from Zimbabwe in November 2012. Prior to joining Renaissance Partners, Mrs. Kwangwama worked for Old Mutual Properties where she was a Property Investment Analyst from 2006-2008. Mrs. Kwangwama began her career in 1997 at the City of Harare as a Property Valuer where she was responsible for Council's Estate Management and valuation of properties for rating purposes. In 2000, she joined the University of Zimbabwe as a Lecturer in the Department of Rural and Urban Planning. While lecturing at the University of Zimbabwe, she was engaged as a part time Researcher in property investment and development by CB Richard Ellis in 2006. Mrs. Kwangwama is a Corporate Member of the Zimbabwe Institute of Regional and Urban Planners (ZIRUP). She is also registered as a Valuer with the Valuers' Council of Zimbabwe and a Registered Estate Agent. Mrs. Kwangwama is currently enrolled with the University of Zimbabwe for a Doctor of Philosophy in Planning and Real Estate.

Brilliant Mavhima holds a Bachelor's degree in Rural and Urban Planning and is currently a Master student at the University of Zimbabwe studying rural and urban planning. He is currently a graduate teaching assistant at the same institution. His focus is in urban design. He spends most of his time researching on urban design as well as designing building plans for different clients.

Brilliant has 3 publication, 8 papers in press and 2 book chapters in press.

Charity Manyeruke is an Associate Professor and Dean of Faculty of Social Studies, University of Zimbabwe. She holds a DPhil (International Relations and Political Science), MSc (International Relations), BSc (Political and Administrative Studies), University of Zimbabwe, IPMZ (Human Resources), LCCI Diploma (Public Relations) and Law and Management courses (UNISA). Her research interests are politics and natural resources management, international relations and the politics of gender.

Christopher Mabeza is an independent consultant. He holds a PhD from the University of Cape Town, South Africa, where he was awarded an Andrew Mellon doctoral fellowship. Subsequently, Dr Mabeza was appointed a research fellow at Rhodes University where he did extensive fieldwork in the rural Eastern Cape of South Africa. He was part of a research think tank named Amanzi for Food. Dr Mabeza is a co-recipient of the Rhodes University Vice-Chancellor's Distinguished Award for Community Engagement, 2017. Chris is very passionate about the impacts of climate change on rural development. To that end, he is writing a book on rural development, which grapples with "asking what matters, not what's the matter". Dr Mabeza is also the author of the following books: *The Clash of the Titans and Other Short Stories, Water and soil in holy matrimony? A smallholder farmer's innovative agricultural practices for adapting to climate in rural Zimbabwe, Memoirs of an Unsung Legend, Nemeso,* and *Living with the Anthropocene blues: Adaptation to climate change in Zimbabwe* (in press).

Elmond Bandauko is a Consultant and Research Associate with the Development Governance Institute (DEGI), a Harare based consulting and development research firm. He holds a Master of Public Administration (MPA) with specialization in Local government from the University of Western Ontario (Canada) where he studied as an African Leaders of Tomorrow (ALT) Scholar. He did his BSc. (Hons) in Rural and Urban Planning from the University of Zimbabwe. His interests are urban policy and governance, urban resilience, participatory policy making, policy innovation and policy diffusion, public management, program and policy evaluation, collaborative governance and the politics of urban development in cities of the global south. His co-edited book is, *'Peri-Urban Developments and Processes in Africa with Special Reference to Zimbabwe'*, which is published by Springer International Publishing. His academic publication record also includes over 18 book chapters and 20 articles in international journals.

Ignatius Gutsa is currently a Senior Lecturer in the Department of Sociology, University of Zimbabwe. He holds a PhD in Anthropology from the University of Witwatersrand, an M.Sc. in Sociology and Social Anthropology and B.Sc. (Hons) Sociology from the University of Zimbabwe. His research interests are in ageing, climate change, livelihoods and rural development.

Innocent Chirisa is a full professor at the Department of Rural & Urban Planning, University of Zimbabwe. Currently is the deputy dean of the Faculty of Social Studies at the University of Zimbabwe and is a Research Fellow at the Department of Urban and Regional Planning, University of the Free State, South Africa. He holds a DPhil in Social Studies, M.Sc. (Planning), B.Sc. Honours in Rural & Urban Planning all from the University of Zimbabwe and a post-graduate Diploma in Land Management and Informal Land Resettlement from the Institute of Housing and Urban Development Studies, Erasmus University, The Netherlands. His research interests are systems dynamics in urban land, regional stewardship and resilience in human habitats.

Joseph Kamuzhanje is a Professor of Practice in Urban and Regional Planning with the University of Venda. He has over 25 years of experience in Rural and Urban Development. He holds a BSc Rural and Urban Planning (RUP) from the University of Zimbabwe, an MSc in Regional Development Planning and Management from the University of Science and Technology, Kumasi, Ghana. He worked for the Department of Physical Planning for 15 years, for humanitarian and development non-Governmental organisations for 10 years and is currently working as NGO and Projects Executive for Coopers Zimbabwe. Prof Kamuzhanje has a keen interest in community based, community centred and community led sustainable and resilient development interventions. He is also interested in understanding the frame conditions for the transition of communities and institutions from relief to development.

Julius Musevenzi is a senior lecturer in the Department of Sociology, University of Zimbabwe. He holds a PhD in Sociology and Development Studies from the Nelson Mandela Metropolitan University in South Africa, MSc in Sociology and Social Anthropology, BSc Honours in Sociology from the University of Zimbabwe. His research interests are in rural livelihoods development and changing trends, resilience and survival strategies.

Liaison Mukarwi holds a B.Sc. Honours Degree in Rural and Urban Planning from the University of Zimbabwe. He is currently practicing as a Town Planner at Human Settlements Experts (Pvt) Ltd in Zimbabwe. Liaison is a freelance researcher whose researches focus on Urban Management and Governance, Environmental Design, Urban Planning Practice, Housing and Community Issues and Transport and Sustainability issues. He had published more than several journal articles and book chapters. Liaison participated in various academic researches as a research assistant.

Memory Mpambela is a postgraduate student in the Department of Social Work, University of Zimbabwe. She is also a graduate teaching assistant at the same institution. Her research interests are in women empowerment, child protection and social development.

Nicq C.I Paradza is a Town Planner at Pearlville Land Developers in Zimbabwe. He is a holder of Bachelor of Science (B.Sc.) Honours Degree in Rural and Urban Planning with the University of Zimbabwe. He specialises in Construction Engineering. He has 2 years of experience in land development feasibility studies and proposals. His research interests are design of land uses and the built environment, and resilience in human environments.

Patrick Chiroro is a Professor of Psychology who has taught at universities and conducted research studies in Zimbabwe and South Africa. He is a former lecturer at the Psychology Department and Deputy Dean for the Social Science Faculty at the University Zimbabwe. He was also a senior lecturer and professor at the University Pretoria in South Africa. He was also specialist research consultant for various state and non-state organisations in South Africa. He is also the Managing Director at Impact Research International, which operates in South Africa and Zimbabwe among other countries in Southern Africa.

Phineas T Dohwe is an passionate and experienced regional and urban planner with 24 years' of solid and practical experience in the built environment, land use and development planning. He has since 1993 and continues to be involved in several land use planning projects in the Built Environment from conception to implementation and to compliance. Phineas specialises in client advice as well as fostering Local Authorities buy-in for proposed development projects especially innovative projects that introduces new ground in planning. He is a Corporate Member of the Zimbabwe Institute of Regional and Urban Planners. As a member of the Institute he has been actively involved in the business of the Institute through participation at the respective Annual Schools, through chairing sessions, making presentations and leading thematic sessions. He has twice held the position of 1st Vice President as well as a two term President of the Zimbabwe Institute of Regional and Urban Planners for the year August 2016 to August 2017 and August 2017 to August 2018. Phineas is a part time Lecturer at the University of Zimbabwe, Department of Regional and Urban Planning since the year 2003 teaching planning courses with a specific bias in Urban Development Planning Design and Management. Currently, he is an Associate Director and a Team Leader for the Development Planning Division with Arup Zimbabwe (Pvt) Ltd. Phineas holds a Honour's and a Master's of Science Degrees in Regional and Urban Planning from the University of Zimbabwe qualification attained in the years 1992 and 2004 respectively.

Samson Mhizha is a lecturer in Developmental Psychology, Social Psychology and Cross-Cultural Psychology at the Department of Psychology at the University of Zimbabwe. Research interests are in topics around children and youths in difficult circumstances, psychology of grief, influence of religion and culture on psychological functioning and family studies. Samson holds an MPhil and BSc Hons in Psychology from the University of Zimbabwe and is currently working on a DPhil Project on the lived experiences and resilience pathways among street children who have gone through family reunification in Zimbabwe. He has published several articles on Street Children and religious functioning.

Vincent Mabvurira is a Senior Lecturer in the Department of Social Work, University of Zimbabwe. He is a holder of a Doctor of Philosophy in Social Work from University of Limpopo, South Africa. He also holds a Master of Social Work degree and a Bachelor of Social Work Honours Degree both from the University of Zimbabwe. His research interests are in child welfare, indigenous knowledge systems, climate change and religion and spirituality.

Table of Contents

Chapter 1: Community Resilience under Urbanisation and Climate Change – An Overview 1
Innocent Chirisa, Brilliant Mavhima & Archimedes Muzenda

Chapter 2: Consilience as the Basis For Community Resilience: Lessons for Zimbabwe 17
Innocent Chirisa, Nicq Paradza & Liaison Mukarwi

Chapter 3: Vulnerability to Climate Change and Resilience of Child-Headed Households in Buhera District 35
Vincent Mabvurira & Memory Mpambela

Chapter 4: Urban Resilience in Cities of the Developing World with reference to Harare, Zimbabwe 53
Phineas T Dohwe & Ndarova Audrey Kwangwama

Chapter 5: Resilience: An Account of the Survival and Lifestyles of Street Children in Harare 95
Samson Mhizha & Patrick Chiroro

Chapter 6: Community Resilience and the Sustainable Development Goals in Zimbabwe 123
Joseph Kamuzhanje

Chapter 7: Everyday Local Level Sources of Weather Forecasting in Rural Zimbabwe in the Face of Climate Change 143
Ignatius Gutsa

Chapter 8: Thwarting the Sword of Damocles: Community Resilience Challenges in the Age of the Anthropocene 159
Christopher Mabeza

Chapter 9: The Politics of Community Resilience: A Closer Look into the Settlement Hierarchy of Zimbabwe 177
Charity Manyeruke & Archimedes Muzenda

Chapter 10: Externally-Fostered Sorghum and Millets Production in Semi-Arid Regions of Zimbabwe 201
Julius Musevenzi

Chapter 11: Havana (Cuba) and Harare (Zimbabwe) as Innovative Hubs of Resilient Systems in Urban Food Security 221
Innocent Chirisa & Elmond Bandauko

Chapter 1

Community Resilience under Urbanisation and Climate Change – An Overview

Innocent Chirisa, Brilliant Mavhima & Archimedes Muzenda

Introduction

This book is about exploring the vulnerabilities and resilience capacities that emanate from urbanisation and climate change. It asserts, urbanisation and climate change have been instrumental in shaping human settlements and communities. The pattern has been particular in the global south were urbanisation is rapid and agro-based societies are significantly impacted by climate change. Community resilience has gained momentum in recent years and it is interchanged with sustainability. It has become another buzzword to dominate human settlements and climate change mitigation discourses. As a new buzzword in human settlements, resilience has been mistakenly interchanged with sustainability with a risk of replacing it. The rise of urbanisation and intensifying impacts of climate change have increased the uncertainty, by increasing the essence of resilience in social settings.

In Zimbabwe, resilience has not been conceptualised adequately. The inadequacy is attributed particularly to the nature of capacity building being spearheaded by development partners such as Non-Governmental Organisations (NGOs) and International Organisations. The resilience capacity building has been focusing in most vulnerable communities such as drought stricken communities and urban informal settlements. The nature of humanitarian intervention coming after a catastrophe, resilience in Zimbabwe has risked becoming post-disaster planning. Therefore, resilience in Zimbabwe is characterised as reactive rather than proactive. Globally, the notion of self-organisation and self-reliance of communities is central to resilience concept. While this has been advocated in most countries, in Zimbabwe, poor capacity of public institutions became an influencing factor for self-reliance of communities. The book explores the use of indigenous knowledge and survival of vulnerable groups. In humanitarian intervention, nevertheless, the notion of self-organisation is still constrained by dependency syndrome, partly attributed to lack of capacity building for transformative capacity.

The transfer of responsibility from government to the individual and communities with inadequate agency provokes connotations of neoliberal state. This derelict of duty by government institutions can further erodes the existing resilience capacity as they get more responsibility. It is argued that "by rolling back the state's support for vulnerable communities in the name of resilience is a misguided translation of self-organisation in ecological system into self-reliance in social systems" (Davoudi, 2012: 305). This translation provokes sentiments of a neoliberalism in social development and the kind of social Darwinism.

Defining community resilience proves to be as elusive as the terms community and resilience are both contested. The concept of community resilience refers to the capacities and capabilities of a community to 'prevent, withstand, or mitigate' any event that negatively disrupts its form and function (Ahmed, 2004; Islam *et al.* 2014). These disruptions while predominantly derive from external shocks that include social, political or environmental changes (Adger, 2000), the disruptions can also come from the community's internal evolutionary actions of vulnerability (Wilson, 2012). Contrary to the hard systems resilience, as a descriptive concept with precise definition, meaning and quantitative operationalisation, community resilience as resilience of soft systems can be ambiguous, malleable, intangible, difficult to quantitatively measure and is normative (Brand et al. 2007). As a normative concept, dealing with resilience of a community has been difficult, so has been defining and identifying resilient actions conceptually, modelling its behaviour in a single framework operationally and even empirically measuring, collecting and analysing data on resilience of communities.

Originating from sciences of mathematics and physics and ecology as the ability to return to equilibrium after a displacement, the evolution of the concept has tried to balance the natural sciences and social sciences ((Adger, 2000; Norris *et al.* 2008; Reid *et al.* 2013). Emanating from the socio-ecological system resilience that fails to

2

conceptualise the totality of the role of human agency factors in the resilience. Therefore, while traditionally, resilience theorists gave less focus on power relations, politics and culture, the social resilient theorists, emphasise the importance of governance and social construct in conceptualising community resilience (Adger *et al.* 2000; Wilson, 2012a). Stemming from different disciplines, resilience entails different meaning from natural sciences, ecological sciences to social sciences. In 1973, a Canadian theoretical ecologist, Crawford Stanley Holling made a distinction between ecological and engineering resilience. Nevertheless, application of resilience in social sciences is a slippery slope. It is argued that "applying the framework of ecological resilience to human institutions and governance processes generates paths to greater understanding as well as dead ends" (Swanstrom, 2008:.6)

In the myriad of the elusiveness of resilience as a concept, three 'enablers' exists that improves the resilience of a community. It illustrated that the three forms of inputs into resilience of a community are physical, procedural and social enablers (McAslan, 2010). Physical enablers provide the *means* to survive and recover; procedures, policies and plans provide *ideas* on how to survive and recover; while social cohesion provides the *will* to survive and recover (Figure 1.1).

Looking at social enablers in communal areas, out-migration to urban areas, resettlement areas and to neighbouring countries has reduced the capacity of social enablers to overcome disruptions. As the able-bodied population and male population migrate to look for better opportunities and retain benefits to the population that enhance the physical enablers of communal areas they have traded off this with the social enablers of the communities. The overall resilience of a community is determined by the overall strength of the three types of enablers, procedural, social and physical enablers. Procedural enablers nevertheless prove to be critical for the transformative capacity of communities.

Figure 1.1: Enablers for Community Resilience
(Adapted from IFRC, 2012)

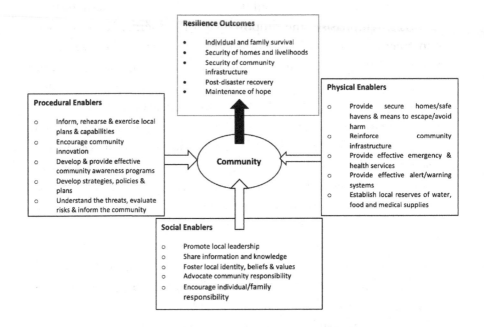

The Good Currency of Community Resilience

The interconnectedness of human settlements cause by globalisation has intensified the connectivity paradox. The more connected the human settlements they are the more vulnerable they are to socio-economic shocks that spread across the globe beyond boundaries. The human settlements evolution adds the impacts of climate change that is ravaging livelihoods of agro-based communities particularly in developing countries. The uncertainty that has increased emanating from climate change has called for a new thinking in how environments respond the uncertainty. The impact of climate change has expanded beyond the traditional natural disaster occurrences that originally impacted ecology. Economic, social and political consequences have concretised the need for resilience in social sciences. These trends have culminated to resilience becoming a desirable attribute in the age of uncertainty. Therefore, it has become an idea of good currency. As powerful for public policy formulation, an idea" in good currency" has been characterised as an idea that *"change[s] over time; obey[s] a law of limited numbers; and lag behind changing events*" (Schön, 1971: 36). The emergence of resilience as a buzzword in social sciences and human settlements vocabulary needs to be taken with caution regarding its meaning and application. Is it going to risk being just another policy buzzword? Various applications vulnerabilities resilience capacities are interrogated in efforts to assess its application in the context of Zimbabwe.

Key Contentions of this Book

The aim of this book is to bring various case studies in Zimbabwe that presents community resilience to various vulnerabilities and resilience capacities. What the case studies explored in this book have in common, is that they discuss different context to which community resilience subsists and how various communities have different resilience capacities: absorptive, adaptive and transformative capacities. Five contentions are discussed in the book's chapters.

Conceptualising resilience from the ecological science to social sciences is a slippery slope. The book explores the conceptual underpinnings of community resilience in Zimbabwe drawing from the interdisciplinary transfer, ecological to social settings. It is asserted that "applying the framework of ecological resilience to human institutions and governance processes generates paths to greater understanding, as well as dead ends" (Swanstrom, 2008: 6). This book explores the reasons to be optimistic and pessimistic in the conceptualisation of community resilience. It sets basis for discussions on the variations of community resilience in both settings and forms. In Chapter 2; Chirisa, Paradza and Mukarwi discuss consilience as critical for building community resilience towards confronting climate change-induced challenges. Conceptualising resilience from ecological science to social science also has political overtones. As Manyeruke and Muzenda argue in Chapter 9, the conceptualisation in social sciences carries some overtones regarding definition of communities' boundaries, determination of vulnerabilities which lead to exclusionary risks in social communities. They also identify the political connotation of bouncing back ability as status quo of power.

5

Second, various capacities of community resilience that are absorptive, adaptive and transformative significantly influence the existence of communities and their governance structures. Deriving from ecological resilience which emphasise equilibrium as critical to resilience (the bouncing back ability) the book explores further the emergence of transformative resilience and its importance to the continual existence of communities in the age of increasing uncertainties and vulnerabilities. In Chapter 6, Kamuzhanje interrogates the need for evolution in development assistance from the current absorptive and adaptive humanitarian assistance to building of transformative resilience capacities. Manyeruke and Muzenda in Chapter 11 identify the political connotations associated with conceptualisation of resilience in social science disciplines and in Zimbabwe. They identify maintenance of status quo in absorptive and adaptive capacity and controversial political instability associated with the transformative capacity.

Third, indigenous knowledge is a critical resource for community resilience against climate change. Indigenous knowledge has always been used by local communities to adapt to changing local climates, particularly in early warning systems and weather forecasts. It has become instrumental with the increasing impact of climate change and uncertainties in the local environment. Therefore, indigenous knowledge has been promotive, absorptive, adaptive and transformative capacities against impacts of climate change. In Chapter 2, Chirisa, Paradza and Mukarwi also conceptualise the use of climate change resilience knowledge in both rural and urban contexts. Gutsa, in Chapter 7, examines the experiences of local level reading of the weather, seasons and climate change by households in Goromonzi District through use of indigenous knowledge and the emergence of religious prophesies in weather forecasting.

Fourth, cities have been less regarded as resources for resilience in Zimbabwe. This emanates from Zimbabwe being an agro-based economy which has been significantly affected by climate change. The increasing urbanisation nevertheless has not been realised as source for strengthening resilience of the community at large. Chirisa and Bandauko in Chapter 11 compare innovativeness between Havana and Harare, capital cities of two countries, Cuba and Zimbabwe, that are vulnerable to economic shocks. They identify

6

variations in how the two cities utilise urban land for agriculture with Havana prospering in urban agriculture to the extent of exportation while Harare faces various setbacks that hinder urban agriculture. In Chapter 4, Dohwe and Kwangwama explore the sustainability and resilience of cities in Zimbabwe. Most development interventions to build resilience capacities of communities have been focusing on rural communities. This is evidenced by Mabeza in Chapter 8, and Kamuzhanje in Chapter 6 on the focus on agricultural productivity of rural communities a key priority for resilience capacity building.

Assessment of community resilience has always focused on overall community against specific vulnerabilities. This book argues that vulnerabilities impact various groups of a community and settlement types differently depending on their resilience capacities. In Chapter 3, Mabvurira and Mpambela examine the vulnerabilities and resilience capacities of child-headed households in Buhera District. They found the households more vulnerable to climate change impacts and characterised by low resilience capacity compared to adult-headed households in the district. Mhizha and Chiroro, in Chapter 5, examine the vulnerabilities and resilience of street children in Harare. They identified street social capital as resilience resource for survival of street children in the streets. Variations of resilience capacities and vulnerabilities also exist across the human settlement hierarchy. Manyeruke and Muzenda, in Chapter 9, discuss challenges of defining communities' boundaries and migration flows that culminates from differences in vulnerabilities and resilience capacities.

Chapter Synopses

Chapter 1: Community Resilience under Urbanisation and Climate Change – An Overview.

Chapter 2: Consilience as the basis for Community Resilience: Lessons for Zimbabwe. This chapter discusses consilience (the unity of knowledge) as a critical reference point for building community resilience towards confronting climate change-induced challenges, including floods and drought, in the planning and management of human settlements. The discourse emanates from disparate and disjointed approaches usually applied by agents and actors in dealing with environmental risks and disasters. Advanced in this chapter is the argument that effective environmental management comes only by harnessing different approaches pigeonholed into the issues whose solution lies in angling them from applying multi-perspectives by multi-stakeholders. Bigotry and disciplinary intolerance are a recipe for disaster. To demonstrate the realities surrounding these fundamental truths, the study engages Zimbabwe as a country suffering from a few weather-related vagaries. These weather-related vagaries are located in various locales defined differently, calling for consilience application to achieve community resilience or at least the building of it effectively.

Chapter 3: Vulnerability to Climate Change and Resilience of Child-Headed Households in Buhera District. Climate change is one of the biggest threats facing global development. Developing countries are more vulnerable due to their low adaptive capacities. Some of the effects of global climate change are evident with increased incidences of droughts, floods, hailstorms, more hot days and heat waves affecting mostly rural inhabitants. These effects have impoverished millions of people around the globe including children. This chapter examines the impact of climate change on child-headed households and their resilience strategies with the intention of informing social work practice in Zimbabwe. The study adopted a qualitative approach and it targeted child-headed households in ward 10 of Buhera District in Manicaland province, Zimbabwe. Data were collected from a sample of 21 children identified through snowball sampling. Semi-structured face-to-face interviews and focus group discussions were used as data collection methods. The study found that child-headed households in Buhera District are besieged by food shortage, domestic water shortage, heat waves as a result of climate change. The children have resorted to child labour, trading of non-wood forest products and spirituality as resilience strategies. Therefore, it is critical for social workers as vanguards of child welfare in Zimbabwe to improve the ability of child-headed households to adapt and mitigate the impact of climate change.

Chapter 4: Urban Resilience in Cities of the Developing World with Reference to Harare, Zimbabwe. This chapter is based on a review of the concept of resilience to inform urban development professionals, academia, government and the general public in understanding the relevance and importance of the resilient human settlement framework within the context of urban planning. This is critical in the face of intensifying urbanisation and the growing resultant challenges. Cities are a culmination of the search by humanity for permanent, safe and secure habitats. This search and desire arises from the lessons learnt from historical settlements which survived, prospered for some time but disappeared upon crossing their carrying capacity threshold. While cities have created a certain level of security, safety and comfort, their growing numbers and sizes, intensified resource use and consumption, environmental impacts have resulted in their resilience capacity becoming questionable. Consequently, this has threatened the future of their citizenry. The chapter reviews literature on the evolution of the concept of resilience and focuses on urbanity and urban resilience. It examines the five pillars and seven building blocks of urban resilience. The chapter reviews research work undertaken by ARUP International Development (2012-2015) to establish a City Resilience Index providing evidenced and measurable indicators for urban resilience using information from six cities from diverse geographical locations which experienced chronic stresses and acute shocks. The City Resilience Index brings out twelve critical factors key to building urban resilience as well as the indicators which can be used by cities universally to measure urban resilience. A case study of urban resilience for Oaxaca City is presented in the chapter highlighting how the city coped and transformed the shocks from a hurricane induced by an El Nino into opportunities for enhancing the city's food security. The chapter discusses urban resilience in Harare on the basis of the identified five pillars of urban resilience. The chapter highlights a myriad of challenges being experienced by the city which have negatively affected its capacity to attain urban resilience. The chapter recommends that the attainment of urban resilience in Zimbabwe hinges on national economic recovery and political tolerance. Urban planning in Zimbabwe should play a pivotal role in guiding urban development. A well planned city with a well-functioning economy and political tolerance and harmony is able to build urban resilience enabling it to cope and transform after experiencing chronic stresses and acute shocks.

Chapter 5: Resilience: An Account of the Survival and Lifestyles of Street Children in Harare. The phenomenon of street children punctuating the cityscape of many urban areas is global, disquieting and escalating. The objectives of this study were to determine the economic activities engaged by the streets children and determine the lifestyles that enabled the economic activities again adopted by the streets children. The study being exploratory and qualitative employed the phenomenological research approach. Data were collected using in-depth key informant interviews. The research revealed that street children engaged in various economic activities including begging, vending, drug peddling. The also engage in stealing, transactional sex, hiring children out, car washing, car guarding, car parking and carrying peoples' luggage. The lifestyles that the street children adopted that helped them in carrying out the economic activities included violence, territoriality, lying and maintaining social networks. The study revealed that street children developed resilience by acquiring street capital as they sought to live and work in the streets and fit into the street economy. The researchers recommend that the government and non-government organisations provide both academic, life skills and vocational education which is individualised, career-oriented and help them to cope with the stresses they face in their challenging lives. Rehabilitation services should also be provided to help them deal with the addictive and crime-prone street lives. Empowerment of families, parents or guardians and communities for better provision for their own children.

Chapter 6: Community Resilience and the Sustainable Development Goals in Zimbabwe. The community development discourse is gradually shifting from humanitarian to resilience building. In the middle, the dialogue has also included disaster risk reduction and management. However, reducing the disasters or managing them is not good enough. Other than for a community to 'bounce back' after a disaster, the practice does not necessarily build capacity of communities to withstand other future disaster occurrences. There are several challenges that poor and vulnerable communities face as they attempt to improve their well-being. These challenges are both internal and external to the communities. Most of the humanitarian and recovery responses focus mainly on the absorptive and adaptive capacities of the communities. They rarely expose the communities to transformative capacities that should graduate communities to a higher level of resilience. Other arguments exist that institutions and structures that are supposed to support the communities in their struggle for resilience are no longer relevant especially for the situation that obtains in Zimbabwe. Sustainable Development Goals (SDGs) provide a scope to address most of the challenges that communities face. Nevertheless, without deliberate effort by communities and development partners to address resilience at all levels, not much would be realised by 2030. The chapter is structured such that it provides brief theoretical understanding of the key areas of resilience building. It then addresses the challenges that the author has encountered in the last 25 years of community development work. Relevant case studies are used to indicate that with the right approach, it is possible to build community resilience.

Chapter 7: Everyday Local Level Sources of Weather Forecasting in Rural Zimbabwe in the Face of Climate Change. This chapter examines the experience of local level reading of the weather, seasons and climate change by elderly women heads of households in Gutsa Village Domboshava Communal Lands, Goromonzi District. The methodological approach draws from ethnographic field research which included the use of life-history interviews, Focus Group Discussions and participant observation for close to nineteen months in the study village. Findings show that in the study village various sources of local knowledge are used for weather forecasting. Elderly women use their local stocks of knowledge for local level reading and forecasting of the weather, seasons as well as understanding climate change and how humans can directly influence the weather. Understanding and reading the weather is mainly achieved through examining the behaviour of flora and fauna. Increasingly there has emerged the use of a new weather forecasting technique in the form of prophecy from Independent African Churches.

Chapter 8: Thwarting the Sword of Damocles: Community Resilience Challenges in the Age of the Anthropocene. The threat of climate change Armageddon hangs menacingly above our heads like the sword of Damocles. The signposts are all around us: increased rainfall variability, rising temperature, increasing poverty, perennial food shortages and rising inequality. Building resilience to shocks and stressors among rural communities is now the rallying cry for stakeholders in the rural development discourse. Technical fixes are said to be the panacea to food insecurity in rural Zimbabwe - a familiar a plot, in a habitual setting. But we have entered a new era of complexity. Building resilience in the midst of complexity means much more than technical fixes. Building resilience means a paradigm shifting revision of perennial food insecurity in rural Zimbabwe. Of all rural development narratives in Zimbabwe, none so epitomises the perennial food insecurity as flawed interventions in the wake of a changing climatic environment. Smallholder farmers in rural Zimbabwe, mainly practise rain-fed agriculture but yields have been low. This has been exacerbated by rainfall variability. The rural communities employ a suite of strategies mainly premised on water conservation in order to adapt to a changing climatic environment. The research focused on ethnographic data generating techniques.

Chapter 9: The Politics of Community Resilience through the Settlement Hierarchy of Zimbabwe. In human settlements development, community resilience has become critical issue in confronting uncertain disruptions in the post- "predict and prevent" era. This chapter explores the politics of community resilience as it applies to various settlement hierarchy in Zimbabwe. It assesses the vulnerability and resilience capacity of urban, peri-urban, resettlement and communal areas. The chapter argues the various settlements hierarchies in Zimbabwe have different levels of vulnerability to disruptions within their environment and have different levels of resilience capacity to respond the disruption. To examine critically the variations of resilience capacities and vulnerabilities, the chapter applies a livelihoods framework to explore and assess livelihoods of communities as they relate to resilience capacity. The chapter using a reductionist approach further discusses the conceptual components of community resilience as it relates to assessing and programming resilience. It identifies three types of resilience enablers; physical, procedural and social enablers that rank urban settlements as the most resilient and resettlement areas least resilient while peri-urban and communal areas rank second and third respectively. The various communities face varying vulnerabilities regarding their configuration and security. It further asserts that adversities the communities in various settlement hierarchies' face have altered their functionality at the detriment of the sustainability of these communities. Delineating from the various settlement hierarchy, it identifies various political overtones associated with resilience capacity building as central notions of power, authorities and resource control. It argues that high levels of vulnerability do not automatically result in low levels of resilience.

Chapter 10: Externally-Fostered Sorghum and Millets Production in Semi-Arid Regions of Zimbabwe. This chapter brings out the different perceptions and the debate over small grains production as a response to climate change in semi-arid regions of Zimbabwe. It analyses the external support towards small grains (sorghum and millets) as a mitigation measure to the impact of climate change to food security. The study used in-depth interviews and selected participatory methods with the rural poor in selected in Mwenezi and Chiredzi districts. The study finds that the externally fostered production of small grains resulted in increased output of sorghum but farmers have failed to consume it due to various reasons. The study also shows that wrong sorghum varieties were produced leading to huge stocks of red sorghum that could not be consumed nor marketed to generate income. Comparing the new promoted varieties to their traditional land races, climate change was considered a rhetoric. For most farmers it is a political tool by NGOs to influence a shift in small grains varieties that are of no help to the target beneficiaries. For rural communities, small grains production may not have a relationship with climate change as depicted in the advocacy messages by various NGOs. The chapter concludes that adverse perceptions on climate change are influenced by the various adaptation strategies particularly those externally fostered if they fail to produce the desired results. Climate change understanding among the rural communities becomes defective.

Chapter 11: Havana (Cuba) and Harare (Zimbabwe) as Innovative Hubs of Resilient Systems in Urban Food Security. This chapter seeks to advance the argument that strenuous and little performing economies can be a breeding ground for innovative ways towards survival and growth in food security for urban residents. Naturally, when people are 'cornered' by circumstances beyond control, necessity-wise, innovation as the mother of invention come in. This study is an attempt to draw lessons on survival strategies of residents in two cities; Cuban capital, Havana and the Zimbabwean capital, Harare. The two cities have succumbed to multiple economic crises emanating from the closed nature of their economies being in dissonance with the international community. Both Harare and Havana 'fell victim' 'sanctions' and trade embargoes. Little study, if any, has been made so far to explain fully the dynamics of urban farming as an outcome of the unfavourable macro-economic environment. There is inadequate scholarly literature to show urban farming as a survival strategy for urban households in both Havana and Harare. Using literature review and document analysis, this chapter shows that some of the innovations done by households is to reduce transport costs of food by growing it within city boundaries. This, in a way, has had a greening effect to the cities thereby play a pivotal role as carbon sinks. In addition, some households, particularly in Havana, have used the vertical space including rooftops to grow their food. However, in Harare, encroachment into wetlands is prominent in urban farming as farmers seek to utilise them at the detriment of environmental sustainability. Some stakeholders regard the definition by the environmental regulatory body, the Environmental Management Agency (EMA) to lack clarity and proper criteria. The overall food production net effect nonetheless, has ensured much of the existing spaces in the cities hence supply of fresh produce to the cities.

References

Adger, W.N. (2000) Social and Ecological Resilience: Are They Related? *Progress in Human Geography* 24, 347–364.

Ahmed, R.; Seedat, M.; van Niekerk, A.; Bulbuli, S. Discerning community resilience in disadvantaged communities in the context of violence and injury prevention. *South African Journal of Psychology* 2004, 34, 386–408

Brand, F.S.; Jax, K. Focusing the meaning(s) of resilience: Resilience as a descriptive concept and a boundary object. *Ecol. Soc.* 2007, 12, 23.

Carpenter, S.R, Westley, F. & Turner, G. (2005) Surrogates for resilience of social–ecological systems, Ecosystems, 8(8), pp. 941–944.

IFRC (International Federation of Red Cross and Red Crescent Societies). *Understanding Community Resilience and Program Factors that Strengthen Them: A Comprehensive Study of Red Cross Red Crescent Societies Tsunami Operation*; IFRC: Geneva, Switzerland, 2012

Islam, M.S.; An, Q.R. Climate Change and Urban Resilience: The Singapore Story. In *Globalization, Development and Security in Asia* (Vol. IV); Li, J, Ed.; World Scientific Publishing: London, UK, 2014; pp. 205–220.

Norris Fran, H.; Stevens, S.P.; Pfefferbaum, B.; Wyche, K.F.; Pfefferbaum, R.L. Community resilience as a metaphor, theory, set of capacities and strategy for disaster readiness. *American Journal of Community Psychology*. 2008, 41, 127–150.

Reid, R.; Botterill, L.C. The Multiple Meanings of 'Resilience': An Overview of the Literature. *Australian Journal of Public Administration*. 2013, 72, 31–40.

Simin Davoudi , Keith Shaw , L. Jamila Haider , Allyson E. Quinlan , Garry D. Peterson , Cathy Wilkinson , Hartmut Fünfgeld , Darryn McEvoy , Libby Porter & Simin Davoudi (2012) Resilience: A Bridging Concept or a Dead End? "Reframing" Resilience: Challenges for Planning Theory and Practice Interacting Traps: Resilience Assessment of a Pasture Management System in Northern Afghanistan Urban Resilience: What Does it Mean in Planning Practice? Resilience as a Useful Concept for Climate Change Adaptation? The Politics of Resilience for Planning: A Cautionary Note, Planning Theory & Practice

Swanstrom, T. (2008) Regional resilience: A critical examination of the ecological framework, IURD Working Paper Series (Berkeley, CA, Institute of Urban and Regional Development, University of California).

Wilson, G.A. Community Resilience and Environmental Transitions; Routledge: London, UK; New York, NY, USA, 2012a.

Chapter 2

Consilience as the basis for Community Resilience: Lessons for Zimbabwe

Innocent Chirisa, Nicq Paradza & Liaison Mukarwi

"The search for consilience might seem at first to imprison creativity. The opposite is true. A united system of knowledge is the surest means of identifying the still unexplored domains of reality. It provides a clear map of what is known and it frames the most productive questions for future inquiry. Historians of science often observe that asking the right question is more important than producing the right answer. The right answer to a trivial question is also trivial, but the right question, even when insoluble in exact form, is a guide to major discovery. And so it will ever be in the future excursions of science and imaginative flights of the arts."

- Edward O. Wilson (1999:326)

Introduction

The importance of local knowledge in building sustainable communities in Zimbabwe has been neglected and is fast disappearing in favour of scientific solutions. The scientific ways in confronting climate change are more effective but without the local support, they tend to lose the battle. Edward O. Wilson (1999:326) elaborates the notion that knowledge is the means by which men and women deal critically and creatively with reality and discover how to take part in transformation of their world. He stresses the collaboration among the natural sciences and the humanities (or the social sciences), focused on the study of human perceptions and actions on climate and environmental change in the past. Recognising and valuing knowledge, scientific and traditional (indigenous), will help improve resilience to the impact of disasters and the effects of climate change among global populations. Climate change has threatened human race. It is defined by increasing global temperatures, rising sea levels and changing rainfall patterns and increase in the frequency and severity of storm surges, floods, droughts and heat waves (Kumar, 2014).

In addition, agricultural production is declining, freshwater is becoming scarcer and infectious diseases are on the rise with the effect of degrading community livelihoods and wellbeing. Although indigenous peoples' "low-carbon" traditional ways of life have contributed little to climate change, indigenous peoples are the most adversely affected by it (Sonia et al. 2012). This is largely a result of their historic dependence on local biological diversity, ecosystem services and cultural landscapes as a source of nourishment and well-being (ibid.). In this view, the importance of integrated knowledge on climate change adaptation cannot be overemphasised. Adaptation strengthens the resiliency of communities and increases their capacity to deal with threats (Audefroy and Sa´nchez, 2017). The participatory approach to adaptation is essential for it engages the community. It is at community level that climate change adaptation will be most successful (ibid.). This chapter seeks to discuss consilience (the unity of knowledge) as a critical reference point for building community resilience towards confronting climate change-induced challenges that include floods and droughts, in human settlements planning and management. The discourse emanates from the disparate and disjointed approaches usually applied by agents and actors in dealing with environmental risks and disasters.

Literature Review

This section explores analytically the literature on the role of knowledge systems on climate change resilience in urban and rural areas towards a comprehensive outlook. Resilience is defined as the capacity of a system and community exposed to hazards to resist from the impacts of a climate change (United Nations International Strategy for Disaster Reduction (UNISDR, 2009). Climate change is a stern dilemma in many parts of the world. There are visible disastrous impacts resulting from climate change which include, among others, rising temperatures, extreme rainfall, poverty and droughts. Local knowledge is an important resource that makes community more resilience to the impacts of climate change among other resources. Therefore, this review explores deeper different cases from global to local level on the subject handy. In addition, the impetus of this reassess emanates from global recognition of local knowledge systems for climate change resilience (UNFCCC, 2013).

In 1998, Wilson propounded the Unity of Knowledge Theory. The main component of this theory relies on the possibility and dynamics in intertwining environmental policy and social sciences (Wilson, 1998). From the theory, history could be understood mathematically to predict the future in an urban setup. The theory also alludes the need for scientific discovery or count for zero. To make such discovery in science set the status forever. The theory regard science as not yet reached the edges of humanities. Hence, people must be in a position to follow a thread from element to culture. The regard of culture as created by shared mind and each mentality is the product of hereditarily structured human brain. A connection exists between genes and culture. Nevertheless, the linkage is flexible to a degree still mostly unmeasured. This dependence on folk knowledge to establish how people think through social scientists miscalculate the potential of Marxism and underestimate civilisation as a bind (Wilson, 1998) Therefore, this research is modelled on consilience: the knowledge theory.

There is a profuse literature on the role of knowledge systems on climate change resilience in urban and rural areas in different countries. In a review of 25 adaptive management regimes in USA's riparian and coastal ecosystems, only two strategies on knowledge systems were found to be fighting to fit in this system (Walters, 1997). Programmes were poorly focused to model development rather than field-testing and application. It is noted that lack of public participation hinders the programmes. Identified also are the factors that lead to the let-down in the beginning of adaptive management by top decision-makers, namely the perceived short-term expenses, risk of doing experiments and the lack of participation from stakeholders.

In Nepal, South Asia, for example, rural communities have inadequate access to water for drinking and irrigation. Nepal is characterised by high rates of poverty, erosion and deforestation. To get rid of the impacts, the diverse ethnic and social groups have developed rich local knowledge to adapt to climate changes through managed use of natural and community-built resources (Sherpa et al. 2013). It is also affirmed that social groups in Nepal adapted to the stresses emerging from climate changes of different forms. The comprehensive consideration of the functions of interconnected human-environment which people live promote the success of the programme (Gurung, 2005). People's knowledge in accessing and managing services from ecosystems is also highlighted. Combined with strong social networks that people develop from an integral part of their adaptive culture and identity, it helps in developing mechanisms for adjusting to stress and improving resilience capacity towards a consilience (Gurung, 1994). There are trends and gaps in Nepal on the knowledge systems on climate change resilience (IPCC, 2007; Table 1).

From Table 1, Nepal identifies with Indigenous and Local Knowledge (ILK) systems that have been ignored for long but gained value recently (MoSTE, 2010). Similar is the case in many other developing countries because of inadequate scientific knowledge on climate change or lack of thereof. More so, the fundamental drive of using ILKP lies in reducing vulnerability that emerges from the intersection on exposure (IPPC, 2007; MoEnv, 2010). In Indonesia, different researchers have been researching on the diverse knowledge systems on climate change towards consilience. One research identified the use of indigenous knowledge in reducing the impact of climate change, flooding. Local communities passed a rule that governed settlements establishment around river catchment areas as adaptive resilience to the devastating hazard. In addition, the study shows that people are forbidden to build houses closer than 100m from huge river's bank and 50m for minute rivers (UNESCO, 2004).

In many developing countries, knowledge systems on climate change resilience is very poor. Contributing causes to such inadequacy include external and internal forces such as technological inadequacy and shortage of funds for awareness raising to different groups of people. The resilience of cities is not exclusively dependent on climate change adaptation of single infrastructure elements. It depends on the quality and performance of the overall urban form and system (Brown et al. 2012a).

Table 1: Trends and Gaps in the Use of Knowledge Systems for Resilience in Nepal (IPCC, 2007)

Trends and gaps	Forecasting and early warning	Vulnerability assessment	Adaptation planning	Implementation
Thematic sectors:	Trend: at local level, Indigenous and Local Knowledge (IKL) holders and traditional social institutions are using ILK to forecast rainfall and droughts	Trend: ILK is used mostly by INGOs, NGOs and cobs to carry out participatory vulnerability assessment;	Trend: a large number of local adaptation plan of actions and community adaptation plan of action have been prepared by development agencies using participatory processes which includes ILK	Trend: 1. since very few LaPas and capes have gone into implementation, it is not clear how different agencies, if any, are using ILK or Itch in implementing adaptation plans
Local water management systems	Gaps: dam and its early warning division do not incorporate ILK in weather and food forecasting or early warning in case of extreme climatic events	Gaps: the framework consists of a series of steps to carry out vulnerability assessment and service delivery; the gap remains in not mentioning the application of ILK in visioning and planning suitable adaptation options	Gaps: the NGO has prepared Napa, which does not explicitly require application of indigenous knowledge and practices for local Level planning (that is LaPas).	2. department of water Induced disaster Prevention, dept. of Local Infrastructure Development and Agriculture Roads and Department of Forest do use some local technologies in their work, albeit minimally

To improve resilience to climate change in Tanzania, Temeke Municipal Council established mangrove rehabilitation schemes inter alia Mtoni Kijichi, Mbwamaji South Beach, Kimbiji and Pulia areas (Laros et.al, 2013). The schemes were associated with rather low costs employment opportunities and environmental protection benefits for the local communities. More so, this is a part of the broader Marine and Coastal Environmental Management Programme (MACEMP) which aims to promote sustainability and poverty alleviation. However, some scholars have identified lack of regular monitoring as a hindrance to the success of the communities renewed through this programme (Laros et.al, 2013).

In future, climate in Zimbabwe will comprise increasing temperatures and even lower rainfall. This is evidenced by shifting and changeable rainfall patterns and periods of drought resulting from the El Niño-Southern Oscillation (ENSO) (ALM UNDP, 2009; MENRM, 2013). More so, water stress is expected mostly to increase the vulnerability of agricultural production, worsened by Zimbabwe's reliance on rain-fed agriculture (HBS, 2010). Urban communities in cities such as Harare, Bulawayo and Masvingo have become increasingly dependent on urban agricultural produce for survival. An estimated 56% of urban households grew maize in 2008 and 2009 in these cities (Brown et al. 2012b). However, for the past few years, drought affected these urban areas and in rural areas for example Chivi, Gokwe and Zaka. Hence, knowledge systems are vital to climate change resilience on the disastrous hazard, drought.

To be resilient to climate change impacts, in June 1992, Zimbabwe signed the UNFCCC and endorsed it on 3 November 1992. In addition, the Second National Communication to the UNFCCC was published in January 2013. The Ministry of Environment and Natural Resources Management (MENRM) initiated the preparation of a National Climate Change Response Strategy (NCCRS). This involves a broad range of stakeholders led by a National Task Team on Climate Change reporting to the Office of the President and Cabinet to adapt impacts of climate change (Laros et al. 2013).

Box 1: Case Study: Coping with Drought and Climate Change project in Chiredzi District, Zimbabwe (Adapted from Laros et al. 2013)

The Coping with Drought and Climate Change project is a joint Government of Zimbabwe (GoZ)-United Nation Development Program (UNDP) that response to the climate change challenges within the agriculture sector. The goal of the project was to enhance the capacity of agricultural and pastoral livelihood systems in Zimbabwe to adapt to climate change. The main objective of the project was to demonstrate and promote adoption of approaches for adaptation to climate change. This was targeting poor rural communities in the agriculture sector in vulnerable areas of Chiredzi District (Zimbabwe) as a national model.

To achieve this, the project is structured around four main clusters as follows:

Cluster 1: develop local capacity to expand the knowledge base on climate change for effective adaptation in the agriculture sector. Communities' perceptions of risk and access to information play a role in determining appropriate response a greater willingness to response appropriately to climate related risks.

Cluster 2: Implementing a range of viable pilot demonstration measures in response to identified climate risks

There are strategies formulated which include: risk avoidance on for example livelihoods; risk reduction through irrigation conservation farming and optimizing choice of crop varieties among others. Also, risk transfer (insurance), managing residual risk (for example drought preparedness plans).

Cluster 3: Developing local capacity to use climate early warning system to strengthen livelihood strategies; training farmers and extension services.

Cluster 4: Disseminating project generated lessons to the public.

However, these policies are insufficient in the catastrophes of climate change impacts. Therefore, specific gaps related to climate change adaptation policy in the key areas of poverty alleviation need to be addressed. In addition, enabling provisions of the Environmental Management Act, entails the development and implementation of Local Environmental Action Plans. However, they do not set down the capability and essence of such plans to make sure that climate change issues are addressed effectively (HBS, 2010b). The external environment also affects the implementation of these plans negatively. Furthermore, knowledge systems to climate change resilience need to encompass all stakeholders especially those directly affected by the climate change disasters such as drought. The gap between drafted plans and implementation is increasing nevertheless. This is attributed to inadequate funds a result of economic melt-down abuse of public offices by officials. In areas such as Chiredzi, different strategies were formulated to cope with drought and climate change. A case study to explain the draft of the strategy is presented in Box 1.

Since 2013, many climate catastrophes occurred in Chiredzi district regardless of the knowledge systems available in the community. Between 2013 and 2016, the low rainfalls that prevailed were adapted through changing crop types. However, in 2017, due to climate change that led to excessive rains, many people lost their crops, livestock, homes and lives. This signalled poor resilience to flooding. Lack of adequate monitoring and regular scientific forecasts (to enable generation of new knowledge) in the 2013 strategies were main causes of the losses. This stresses the importance of knowledge systems on climate change resilience. This study examined a global viewpoint with less attention given to developed countries. Less focus on developed countries is because of their advanced technology among other complimentary conditions that makes them more resilient to natural disasters than developing countries. Indonesia, Nepal, Tanzania and Zimbabwe received meticulous expression as typical developing countries. Moreover, from the literature it was observed that although knowledge systems play a vital role in climate change resilience, other external and internal forces, for example, corruption and lack of funds, hinder this role. The whole knowledge systems is greater than the sum of its parts. Therefore, countries must engage in vast strategies that seek to make people adapt the impacts of climate change.

Local knowledge systems are ever more familiar and are always brought forward as source of information on ecosystem dynamics and sustainable practices. This is a potential attribute often, less considered in decision-making on ecosystem management beyond local level. The Multiple Evidence-based Approach proposes parallels where the local and scientific knowledge systems make equal useful evidence for interpreting conditions and change. In some instances, there is a causal relationship between the scientific and local knowledge that is relevant to the sustainable governance of ecosystems (Tengo et al. 2013). It is argued the approach draws on creative writing emphasising the equivalent environment of various knowledge systems. There is also need to move away from translating knowledge into one coinage (Berkes, 2007). Therefore, integrating local knowledge into science through unidirectional validation processes. Local and scientific knowledge systems are different expressions of practical knowledge systems which make balancing evidence for interpreting conditions and change. People aimed at building dialogue in a way to mobilise existing knowledge for assessments and improved policy. Different criterion of legalisation should be applied to data and information originating from different knowledge systems. The aim is to make an equal starting point for mutually agreed ways to proceed, including the potential for co-production of understanding. The balancing outlook will contribute to build resilience and capacity for transformation that includes empowerment of local communities (Tengö et al. 2013).

Results and Discussion

This study examined the unity of knowledge as a theoretical framework for the subject. It also reviewed literature on the role of knowledge systems on climate change resilience in urban and rural communities in the Zimbabwe context. Local communities particularly the poor with low adaptive capacity suffered most from the impacts of climate change. . Hence, a comprehensive approach towards knowledge systems is needed to adjust to the impact of climate change. In Zimbabwe, rural communities such as Zaka, Chivi and Bikita engage in various adaptation activities to the ravages induced by climate change. The use of conservation farming practice of zero tillage dubbed *"Dhiga udye"* (Dig for you to eat) is pivotal resilience strategy. Communities also use social capital harnessing, diversified livelihoods and drought resistant cropping among other practices as resilience strategies. Urban communities of Zimbabwe adopt several schemes that are directly relevant to climate change resilience. These include innovative housing projects of integrating solar roofing sheets which supply energy to households as well as feeding into the electricity grid. A detailed analysis of the local based knowledge systems to climate change adaptation is as presented in the forthcoming sections.

Rural areas that fall under region four and five in Zimbabwe, naturally, receive low rainfall and are more prone to droughts. These regions have been a home to famine and water shortages due to climate change. Asserting how climate change is radically reversing and slowing down poverty by eroding the source of livelihood of poor rural communities, agriculture (Slater et al. 2007). Communities in Bikita, Zaka and Chivi are among the victims. However, communities in these areas have engaged in climate resilience practices presented in forthcoming paragraphs.

Farmers are using a conservation farming technique dubbed *"Dhiga Udye"*. This is a zero-tillage approach to agriculture seeking to maximise moisture availability in the dry regions that receive low rainfall. Despite being a traditional practice, agricultural research organisations are spearheading this approach which is also promoted by agriculture research institutes and NGOs like CARE Zimbabwe. It is highlighted that *Dhiga udye* (conservation) farming has been adopted as a solution to drought in rural communities such as Chivi and Zaka among many other rural areas in the dry regions. These rural people are adopting farming practices that preserve delicate soils and improve its fertility. Many farmers are receiving bumper harvest from this system. After harvesting, the local people gather on an event called "Field Day" to celebrate those with higher yields and to discuss the way forward in the following season (Gukurume et al. 2012).

Some farmers are using their traditional knowledge to farm on wetlands *(matoro)*. They plant early on the wetlands before the rains fall to allow enough time for the crops to grow ahead of the waterlogging period. This farming practice is making farmers realise a good harvest (Gukurume et al. 2012). Wetlands can hold moisture for a long period of time as compared to an ordinary soil type. The farmers cultivate their fields before the rain and they use short term variety that can be mature early while the wetland still embraces its moisture. Furthermore, people in rural areas such as Zaka and Chivi dig holes inside a river which is called *mufuku*. This is mostly done in summer when water levels drop below the river surface to get water for drinking, washing and other domestic uses. Water from these river water holes can also be used to irrigate their gardens where they grow vegetables and maize. The people normally cover this hole by sand or any shade after using it. Technically, this is done to stop wild animals from using the same source of water but also helps in reducing evaporation.

Rural livelihood diversification can be defined as the process by which households build a diverse collection of activities and social support capabilities for survival and to improve their standard of living (Ellis, 2000). Many farmers in Chivi, Zaka and Bikita communities responded to climate change by diversifying in farming. Farmers are growing crops that include maize, millet, rapoko, sorghum, sweet potatoes, cowpeas, ground nuts, round nuts and water melons among other crops. Scholars have argued, the uncertainty brought by climate change such as drought occurrences, encouraged the community to obtain various contingent responses to drought with a combination of diversification of crops. On top of cropping a variety of crops, the people have adopted diversified lifestyles where they are no longer depending on farming only but include other socio-economic activities for survival. It is observed that communities in Bikita benefit from drought resistance crops in many ways such as brewing traditional beer dubbed 'seven days beer' for its brewing process takes seven days. The beer is a source of income that communities use in several functions such as *kurova guva* (a traditional ritual) and *mukwererere* (rainmaking ceremony) (Chenje and Solar, 1998). He also argued that due to regular decrease in agricultural productivity, several households rely on a diversity of economic activities within a year. Diversification of livelihood activities widen the local communities' sources of income thereby improving food security and livelihoods sustainability. In this realm, communities engage into menial jobs within and around the rural communities such as *maricho* (rural piece work) and firewood trading among many other off-farm activities (Gukurume, 2012). Some families also depend on remittances from their kins working in urban areas in the country or abroad.

In Bikita, networks exist among rural communities that are very poor. The networks include various stakeholders such as NGOs supporting communities with adaptation strategies. Examples are the new cropping systems introduced by CARE International in Bikita,

Chivi and Zaka (Gukurume, 2010). Social capital in areas such Bikita promoted community cohesion within many villages which enabled the communities to withstand the effects of droughts. Social cohesion includes characteristics such as sense of common belonging. Cohesion assist the community in adaptation and absorbing shocks that confront peasant farmers in Bikita. Sharing of scarce resources such as water and food facilitate the cohesion. For example community members with boreholes would allow fellow members without to fetch water free. Therefore, social networks promoted adaptability of these communities during successive droughts that threaten their livelihood. The *Zunde raMambo* practice is also an indication of the importance of community cohesion in Zaka, Chivi and Bikita (ibid.). *Zunde raMambo* means collective production of crops at the chief's fields by all the subjects under a chief jurisdiction. It is also argued that long ago *Zunde raMambo* was used not only to produce communal crops for food security, but also as a social, economic and political rallying-point for the neighbourhood (Dhemba et al. 2002). Therefore, it can be safely asserted that *Zunde raMambo* as a safety net, protected communities during drought seasons. The rural communities also started cooperatives in farming and other related projects. They pool resources such as labour for a common good. For example, in Bikita, NGOs such as CARE Zimbabwe promote a financial savings practice dubbed, *"Mukando/ Raundi"* (monthly subscriptions). In this practice community members give one another an agreed amount monthly to cater for their needs a practice local communities describe as *"Kufusha Mari"* (monetary preservation)

Science has it on record encouraging the farmers to grow drought tolerant varieties, most of which are now hybridised varieties. However, the local communities in Bikita, Buhera, or Chiredzi among other rural areas in the low rainfall regions have already been producing drought tolerant food like rapoko, sorghum and millet (Gukurume, 2010). These crops had been passed from generation to generation, their ancestors grew these crops producing a bumper harvest. Such crop varieties are used in traditional ceremonies such as *mukwerera* (rainmaking ceremony), *biras, kurova guva* and *marombo* (all these are Shona traditional rituals). These traditional ceremonies require local communities to brew traditional beer and consume

28

traditional food such as sadza made from millet or sorghum meal. These are climate change adaptation measures emanating from indigenous knowledge and practices. Improvements are there to include newly established drought tolerant crops varieties but the gist has been established a long time ago within the traditional systems. Some local people have knowledge that these traditional varieties like millet do not succumb to pest or insects during production and storage of the harvest. Many villagers, especially the elderly, prefer to grow these drought tolerant varieties for their resistance to diseases and pest. For example, millet is regarded as resistant to weevils (*zvipfukuto*) (Ellis, 2000). Other than significant production in drought seasons, these crops reduce the need for preservation chemicals thereby ensuring food security among local communities without scientific methods of production (Ellis, 2000).

Climate change also impinges urban communities in Zimbabwe. However, urban communities adopt various climate change resilience practices presented in forthcoming paragraphs.

In Zimbabwe, local governments are required to develop Local Environmental Action Plans (LEAPs) in partnership with the Environmental Management Agency (EMA) (a government agency responsible or environmental management and protection) (Laros, 2013). These Action Plans brought the prospects for integration of climate change into local planning in urban communities such as Harare and Mutare. LEAPs stem from Agenda 21 which is focus on environmental, health, cultural, education and housing sectors. A City-Link Project existed, as a partnership between City of Mutare and City of Harare. It resulted into schemes that are directly relevant to climate change as mentioned earlier, innovative housing project that integrate solar roofing sheets which supply energy to households and feeding into the electricity grid, There was also a Re-Greening Programme in Mutare urban developed to protect green belts and recreational areas. The Department of Housing and Social Amenities looks after the maintenance of the green belts. The department in collaboration with urban communities committed to a significant tree-planting programme. More so, protection of forest areas within the green belt and nearby mountain areas is being undertaken in partnership with the EMA. Some people are being employed by the public works programme to assist in keeping drainage areas free from weeds. This is an ecosystem-based adaptation project that can generate income for the unemployed (Laros, 2013).

The urban environment, due to the intensity of development and concentration of people, is more subject to degradation. There is great need for conservation of the urban ecosystems so as to avoid upsetting the natural environmental processes like climate and weather systems. One research identified that the City of Mutare partnered Environment Africa implementing an urban conservation farming project. This project trained community groups in 15 different communities of the city in conservation farming practices (Laros, 2013). Introduced in 2009, the project supports over 500 people who are dependent on urban farmers. Conservation agriculture is well established in Zimbabwe. In 2004, the government set up the Conservation Farming Task Force. It is asserted that "it has consistently increased average cereal yields by 50 to 200% in more than 40,000 farm households with the yield increase varying by rainfall regime, soil types and fertility and market access" (Twomlow, 2008:1). Rather than simply handing free seed and fertilizer inputs to farmers, teaching farmers the principles of conservation agriculture enables them to apply inputs (water, fertiliser and seed) more efficiently. The pursuit of input-use efficiency provides higher and more sustainable productivity gains needed to achieve better food security in drought-prone farming systems."

Conclusion and Way Forward

The study concludes that weather-related vagaries are located in various locales defined differently, calling for consilience application to achieve community resilience or at least the building of it effectively. In this process, indigenous knowledge is widely accepted as an alternative way of thinking that evolves over time to safeguard local communities from impacts of climate variations. The modern society dominated by science. However, indigenous knowledge is regarded non-scientific basing on attributes of its oral transmission. Indigenous knowledge is also as scientific as it evolved on the same principles of experiments and trial and error methods which are widely followed in sciences. This discourse observed the disparate and disjointed approaches applied in country's environmental risks and disasters. Bigotry and disciplinary intolerance are a recipe for disaster; there is need to harness different approaches to pigeonhole into the issues whose solution lies in applying multi-perspectives by multi-stakeholders.

The local knowledge systems are ever more familiar and brought forward as sources of appreciative on ecosystem dynamics and sustainable practices. People need to build dialogue in a way to mobilise existing knowledge for assessments and improved policy. Different criterion of legalisation should be applied to data and information originating from different knowledge systems. The aim is to make an equal starting point for mutually agreed ways to proceed, including the potential for co-production of understanding. The balancing outlook will contribute to build resilience and capacity for transformation that includes empowerment of local communities. Five lessons can be derived from this study.

Lesson 1: Zimbabwe is a cultured country where ethnic norms, values and principles are upheld. In this realm, rural communities should learn that social cohesion can assist adaptation and absorption of shocks that confront peasant farmers. This is facilitated through the sharing of scarce resources such as water and food.

Lesson 2: To translate consilience to resilience, local and indigenous knowledge can be used to acclimatise to the impact of climate change using little funds if any.

Lesson 3: Ecosystem-based adaptation projects in Zimbabwe can create employment that can improve the livelihoods of many Zimbabweans and acting as a safety net in this era of climate change and variability.

Lesson 4: Indigenous knowledge can provide invaluable information about the local context. The non-formal ways of disseminating indigenous knowledge can serve as a model for education about climate change adaption in Zimbabwe.

Lesson 5: Effective governance is both a prerequisite and a measure of development in a climate change adaptation and mitigation. Good governance improves working relations in formulating and administering climate change responses. This is particularly true for green growth under resilience. For green growth

31

to reduce poverty, it is important to take into account the needs and interests of poor and vulnerable people in Zimbabwe.

References

ALM UNDP (2009). *Zimbabwe Country Profile*. Adaptation learning mechanism. UNDP. Retrieved 13 July 2017 from: www.adaptationlearning.net/zimbabwe/profile

Audefroy, J.F. and Sa´nchez, B.N.C. (2017). Integrating local knowledge for climate change adaptation in Yucata´n, Mexico. *International Journal of Sustainable Built Environment*, xx (xxx), 1-10.

Berkes, F. (2007). Sacred Ecology (2nd ed, p. 336). New York: Routledge.

Brown, A. Dayal, A. and Rumbaitis Del Rio, C. (2012a). *From practice to theory: emerging lessons from Asia for building urban climate change resilience. Environment and Urbanisation* 24: 531-556.

Brown, D, Rance Chanakira, R, Chatiza, K, Dhliwayo, M, Dodman, D, Masiiwa, M, Muchadenyika, D, Prisca Mugabe, P. and Zvigadza, S (2012b). *Climate change impacts, vulnerability and adaptation in Zimbabwe. IIED Climate Change Working Paper No. 3*, October 2012.

Chenje, M and Solar, L. (1998). *State of the Environment. The Zambezi Basin*, University of Zimbabwe. Harare.

Dhemba, J. (2002). *Phase II: Zunde raMambo and Burial Societies.* Journal of Social Development in Africa, Vole 17 No 2 pp 132 -156.

Ellis, F (2000). *Rural Livelihoods and Diversity in Developing Countries*. Oxford: Oxford University Press.

Gukurume S (2012). *Climate Change, Variability and Sustainable Agriculture in Zimbabwe's*

Gukurume, S. (2010*). Conservation farming and the food security-insecurity matrix in Zimbabwe: A case study of ward 21 Chivi rural*. Journal of Sustainable Development in Africa (Volume 12, No.7, 2010) pp 40-52.

Gurung, B (1994*). A cultural approach to natural resource management: a case study from eastern Nepal: Summary report of FAO regional expert consultation on non-wood forest products: social, economic and cultural dimensions.* Rome: Food and Agriculture Organisation

Gurung, O (2005). Concepts and methods of common property resource management. *Dhaulagiri Journal of Sociology and Anthropology*, 2, 63-64, Gautama, T. R. et.al (eds.) department of Dhaulagiri Journal of sociology and anthropology.

Heinrich Böll Stiftung Southern Africa (HBS). (2010b*). Climate Change Vulnerability and Adaptation Preparedness in Southern Africa – Zimbabwe Country Report 2010, Report prepared by Tigere Chagutah.*

IPCC (2007a), *Climate Change 2007: Impacts, Adaptation and Vulnerability - Summary*

Kumar, V. (2014). Role of Indigenous Knowledge in Climate Change Adaptation Strategies: A Study with Special Reference to North-Western India. Journal of Geography and Natural Disasters, 5(1), 1-5.

Laros M, Birch S, Clover J. And ICLEI-Africa (2013). *Ecosystem-based approaches to building resilience in urban areas: towards a framework for decision-making criteria*, EThekwini

Ministry of Environment (2010). *Climate change vulnerability mapping for Nepal.* Kathmandu: government Of Nepal, ministry of environment.

MoSTE (2010). *National adaptation program of action to climate change.* Kathmandu.

Rural Communities, Russian Journal of Agricultural and Socio-Economic Sciences, 2(14)

Sherpa, P. D. and Sherpa, G. (2013). *Revitalizing customary governance and strengthening traditional knowledge on natural resource management in Nepal. Indigenous peoples, forests and REDD plus: Sustaining and enhancing forests through traditional resource management,* 2, 195-2

Slater, R.; Peskett, L.; Ludi, E.; and Brown, D (2007). *'Climate change, agricultural policy and poverty reduction – how much do we know?',* Natural Resource Perspectives, 109.

Sonia L, Meg, P, Knut, O. and Kofoda, F. (2013).The role of culture and traditional knowledge in climate change adaptation: Insights from East Kimberley, Australia. *Global Environmental Change* 23(3) 623–632.

Tengö, M, Brondizio, E. S, Elmqvist, T, Malmer, P. and Spierenburg, M (2014). *Connecting Diverse Knowledge Systems for Enhanced Ecosystem Governance: The Multiple Evidence Base Approach. Ambio.* Stockholm: Stockholm Resilience Centre.

Twomlow, S, Urolov, J.C, Jenrich, M. and Oldrieve, B (2008). *Lessons from the field – Zimbabwe's Conservation Agriculture Task Force.* Journal of SAT Agricultural Research 6.

UNESCO (2013). *Impacts and adaptations to climate change: Observations and experiences of the local community of Lifuka/ Ha'apai in the Kingdom of Tonga by VikaLutui.* The United Nations: The United Nations Educational, Scientific and Cultural Organisation.

UNFCCC Secretariat (2013). *Report on the technical workshop on ecosystem-based approaches for adaptation to climate change. Note for the 38th Meeting of the Subsidiary Body for Scientific and Technological Advice,* UNFCCC

UNISDR (2009). *Terminology on Disaster Risk Reduction.* Geneva: UNISDR. Retrieved: http://www.unisdr.org/we/inform/terminology (25/05/2017)

Watts, M (2000). Political Ecology, in Sheppard, E. and Barnes, T. (eds.), *The Companion of Economic Geography,* Oxford: Blackwell, pp. 257–74.

Wilson E, O (1998). *Consilience: The Unity of Knowledge.* New York: Vintage Books.

Chapter 3

Vulnerability to Climate Change and Resilience of Child-Headed Households in Buhera District

Vincent Mabvurira & Memory Mpambela

Introduction

The main thrust of this chapter is on the direct and indirect impacts of climate change on child-headed households in rural communities in Zimbabwe with aim of informing social work practice. The study also identifies the resilience strategies of child-headed households besieged by the effects of climate change. Climate change is controversial and a cause of disagreement as there are differences in opinions amongst scholars as to what climate change is. It is defined as a process of global warming, that emanate from greenhouse gas emissions generated by human activity (Gukurume, 2013). On the other hand, the phenomenon is also defined as the long-term significant transformation in the 'weather average' that a given region experiences (Manyatsi, 2010). The problem of climate change has led to excessive use of natural resources-ecological overshoot (Peeters, 2012). Planetary warming because of climate change has led to ecological changes such desertification, floods, droughts, heat waves, rising see levels and many others. The impact of climate change is increasing the vulnerability of people in Zimbabwe especially people in the rural areas. Regardless of climate change affecting all communities in Zimbabwe, vulnerable groups such as child-headed families, people living with disability and children are the most affected groups. The reliance of Zimbabwe's economy on rain fed agriculture is worsening the plight of the rural people as they heavily rely on natural rains.

The devastating impact of HIV and AIDS has been labelled as the main cause of child-headed households in Africa particularly in the Sub Saharan Africa. These vulnerable children suffer a double blow as they have to cope with the orphanhood and climate change at the same time. As children are also among the vulnerable groups that are threatened by climate change (Manica Post, September 2016), incidences of malnutrition have increased and school dropouts are expected to increase (UNICEF, 2014).

The impact of climate change are felt more by the world's poorest regions. Many developing countries have agricultural dependent economies (Dominelli, 2011). It is noted that Zimbabwe's high dependence on rain fed agriculture and climate sensitive resources makes it particularly vulnerable to climate change. Rural communities are the hardest hit as they rely mainly on agriculture for their survival due to skyrocketing levels of unemployment and lack of adequate resources and income to supplement their food security (Chagutah, 2010). The dry spells, which are a major common problem caused by climate change in Zimbabwe. They lead to low levels of food production and are inextricably linked to widespread poverty and food insecurity in the rural areas (Gukurume, 2012). Other problems include flooding, for example the Tokwe Mukosi incident, heat waves and shifting of seasons. Climate change also has a negative impact on the health of people. The heat waves cause headaches and in severe cases stroke and death. As a result, the economically active population is lost most due to the high risk of exposure in their quest for livelihood. These problems associated with climate change have presented overwhelming stress on the social work professionals to come up with measures to mitigate them. Addressing climate change has become a challenge for mainstream social work (Dominelli, 2011).

Conceptualising Resilience

Resilience is a complicated term used in many areas such as ecology, engineering, psychology and development studies. Resilience as a concept originated from the late 1970s remarked by work of some psychiatrists asserts that resilience dates to the Second World War when clinicians noted more psychological damage in some evacuated children than in those who stayed at home to face some bombings (Garmezy, 1983; Glover, 2009). Resilience is defined as a human capacity (individual, group and/or community) to deal with crisis, stressors and normal experiences in an emotionally and physically healthy way; an effective coping style (Barker, 2003). Disruption system's capacity to 'bounce back' after a disruption also entails resilience. Resilience is also defined as a successful adaptation to life task in the face of social disadvantage or highly adverse conditions (Windle, 1999). It is a two-dimensional. It concerns exposure to adversity and the positive adjustment outcomes of that adversity. This implies the existence of impact of a risk cause and adaptation capacity of an individual. Resilience as contextual must be understood as multi-dimensional, varying across time and circumstances. Three factors influence resilience of an individual. Internal environmental and outcome of individual's interaction with the environment. (Tousignant and Sioui, 2009). Internal factors include internal locus of control, perseverance, emotion management, optimism and sense of humour, self-efficacy and the ability to solve problems. It is observed that individual factors such as genetic characteristics, personality traits and intelligence quotient also influence resilience. Environmental factors such as the family, peers, religion, the community and social support significantly influence an individual's resilience. Resilience is a long process of interaction between an individual and his environment, to face adversity and lead to emergence of moral strengths and a sense of optimism (Tousignant and Sioui, 2009; Pienaar, 2012).

Theoretical Framework

The study was informed by the resilience theory. The resilience theory was coined in 1973 by Holling who denoted it to determine the persistence of relationships within a system (Daniel, 2011). It is a measure of the ability of these systems to absorb changes of state variable, driving variables and parameters. The theory has its foundation in systems thinking. The foundation also include complex systems theory and focuses on understanding the characteristics of change and the interactions between human and natural systems. It is further asserted that resilience theory aims to understand three fundamental themes. First, the characteristics of stability, resilience and change from one state to another in systems with multiple stable states. Second, is cross-scale interactions the third theme is adaptive change and learning using the heuristic model or metaphor of the adaptive cycle (Gunderson *et al.* 2002).

Literature Review

Climate change is causing unprecedented, unpredictable and irreversible changes to the earth's ecosystem at an alarming rate. It affects a wide range of sustainable development issues such as health, food security, employment, livelihoods, gender equality, education, housing either directly or indirectly (Sugirtha and Little Flower, 2015). Climate change is not an isolated phenomenon but is part of interrelated problems such as urbanisation, industrialization and armed conflicts. Climate change is mainly affecting four dimensions of food security in many countries. These are food availability, food accessibility, food utilisation and food systems (FAO, 2016). Climate change has seen Zimbabwe experiencing erratic seasonal rainfalls and shifting of seasons and extreme weather conditions in the form of floods and droughts, which have consequently disrupted the agricultural system. This has a head on effect on the economy as the country is largely dependent on the agricultural sector and it is also the main source of livelihood for the majority of Zimbabweans as a huge percentage of the population resides in the rural areas and rely on agriculture. Farmers represent 62% of the Zimbabwean population (Brown et al. 2012). The situation is aggravated by the fact that majority of the people rely on rain fed agriculture and natural ways of enhancing soil quality as they lack the necessary resources such as irrigation infrastructure and fertilizers, which has grossly lowered food production.

It is noted that over one billion children live in flooding zones and over one hundred and sixty thousand children live in drought severity zones. In any bad circumstances it must be noted that children are the most affected. They bear the burden of risk situation because of their vulnerability. Infrastructure that is very critical in children's well-being will be affected by such climate change. Schools, health facilities and homes are destroyed by floods at an alarming rate (UNICEF, 2015). When climate change is not attended to, children from poor regions are the most affected.

Children are an especially vulnerable group and are at increased risk from disease, under-nutrition, water scarcity, disasters and the collapse of public services and infrastructure resulting from extreme climatic change events. It must be noted that 73.5 per-cent of the children's population in Zimbabwe live in the rural areas (ZIMSTAT 2012). The over dependency of rural people on communal farming means that with decreased crop production, food insecurity and hunger most children are at risk of being impacted negatively by climate change. It is reported that under nutrition is a major public health problem in Zimbabwe especially among rural children (Food and Nutrition Council, 2010).

Access to clean water is crucial to wellbeing and development of children hence with drought that was experienced in 2016 saw most rural people resorting to unclean water. This exposes many children to disease. It must be noted that in most rural areas laundry and bathing is done in the rivers, with the shortage of water people resort to drinking river water of which maybe up stream others are busy doing their laundry. Unsafe drinking water put children at risk of contracting water borne diseases. As speculated, climate change will make clean water and sanitation facilities more difficult to access. As a result, it will be difficult to tackle diarrhoea that is regarded as one of the major killers of children (Chingwenya et al. 2008).

The other critical impact of climate is unavailability of water for domestic use. Among most communities in Zimbabwe, children actively participate in fetching water for domestic use. As most rivers dry up children have to travel further to collect water. In some cases they have to wake up early in the morning to get water before they go to school. This affects their concentration at school as they will be tired.

Climate change also brings with it diseases especially those that are water borne such as cholera, malaria and diarrheal. It is reported that about 430 000 deaths of which two third are children below the age of five are dying of malaria. In 2015 about 530 000 infants died of diarrhoea at global level (UNICEF, 2015). These figures clearly show the severity of climate change on children especially those from developing countries. Zimbabwe has also witnessed its fair share of heat waves and floods which have worsened the food and nutrition security crisis as these destroy crops and infrastructure, livestock and cause soils erosion leading to land degradation.

Of the one third of all people who rely on farming as a means of livelihood, more than 60% own livestock (FAO, 2016). Livestock buttresses their food security in the face of climate shocks, are a means of farming, milk, meat and a source of income. However, much anecdotal evidence has shown that climate change has had severe effects on the livestock. Their health has been affected by heat waves and the advent of new pathogens and vectors caused by the rise in temperatures. A lot have perished in floods. Increased dry spells have left others with no water to drink or grazing lands. This has also affected food security as livestock supplement the nutrition of many people.

Another impact of climate change on food security is an increase on food prices which is inextricably linked to low productivity and a decline in yields. The price increase will consequently affect food accessibility especially for poor households and those in the rural areas with no alternative sources of income and they will have to reduce their consumption or rely on food aid (Porter et al. 2014). It is argued that there are certain types of foodstuffs that cannot be produced at household level (Du Toit and Ziervogel, 2004). However, these are acquired through trade or buying. With price increase such kinds of food are likely to become unaffordable. This will have an effect on individual's nutrition as well as health (FAO, 2008). Most child-headed households may not afford the expensive food stuffs hence may be food poor.

Climate change has serious effects on human health. It is recognised as the biggest public health threat of this century (Costello, 2009). There is a growing recognition for the need for greater attention to the health and psychosocial impacts of climate change and related environmental challenges (Kemp and Palinkas, 2015). Although some effects may be advantageous, particularly with regards to temperate countries where temperature increase may lead to milder winters, thereby reducing the deaths caused by immense cold (WHO, 2012). However, some evidence suggests that in overall climate change will negatively affect the health of humans. The impact of climate change on human health is already being felt globally. In its 'World Health Report of 2002' WHO attributes 2.4%

of the diarrhoea experienced across the globe and 6% of the malaria that hit middle income countries to climate change. Developing countries are the hardest hit and more susceptible to climate change induced health hazards this is because of the poor health status, lack of resources and infrastructure, lack of skilled personnel and economic underdevelopment. Malaria claims the lives of many children in sub-Saharan Africa.

Water borne diseases such as cholera are also expected to be more widespread as a result of erratic water supplies. The year 2008 saw Zimbabwe experiencing a cholera epidemic which is said to be the largest outbreak recorded in history. The number of people affected by the epidemic was pegged at 100,000 and those killed at 4,000 (GoZ, 2010). Extreme weather conditions like flooding have the potential of cross contaminating water and sanitation systems heightening the risk of recurrent cholera outbreaks. Available evidence also suggests that the rise in temperatures caused by climate change will lead to an increase in ground level ozone. This will have severe effects on the respiratory system and lungs and individuals with pre-existing cardio and respiratory conditions are more at risk (Brown et al. 2012).

Social work and climate change

Though climate change is one of the most topic cross-cutting issues of the 21st Century, social work has given the problems little attention (Achstatter, 2014). It is observed that "leaving global warming to scientists is like leaving poverty to economists, mental illness to psychiatrists and crime to the police" (Sugirtha and Flower, 2015:103). Though since its inception, social work has focused on person-in-the environment, the natural environmental has not been given due attention in most cases. Climate change poses threat to human survival needs, physical safety and human rights. The International Federation of Social Workers (IFSW) calls for social workers to recognise the importance of the natural and the built environments on the social environment, to promote sustainable use of natural resources and to ensure that environmental issues gain increased presence in social work education. The Australian Association of Social Workers (AASW) has made it an ethical requirement for social workers to actively promote a health natural environment as part of their commitment to social justice (AASW, 2010: 13).

Currently there is no policy that supports Zimbabweans relying on rain fed agriculture hence social workers have to work for the formulation and implementation of new policies which mitigate and enhance moves of adaptation to climate change. The UNs Intergovernmental Panel on Climate Change (IPCC) spells out that human activities are the major contributor of global warming experienced in the past 50 years. Therefore, to ensure mitigation, social workers have a huge task on their shoulders. Firstly social workers have to conscientise, educate and inform masses about climate changes, its effect and causes. This is so because armed with information people can be empowered and can also assist in the mitigation of climate change through reducing greenhouse gas emissions, avoiding deforestation and protecting green lands. Social workers also have to work towards the adaptation and strengthening the resilience of communities. To achieve this, they have to come up with innovative ways of curbing against the calamities brought by climate change. Rural people can be taught on how to diversify their livelihood and sources of income as a buffer against shocks from climate change and protection of their food security.

Social workers who have been involved in environmental causes and who strive to fight environmental degradation have assumed the name green social workers. green social work is defined as "a form of holistic professional social work practice that focuses on the: interdependence amongst people; the social organisation of relationships between people and the flora and fauna in their physical habitats; and the interactions between socio-economic and physical environmental crises and interpersonal behaviours that undermine the well-being of human beings and planet earth. It proposes to address these issues by arguing for a profound transformation in how people conceptualise the social basis of their society, their relationships with each other, living things and the inanimate world" (Dominelli, 2012). Social work can play a leading role in addressing the human impacts of environmental change in four major areas; (1) disaster preparedness and response (2) population dislocation (3) community-level organising and development aimed at strengthening local and regional capacity to respond to global environmental change particularly in urban settings and (4) mitigation, advocacy and practice engagement in addressing the underlying causes of environmental change (Boetto and McKinnon, 2013; Kemp and Palinkas, 2015).

Methodology

This study followed a qualitative research approach. Qualitative research is concerned with exploratory research which seeks to understand underlying reasons and motivations of human behaviour (Yeasmin and Rahman, 2012). The study adopted a case study design where data was gathered through semi-structured face-to-face interviews and focus group discussions. The population of the study comprised of persons below the age of 18 years who were serving as household heads. A sample of 21 child households' heads was selected for the study through snowball sampling technique. Thematic content analysis was used to analyse the data. The study was carried out in ward 10 of Buhera District under Chief Chimombe. The ward has a total population of 5 865 and 288 food poor households and a food poverty prevalence of 20.9% (UNICEF, World Bank and ZIMSTATS, 2016). The district is experiencing serious impacts of climate change as evidenced by many families that are in need of food aid (World Food Program, 2016). Buhera district is also one of the rural areas hardest hit by HIV and AIDS pandemic leaving many children orphaned and resulting in many child-headed households. The overall poverty prevalence in Buhera is 78% (UNICEF, World Bank and ZIMSTATS, 2015).

Results and Discussion

Twenty-one children participated in the study and of these 14 were girls while 7 where boys. This may suggest that there are more female child-headed of households in Buhera District. Being the head of household does not imply being the eldest child in the family as the eldest child might be staying somewhere for whatever reason. The children ranged in age from 13 to 17 with a mean age of 15 years.

43

Only 9 of the respondents reported that they were attending school regularly.

The research discovered that child-headed households are experiencing a number of challenges due to climate change. The main challenges that were highlighted by the respondents include food shortage, shortage of water, dropping out of school, heat rash and floods. However, there was not much difference with challenges faced by rural people in general.

Food shortage was the first impact of climate change that was reported by all child household heads. The drought that occurred during the 2015/16 farming season led to most households failing to have a good harvest. In ward 10 of Buhera district, all the households were in need of food assistance. Inadequate food for most families in Buhera presented a double tragedy for minors who must be supported. Seventeen (17) of the child respondents indicated that they were having one meal per day and the remaining few had at most two meals per day. Droughts experienced because of climate change are jeopardising the food security of child-headed households in rural Zimbabwe. This was attested by a child who said the previous season was so bad because rains came late and left so early that they could not harvest anything. Another male child argued that their relatives gave them food. However, in drought seasons they were unable as they would as be struggling to feed their own families. Mealie meal was the most cited food item to be scarce. In Buhera District, the common grown crop is maize hence the erratic rainfall pattern resulted in acute food poverty.

It is of paramount importance to note that due to frequent droughts most water reservoirs are failing to fill up. The droughts resulted in rivers and wells that communities depend on drying up. Most households reported travelling more than 7 kilometres in search of drinking water. Children from child-headed households are among the hardest hit as some of them cannot balance school time and time needed to travel to fetch water. In support of this observation, one respondent asserted that they could not balance school and domestic chores. Their well has dried up and they could not find time to go fetch water. As such, either they dismissed early from school or dropped out completely.

In another interview one child from Chivhaku village reported that she wakes up as early as 3'oclock in the morning to go and search for water with her neighbours from Murove River. Children are exposed to dangerous situations when they woke up early in the morning to fetch water. Besides waking up early and travelling long distances to fetch water, children also raised concerns of water being unsafe for consumption. Another child household head reported that they fetch water from open surface or river. In one research on climate change, it was discovered that the capacity of most dams will decrease and rain seasons will be very shorter (Brazier, 2015). These findings are in line with this study's observations as most rivers are drying up there by affecting child households. Another research also discovered that about one-third of children in the world do not have safe drinking water (UNICEF, 2014). This research discovered the same notion as children in Buhera District are drinking unsafe water from rivers.

Floods are one of the major causes of death and loss of property in low-lying areas among other climate change impacts (UNDP, 2004). Incessant rain characterised the 2016/17 rain season throughout Zimbabwe. Family members of child-headed households also witnessed flash floods. All the participants reported that they were affected by floods regardless of age and gender. Three families had their crops destroyed by hailstorm. Seven school-going children reported spending more than two weeks without attending school as a local bridge was overflowing. Children are more vulnerable to such natural disasters, as they do not have experience to handle them. Several child-headed families reported losing their property due to floods. It is also identified children as the most victims in any disaster since they depend on adults for protection (UNICEF, 2014). One would only imagine how child-headed households cope with disasters. As a result, child-headed households suffer more than households headed by adults

Most child-headed household engage into economic activities for their livelihood. Hence, some of them dropped from school. Child household heads dropped out of school due to economic hardships that was caused by the impact of climate change. Some of the child-headed households benefit from support of extended families. One of the child household heads narrated that his uncle in the same village was paying school fees for him and his three siblings. However, the drought that struck the district led to his uncle failing to continue to pay fees for even one of his siblings. His uncle relied on market gardening for income generation and due to the drought, no produce was obtained. Another child revealed that he dropped from school to venture into illegal gold mining to fend for the food requirements of the family. School dropping out is a serious challenge facing most children from child-headed households. In some cases, climate change has not directly caused school dropout but it caused support systems to collapse. One girl respondent who had a condition of albinism was forced out of school because she developed skin cancer, which was now causing blindness and pain. She recounted that she was affected by heat rash and due to her participation in food-for-work programme she spends most of her time exposed to sun. She also narrated that she cannot afford the required skin lotion that helps to prevent heat rash. One can argue that climate change has affected children from child-headed households more than any other child. In a similar observation, on 27 October 2015, a national newspaper, The Chronicle featured a story, "Massive School Dropouts a Cause for Concern". This story reported that in the Matabeleland region (one region of Zimbabwe with lower quality of life), at least 6,000 children have dropped out of school. Also, authorities in the region reduced learning hours as some pupils came to class hungry. This is a clear indication that hunger or food shortage plays a significant role on education. One can imagine how children from child-headed households can cope with such harsh climate change conditions.

Heat rash is a red or pink sport, usually found on body parts covered by clothing. It develops when the sweat ducts get blocked and swell and usually leads to discomfort. Heat rush is another impact of climate change among child-headed households. Due to the El Nino that was experienced in 2016, most children were heavily affected. One of the respondents reported that his sibling experienced heat rash. A boy child household head reported that due to lack of finances he failed to purchase the required medication to help his three-year old sister. This clearly shows how vulnerable children are due to climate. Heat rash if unmonitored can develop into skin cancer. Due to inexperience of children who head households they are reluctant to seek help as they interpret the situation as a minor issue that can naturally heal.

A female respondent also reported that because of her albinism condition heat rush affected her severely that she was no longer able to carry out her usual duties. She was then helped to seek medical practitioners by case care workers where she was told that she was now suffering from skin cancer. Unfortunate enough, children from child-headed households receive help when their predicament worsens that is being reactive rather than proactive. Children lack adequate experience to address such hardships caused by climate change. Adult-headed households at least have vulnerabilities monitored before they get worse.

Due to the hardships caused mainly by climate change, child-headed households have some coping mechanism. The resilient theory that was used in this study best explained the continuation of such households despite the challenges.

The challenges posed by climate change led to almost all the child participants to take part into some form of child labour. To mitigate the impact of climate change children were involved in economic activities for their livelihood child labour is any work that deprives a child his or her physical and or emotional well-being including the work interfering with his or her school (ILO, 2012). One of the child household head reported buying and selling sugarcane to compensate for crop failure due to a drought. Some children spend good time of the day driving livestock to water sources, as local rivers were dry. Some community members then paid them for this.

Other child household heads reported that they are into food for work program so that they sustain themselves. Food for work program is a program that was launched by the government whereby local people are engaged in local developmental projects such as road clearance in return for food. It is of paramount importance to note that children are forced into child labour by circumstances hence they end up being injured during the activities. The Herald of March 21, 2012 under the headline "Child labour in Zimbabwe" reported that about 10 percent of children left school to engage in economic activities. The largest composition of these children came from parents who separated and widowed. With this background, one can argue that children from child-headed families end engaging in labour

47

activities and dropping out of school to cope with stresses caused by climate change. The research findings are in line with ILO's (2012) findings that main causes of child labour in developing countries is due to economic hardship. Most children end up engaging in economic activities to supplement their family income.

Almost all the children reported resorted to the collection and consumption of non-wood forest products (NWFPs). NWFPs consist of goods of biological origin other than wood, as well as services derived from forests and allied land uses. The children reported heavy reliance on products such as mushroom, forage, wild fruits and wild rodents and crickets (FAO, 1995; 1999). This was supported by a child who said that they only have something for supper. For lunch they rely on wild fruits as they cannot afford two meals per day".

Another child reported selling crickets, which do well when there is scanty rainfall during the summer season. Findings of the study corroborate earlier studies as gathering of Non-Wood Forest Products (NWFPs) has been found to be an important element in the livelihoods of most rural communities across the globe. It is observed that at global level, more than 2 billion people are dwelling in forests, depending on non-wood forests products for subsistence, income and livelihood security (Vantomme, 2003).

Some children reported leaning on spirituality as climate change wreaked havoc on them. The belief that God will see them through or that their late parents was watching over them played an important role in motivating them amid challenges. Spirituality has been found to be a source of resilience (Wong and Vinsky, 2008; Cascio, 2012). Spirituality can give people strength to go where there is a threat and it gives courage and encouragement amidst suffering and death. Religion can provide a world-view that helps give purpose and meaning to suffering (Martin and Martin, 2002).

Conclusion and Recommendations

Climate change is bedevilling child-headed households in a number of ways. Child-headed households in some rural communities in Zimbabwe are facing challenges in getting food, safe drinking water and attending school because of climate change. They have resorted to child labour, non-wood forest products and spirituality as resilience strategies to cope with the effects of climate change. Effects of climate change such as floods, droughts and hailstorms all require some form of social work intervention. The study proffers the following recommendations:

- Extensive climate change related awareness campaigns targeting the ordinary person, the civil society and the government.
- Government to incorporate a child-centred perspective when it comes to policy-making in a bid to ensure the vulnerabilities of children, especially child-headed households are taken into consideration.
- Government to develop a national climate change framework that will coordinate policy-making as well as implementation.
- Government to work with the private sector to scale up programs that cater for the needs of child-headed families to cushion them from the extra problems caused by climate change.
- Social work education in Zimbabwe should cover topics on green social work to equip professionals to handle climate change issues.

References

Achsatter, L.C .2014. Climate Change: Threats to social welfare and social justice requiring social work intervention. 21st Century Social Justice 1(1): article 4.

Australian Association of Social Workers .2010. Code of Ethics. Canberra, Act.

Barker, R. 2003. *Social work dictionary.* Washington, DC: NASW Press

Boetto, H and McKinnon J .2013. Gender and climate change in rural Australia: A review of differences. Critical Social Work 14(10): 15-31.

Brazier, A. 2015. *Climate Change in Zimbabwe: Facts for Planners and Decision-makers.* Harare, Konrad Adenine.

Brown, D, Chanakira, R.R, Chatiza, K, Dhliwayo, M, Dodman, D, Masiiwa, M, Muchadenyika, D, Mugabe, P, and Zvigadza, S.

2012. Climate change impacts, vulnerability and adaptation in Zimbabwe, London, IIED, 80-86.

Cascio, T. 2012. Understanding spirituality as a family strengthll. *Family in Society Newsletter. Families in Society, 82(1): 35-48.*

Chagutah, T. 2010. Climate Change Vulnerability and Preparedness in Southern Africa: Zimbabwe Country Report. Heinrich Boell Stiftung: Cape Town.

Daniel, D.C.2011. *A Formal theory of resilience.* Germany: University of Munster.

Dominelli, L .2011. Climate change: social workers' roles and contributions to policy debates and interventions. International Journal of Social Welfare, 20 (4): 430-438. doi:10.1111/j.1468-2397.2011.00795.

Dominelli, L .2012. Green Social Work: From environmental crisis to environmental justice. Cambridge, Polity Press.

Du Toit, A. and Ziervogel, G. 2004. Vulnerability and food insecurity: Background concepts for informing the development of a national FIVIMS for South Africa. Available at: www.agis.agric.za/agisweb/FIVIMS_ZA.

FAO.1996. Rome Declaration and World Food Summit Plan of Action. Rome. Available at: www.fao.org/docrep/003/X8346E/x8346e02.htm#P1_10.

FAO. 2008. An Introduction to the Basic Concepts of Food Security. Published by the EC -FAO Food Security Programme. www.foodsec.org/docs/concepts_guide.pdf.

Garmezy, N. 1983. Stressors of childhood. In N Garmezy and M Rutter (eds), *Stress coping and development in children* (pp.43-84). New York: McGraw Hil.

Glover, J. 2009. *Bouncing back: How can resilience be promoted in vulnerable children and young people?* Essex: Barnado's.

Government of Zimbabwe. 2010. Medium Term Plan, January 2010 – December 2015.

Government of Zimbabwe, Ministry of Economic Planning and Investment Promotion, Harare.

Gukurume, S. 2013. Climate change, variability and sustainable agriculture in Zimbabwe's rural communities, Russian Journal of Agricultural and Socio-Economic Sciences, 2(14), pp 89-100.

Gunderson, L. H, Holling. C.S, Pritchard, L. and Peterson, G.D. 2002. *Resilience of large-scale resource systems*. Washington D.C: Island Press.

IPCC. 2007. Climate change 2007: Impacts, adaptation and vulnerability. Contribution of Working Group II to the Fourth Assessment Report of the Intergovernmental Panel on Climate Change. Cambridge, Cambridge University Press.

Kemp, S.P and Palinkas, L.A .2015. Strengthening the social response to the human impacts of environmental change. Grand Challenge for Social Work Initiative, Working Paper 5,

Manyatsi, A.M. 2010. Climate Variability and Change as Perceived by Rural Communities in Swaziland. Research Journal of Environmental and Earth Sciences2 (3): 164-169.

Martin, E. P. and Martin, J .2002. *Spirituality and the black helping tradition in social work*. USA: NASW Press.

Sugirtha J.T and Little Flower F.X.L. 2015. Global warming, climate change and the need for green social work. Indian Journal of Applied Research 5(12):102-104.

UN General Assembly. 2009. Climate change and its possible security implications: Report of the secretary general. http://www.refworld.org/docid/4ad5e6380.html

Tousignant, M. and Sioui, N. 2009. Resilience and Aboriginal Communities in Crisis: Theory and Intervention. *Journal of Aboriginal Health, 2009: 43-61.*

Windle, M. 1999. Critical conceptual and measurement issues in the study of resilience. In M.D. Glantz and J.L. Johnson (Eds.), *Resilience and development: Positive life adaptations.* (pp 161-176). New York: Kluwer Academic/ Plenum.

Wong, Y.R. and Vinsky, J. 2008. Speaking from the margins: A critical reflection on the Spiritual-but-not religious discourse in social work‖. *British Journal of Social work, 39 (7): 1343-1359.*

Chapter 4

Urban Resilience in Cities of the Developing World with Reference to Harare, Zimbabwe

Phineas T Dohwe & Ndarova Audrey Kwangwama

Introduction

Human beings have increasingly become *homo urbanis*. This is largely explained by the roles cities have assumed: engines of economic development providing opportunities for growth (Drobiak, 2012). It has been observed that one hundred ninety three thousand one hundred and seven (193 107) new city dwellers are added to the world's population on a daily basis translating to five million (5 000 000) new monthly urban dwellers in the developing countries and five hundred thousand (500 000) in the developed world (United Nations Global Report on Human Settlements, 2009: 26). It has also been argued that this high level of unprecedented urbanisation has resulted in the transformation of the planet from 10% urban in 1990 to more than 50% in just two decades (United Nations Department of Economic and Social Affairs, 2010 Report). Against this background and context of rapid demographic growth, cities thus are susceptible to both natural and human made disasters.

Urban societies now live in uncertain environments characterised by catastrophic climate events, terrorist attacks, credit crunches, youth riots and mass redundancies (Davoudi, 2012). Some of these uncertainties arise from the rapid growth of cities in hazard prone locations such as coastal locations, the modifications of the built and natural environment through human activities and the failure of authorities to regulate building standards and land use planning strategies. It has been highlighted that that there has been a fourfold increase in the number of recorded natural disasters (801 in 2000, 786 in 2002 and 744 in 2005) since 1975 and a tenfold increase of human disasters from 1975 to 2006 and higher rates reported in Asia and Africa (UN-HABITAT, 2009).

Despite this increase in these natural and human made disasters and uncertainties, cities are expected to continue existing. Without good and proper urban growth management strategies, the shocks and disturbances threaten man's new found habitat with the risk of throwing into turmoil urban living. The concept of urban resilience has gained significant prominence in an effort to identify and implement solutions which address the challenges threatening cities and their citizenry. It has been observed that in the Social Science Citation Index, the annual references to resilience as a topic increased by 400% (Swanstrom, 2008: 4). Urban resilience has emerged as a favourable concept to address the uncertainties and disturbances which cities continue to grapple with (Meerow et al. 2016). The urban resilience concept has been elicited by major urban threats and disasters in the last three decades including the terrorist attacks in New York, the Asian Tsunami and Hurricane Katrina in New Orleans or the bombing attack in London (Drobriak, 2012). The question is how safe and secure from sudden destruction are cities in view of the emerging challenges? How can the concept of resilience be applied to urban planning (urban resilience) in the designing of resilient cities?

Literature Review

The word resilience originates from the Latin word- *resilio* which means to bounce back/spring back (Meerow, Newell and Stults 2016; Davoundi, 2012). It was first applied by scientists in the physical sciences to illustrate the characteristics of a spring, describing the stability of materials and their ability to resist to external shocks. Although resilience has risen to significant prominence, there are a multitude of different definitions and turning any of them into operational tools is a mammoth task. It has been highlighted that after approximately thirty years of academic analysis and debate, the debate of resilience has become very broad to the extent of rendering it almost meaningless (Klein, Nicholas and Thomalla, 2003). Meerow, Newell and Stults (2016) reviewed four decades of academic literature focusing on resilience since 1973 when the concept was introduced by Holling. They observed that the definitions of urban resilience during the four decade period were underdeveloped as they did not clearly respond to critical conceptual tensions evident in the urban resilience literature.

As previously highlighted, the concept of resilience has gained considerable prominence in the last three decades. The concept of resilience in the field of ecology was first introduced by Holling in 1973. He observed that within the context of an ecosystem, resilience is the ability of a system to absorb, change and persist when it experiences disturbances (Holling, 1973). Holling's perception of ecosystem resilience centred on the capacity of an ecosystem to withstand a disturbance without collapsing into a qualitatively different state that is controlled by a different set of processes (World Bank, 2012). He argued that a resilient ecosystem could withstand any shocks, re-bounce and rebuild itself when necessary. When applied to human social systems, resilience has the added capacity of humans to anticipate and plan for the future.

In its work of trying to manage the risks of disasters in East Asia and the Pacific, The World Bank (2012: 3) defines resilience as the capacity of either a system or community/society to cope and recover in a timeous and efficient way from the effects of a hazard. The system's or the community's coping capacity is achieved through preservation and restoration of its basic original structures. The Resilience Alliance (www.resalliance.org) agrees with the World Bank's definition and explains the meaning of resilience within the context of integrated systems of people and nature as: the volume of disturbance a system can cope with, the extent to which a system can reorganise itself after the disturbance and the point to which the system can cope and develop the capacity to learn and adapt.

Literature on resilience identifies the various states of equilibrium of an ecosystem. Three states of equilibrium are identified: single state equilibrium, multiple state equilibrium and dynamic non-equilibrium. The single state equilibrium is described as the ability of a system to revert to a previous equilibrium after experiencing a disturbance (Meerow et al. 2016). Examples of disturbances include a natural disaster such as flooding, or an earthquake or social upheaval crises such as a banking crisis, wars or revolutions (Holling, 1996). It mostly occurs in disaster management, psychology and economics. The single state equilibrium is often regarded as engineering resilience. This is described as a property of a specific material to absorb energy when it experiences deformation elastically and its ability to recover its energy when it returns to its original state. This concept has been applied to psychology and psychiatry where resilience of individuals has been regarded as the ability to deal with changes and events during life course transitions. It has been observed that in the single state equilibrium, resilience is measured by the speed at which the system returns to its state of equilibrium (Davoudi, 2012). The key points emerging from the diverse meanings and frameworks of engineering resilience are summarised as: maintaining, recovering and looking for equilibrium (Chelleri, 2012).

The second state of equilibrium is the multiple state equilibrium often described as the ecological resilience. Meerow, Newell and Stults (2016) highlight that in this case, a system is regarded as having different stable states and when it faces disturbances, it may be transformed by tilting/tipping from one stability domain to another. It has been observed that in engineering resilience, Holling's argument had centred on the system's capacity to reorganise and manage changes in order to maintain the same identity and structure within one state of equilibrium. However, ecological resilience provides a major paradigm shift of resilience regarding ecological recovery of a system's functions, structure and identity after a disturbance to the transformation principle in adapting to the disturbance (Chelleri, 2012). It argues that since systems are complex, the focus should not be on recovery but transformation in adapting to a disturbance.

The third perspective on the state of equilibrium is the dynamic non-equilibrium which is centred on the argument that systems undergo or experience constant change and do not have a stable state. It has been described as the evolutionary resilience which is conceived as the capacity of intricate socio-ecological systems to adjust, become accustomed and change as a reaction to stresses and strains (Davoudi, 2012: 302). The evolutionary resilience perspective regards systems as complicated, curve-linear, able to self-organise and characterised by ambiguity and incoherencies. The evolutionary resilience perspective is a major paradigm shift with respect to the world views of scientists. Davoudi (2012) further argues that unlike the engineering perspective which views the world as orderly, mechanical and fairly predictable, the evolutionary resilience perspective presents the world as chaotic, complex, uncertain and unpredictable. It argues that after experiencing disturbances, the world never returns to its original normal state.

The evolutionary understanding of resilience has been best articulated by Holling's Renewal Adaptive Cycle Model – also known as the Panarchy Model of Adaptive Cycle. This model presents four distinct phases of change in the structures and functions of a system: growth (exploitation phase), conservation (steady state phase), collapse (release phase) and finally the re-organisation phase as illustrated in Figure 1. Davoudi (2012) describes the first stage of growth, the Alpha phase (α), as characterised by the sudden accumulation of resources, competition, exploitation of opportunities, increasing diversity and connections and declining levels of resilience. It is argued that at this stage, the system is in a state of high potential with available resources ready for exploitation and stimulating innovation. As the available resources and opportunities are exploited by early pioneers, the system experiences the first dynamic changes and interactions.

When the dynamic changes and interactions build up, the system experiences the full exploitation - growth phase as depicted by (r) in Figure 1. During the second stage, growth declines with storage of resources for the maintenance of the system which would have reached natural limits of its carrying capacity. Furthermore, the introduction of rules and regulations result in social exclusion, polarisation and stabilisation of the system – the (k) phase characterised by conservation. Davoudi (2012) highlights that this stage is characterised by stability, certainty, a decrease in flexibility and low levels of resilience. In this (k) phase, the system experiences difficulties which result in destruction – marking the beginning of the third stage of Holling's Renewal Adaptive Cycle Model, the creative destruction phase. Romeo-Lankao, Gnatz, Wilhelmi and Hayden (2016) describe the third stage as the release, scatter or collapse phase, Omega (Ω) as shown in Figure 1. It is characterised by chaotic collapse and release of accumulated resources, uncertainty, low but rising levels of resilience. It is argued that at this stage, the system would have been in a state waiting for an accident to happen (Davoudi, 2012). It has been observed that this stage re-opens opportunities for transformation and re-organisation or renewal and this marks the beginning again of the cycle in the Alpha phase (Romeo-Lankao et al. 2016). Davoudi (2012) describes this stage as a time for innovation and transformation where a crisis can be transformed into an opportunity.

Figure 1: Holling's Renewal Adaptive Cycle Model (Romeo-Lankao et al. 2016)

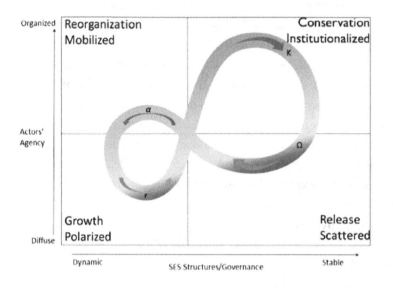

In Holling's Renewal Adaptive Cycle, capacity of the system involves two key stages: the fore loop, from r to k and the back loop, from Omega to Alpha. (Romeo-Kankao et al. 2016). The former is the incremental phase of growth and accumulation while the latter is the phase of rapid re-organisation which results in renewal of the system. It has also been observed that resilience potential varies across the four phases of the Holling's Renewal Adaptive Cycle. It is higher in the renewal and growth phases and lower in the system conservation and collapse phases. Gunderson and Holling cited in Chelleri (2012) emphasize two critical points on resilience theory from the Renewal Adaptive Cycle Model: (i) disturbance is a necessary part of development (ii) renewal (learning and self-organisation for change) is a resilient strategy much more than conservation or bouncing back. It has also been observed that there are several paradoxes in the model including: persistence versus change, flexibility versus efficiency, resilience versus transformation and connectedness versus adaptability. To address these variations, Holling's model is centred on panarchy instead of hierarchy.

The panarchy approach argues that the stages of a system are not sequential or fixed. Instead, a system works in a series of interactive and nested cycles at different scales ranging from small to large, different speeds ranging from slow to fast and different time frames spanning across short to long terms. The evolutionary perspective of resilience is embodied in the panarchy approach which views resilience as a continuous changing process which is not an end state of being but a continuous process of becoming. Davoudi (2012: 304) concludes the analysis of evolutionary resistance: it widens the engineering and ecological perspectives of resilience to include the interaction of "persistence, adaptability and transformability across multiple scales and timeframes."

Urbanity and Urban Resilience

Romero-Lankao, Gnatz, Wilhelmi and Hayden (2016) observe that the term *urban* as a concept has been defined in the context of population size, built environment form and economic function. The first perspective regards urbanity as concerned with a certain number of people within clearly demarcated political and administrative boundaries under the jurisdiction of either local authorities or central government. The second perspective focuses on physical or morphological aspects depicting the physical extent and layout of the built environment, infrastructure and land use zones of a city. The third perspective hinges on urban function defining urbanity as economic and migration interconnections between the urban core areas and their hinterlands. Cities are also viewed as growth machines responsible for social inequality as well as damaging the environment. Romero-Lankao et al. (2016:2) give their last perception of cities as "socio-ecological systems (SESs) either of interacting biophysical and socioeconomic components or social and technical components." They further elaborate that as socio-ecological systems, cities are characterised by five fields: socio-demographics, economy, technology, environment and governance.

Although resilience as a concept originated in the natural sciences in ecological research, it is now applied across diverse disciplines ranging from natural disasters, risk and management, hazards, climate change adaptation, international development, engineering energy systems and planning. The focus of this chapter is on urban resilience in urban planning. The United Nations Global Report on Human Settlements (2009) highlights that urban planning in the context of rapid urbanisation and other economic challenges is not a luxury but a necessity. In the context of urban planning, scholars have coined the term urban resilience. Meerow, Newell and Stults (2016: 39) developed a flexible definition of urban resilience which can be used by diverse disciplines and stakeholders including urban planners: the capacity of an urban system and all its component socio-ecological and socio-technical networks across different spatial levels to sustain or speedily come back to anticipated functions after experiencing a disturbance, to adjust to change and to speedily convert systems that restrict the present and imminent adjustment ability.

The previous definition depicts urban resilience as dynamic with multiple pathways: persistence, transition and transformation. It delineates the complex and adaptive nature of the urban system as composed of socio-ecological and socio-technical networks that span over multiple spatial scales. Urban resilience has been defined as the capability of individual persons, societies, organisations, companies and systems to persist, adjust and develop in the face of any type of chronic stresses and acute shocks which they encounter (ARUP, 2015). Chronic stresses are further defined as slow moving disasters that weaken the fabric of the city while acute shocks are regarded as sudden sharp events that threaten a city as shown in Table 1.

The resilience of social-ecological systems including cities is characterised by three major characteristics: (a) the magnitude of the shock that the system can absorb and remain within a given state; (b) the degree to which the system is capable of self-organization and (c) the degree to which the system can build capacity for learning and adaptation (Folke et al. 2002). The stages of the urban resilience building process are summarised as incorporating coping, transitioning and transformation. The coping stage refers to the capacity of the current system to absorb any experienced shocks and stresses and be able to persist. The transitioning stage focuses on

60

building the urban system's ability to adapt the existing institutions and structures. This stage aims to assert all the usually neglected obligations and responsibilities, for example, participatory decision making process, innovative information and knowledge sharing systems. The final stage, transformation, encompasses the ability of the urban system to set future goals and putting in place the implementation framework which questions the status quo and existing power relationships. In building urban resilience, it has been acknowledged that change is inevitable for all systems. However, the change should be anticipated and managed to ensure persistence of the urban system as well as its continuous positive growth (Pelling, 2011).

Table 1: Chronic Stresses and Acute Shocks (World Bank, 2015: 20)

Chronic Stresses	Acute Shocks
High unemployment	Earthquakes
Overtaxed or inefficient public transportation system	Disease outbreaks
Corruption	Terrorist attacks
Endemic violence	Volcanic eruption
Demographic shifts	Oil spills
Chronic food shortage	Industrial accidents
Chronic water shortage	Labour strikes/unrest

While it is difficult to foretell the future, it is possible for society to monitor the effects of current actions on the environment, develop responses and policy actions and programs that can anticipate and counteract the obvious negative impacts. By so doing, society can equip itself to come up with adaptive measures to deal with the potential turbulences. These would possibly assist in addressing the threats to the future of cities and their effect on the quality of life of their citizens in the face of emerging changes emanating from their development and growth to accommodate increasing population and its growing demands on the environment.

Cities require careful planning and growth management to effectively respond to the emerging changes and challenges. Without careful planning, they risk suffering catastrophic economic and social consequences which will significantly disrupt, alter or bring to an end the "good" urban life. Consequently, there is increasing need to build capacity for greater resilience for the cities to develop strategies for coping with the future shocks and stresses to the urban infrastructure systems. Such challenges are associated with resources depletion and climate change effects arising from city life styles, consumption patterns and waste generation and disposal systems. Cities have to be planned and managed in ways that significantly reduce their dependence on and pollution of finite resources such as land, water and fossil fuels. Proper planning and management enable them to become more self-sufficient and energy efficient in the face of the diverse challenges.

Key Pillars of Urban Resilience

Cities are intricate systems interwoven by diverse social, economic, institutional and environmental threads which affect the welfare of society at large and individual citizens (OECD, 2016). The world's population has experienced significant changes largely driven by urban population growth from one billion in 1950 to approximately six billion in 2050. As already highlighted in this chapter, urban systems face foreseen and unforeseen shocks which result in significant social, economic, environmental and institutional implications. These demand resilient cities with the ability to absorb, adapt, transform, prepare and cope with both the foreseen and unforeseen shocks. This chapter adopts five key pillars of resilience developed by the Disaster, Risk Management, Sustainability and Urban Resilience (DiMSUR), a non-profit, autonomous non-political, regional organisation headquartered in Maputo, with open membership in Sub-Saharan counties. The organisation aims to provide technical assistance and knowledge on disaster risk reduction, climate change adaptation and urban reliance. The five key pillars include urban governance, urban planning and environment, urban economy and society, urban disaster risk management, resilient infrastructure and basic services as illustrated in Figure 1 (Source: DiMSUR 2013).

Figure 2: Five Pillars of Urban Resilience (DiMSUR, 2013: 9)

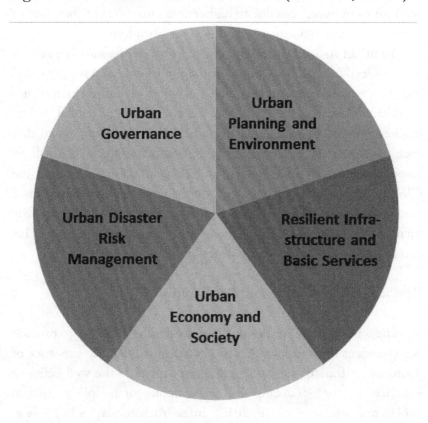

Urban Economy and Society

It has been argued that a city with a diversified industrial base generates more employment opportunities for its population resulting in a stronger revenue base from individual income and corporate taxes (OECD, 2016). A strong revenue base is key to the city's ability to develop resilience against any foreseen and unforeseen shocks. The development of a diversified urban economy is anchored on innovation which generates new products, services and processes. The level of education of the urban population is a critical determinant factor on the capacity of the city to stimulate innovation. It has been observed that in cases where an urban society has a higher concentration of people with tertiary education qualifications, the city experiences higher levels of economic growth and stability (OECD, 2016). For example, developed countries including Japan, Finland

and the United Kingdom have been able to establish more stable economic environments due to higher concentrations of their labour force which attained tertiary education qualifications.

An urban society's inclusiveness and cohesiveness are dependent on the social capital, the urban community's fabric and robust social infrastructure. A city with high levels of socio-economic inequalities is characterised by poor education, health, low social capital, failing businesses and environmental degradation. It has been argued that such a city has a less resilient society which finds it difficult to respond to shocks and stresses. It has been observed that in the Global South, the capacity of the poor and less privileged communities is restricted by their lack of access to the previously mentioned basic services (Yanez and Kernaghan, 2014) This compromises their level of urban resilience.

Resilient Infrastructure and Basic Services

The well-being of any society is measured by its ability to provide basic services to its residents. It has been argued that the existence of protective infrastructure and technology enhances the well-being of a society through reducing the susceptibility of people to certain shocks and stresses (ARUP, 2012). Infrastructure plays a key role in building a resilient city. The state of a city's infrastructure enables the provision of diverse essential services and underpins the level of economic growth. It has been observed that infrastructure as well as technological assets are key in facilitating the mobility of people and resources, exchange of goods and services as well as establishing dynamic connections among different stakeholders (da Silva, Kernaghan and Luque, 2012). A city's well developed infrastructure is constituted by a good transportation system, water and sewage treatment works and reticulation systems and effective storm water drainage. It has been argued that an integrated and interconnected transport system has a network of a wide range of transport modes including rapid bus lines along main transport routes and to ensure low carbon emissions, different transport modes are used including pedestrian cycling routes (ARUP, 2012). The water supply sources should be diverse, adequate and being able to cover distribution in the whole urban area. Drainage of water should be effective and functional to enable rainwater to drain fast to avoid the hazard of flooding in the city.

Urban Planning and Environment

The rapid growth of urban population has resulted in increasing demand for basic and essential services such as housing, food, water and transportation facilities. As already indicated in this chapter, urban planning should no longer be regarded as a luxury activity for the elite but a necessary and requisite activity to guide the growth of a city. An effective urban planning system is evidenced by the development of a city's vision and integrated development strategy as well as regular review of development plans of the city. Cities and municipalities depend on development plans and land use regulations in managing development in areas under their jurisdiction. It has been observed that an integrated urban planning system provides a framework to address diverse issues ranging from climate change and disaster risk management. The existence of up to date development plans aligns the city's various projects and programmes ensuring that they are mutually supportive and reflect on past experiences of the city as well as being resourceful in times of emergencies (ARUP, 2012). For urban planning to be effective, it should be inclusive and engaging residents during preparation and implementation of development plans.

Contemporary urban planning is advocating for compact mixed use developments involving dense development with effective public transportation and where commercial, educational, recreational and community points are located within easy proximity of each other (ARUP, 2012). This enables communities to live, work and play in their environments and minimises the use of the automobile which has created immense challenges for the city ranging from traffic congestion to fuel shortages. Effective urban planning ensures provision of adequate infrastructure including water and energy supplies which can be shared and reticulated in the whole urban area.

Urban Disaster Risk Management

Cities are exposed to diverse shocks and stresses including flooding, storms, heat waves, rising sea levels, droughts, soil erosion, food insecurity and water scarcity (ARUP, 2012). A well -developed infrastructure is critical in risk management and dealing with the shocks. For example a city should maintain large open parks and wetlands to manage and minimise the effects of flooding. Natural barriers and man-made structures are key to manage any possible catastrophic impacts. It has been observed that in earthquake regions, building structures should be retrofitted to reduce and manage the effects of earthquakes (ARUP, 2012). The city should develop an educational programme to provide early warning systems and campaigns regarding rapid responses on earthquakes and other natural and human made disasters.

Urban Governance

Urban governance refers to the relationship between an urban local authority and its residents (Harpham and Boateng, 1997). It has also been defined as the way in which government, the private sector and civil society relate to each other as manifested in the trust given to individuals, multi-stakeholder consultations and making decisions on the basis of evidence (ARUP, 2015). Good urban governance ensures the development of trust, unity and shared meanings and understanding of a city's development path. It has been observed that the key to good urban governance is effective leadership that encourages its citizenry to act together when they experience shocks and stresses.

An effective framework for urban governance allows urban local authorities to make decisions at the local level in an integrated and co-ordinated way through consultation of the diverse stakeholders on the basis of well-established practices and procedures. Good urban governance appreciates the critical role played by locally generated knowledge in understanding shocks and stresses. It promotes relationships across various sectors of the city. This facilitates effective co-ordination of the citizens and promotes easy accessibility to private and public resources during emergencies.

Effective urban governance is evidenced by timely responses of urban local authorities during emergency situations.

Building Blocks of a Resilient Urban System

The building of urban resilience faces a myriad of challenges among them lack of technical capacity and experiences, inadequate information and data as well as meagre financial resources (DiMSUR, 2013). ARUP in its City Resilience Framework (2015) and the OECD (2016) identified seven qualities usually described as the seven building blocks of urban resilience. These include resourcefulness, inclusivity, redundancy, flexibility, robustness, integration and reflectivity as shown in Table 3.

The previously described seven building blocks of urban resilience can be applied to physical and social systems to create disaster-resilient cities. They place emphasis on resilience as an approach which deals with uncertainty. Their argument is centred on the ability of a system to continue existing after experiencing foreseen and unforeseen shocks. It has been observed that cities must be planned with the strength to resist hazards, the flexibility to accommodate extremes without failure and the robustness to rebound quickly from disaster impacts.

In its efforts towards informing urban planning practice on urban resilience in cities on the basis of measurable and evidence based indicators and variables, ARUP International Development embarked on an international study of six geographically diverse cities : Cali in Colombia, Concepcion in Chile, New Orleans in USA, Cape Town in South Africa, Surat in India and Semarang in Indonesia. The basis of selection of the cities was either they had recently experienced a serious shock or suffering from chronic stresses. The main purpose of the study was to identify the critical factors contributing to resilience in urban areas and how urban resilience is perceived by diverse stakeholders in the cities.

Table 4: The City Resilience Index (ARUP, 2015: 26)

Building Block	Description
Resourcefulness	A resourceful urban system recognises alternative ways to use available resources to ensure the restoration of basic and essential services into functionality when a crisis occurs under a very constrained environment.
Inclusivity	Inclusivity refers to broad consultation, involvement and engagement of diverse stakeholders to create a sense of shared meaning and ownership in decision making from policy formulation.
Robustness	A robust urban system entails a well-conceived, designed, constructed and managed system with the capacity to absorb impacts of any foreseen and unforeseen shocks. It bounces back without any significant losses. There should be multiple components or nodes instead of a central node in order to protect against foreseen and unforeseen threats.
Integrated	An integrated urban system brings together a wide range of distinct systems and institutions
Redundancy	Redundancy refers to extra spare capacity of a system purposively created to accommodate any possible disruptions arising from foreseen and unforeseen shocks. Systems should be planned with various nodes to ensure that failure of one component does not result in the subsequent failure of the whole system.
Reflectivity	A reflective urban system uses past experiences to inform future decisions.
Flexibility	A reflective urban system is willing and able to adopt alternative strategies in response to changing circumstances.

Eight city functions critical for urban resilience were identified: delivering basic needs, safeguarding human life, protecting, maintaining and enhancing assets, facilitating human relationships and identify, promoting knowledge, defending the rule of law, justice and equity, supporting livelihoods and stimulating economic growth and prosperity. In this context, the resilience of a city is thus regarded as its ability sustain good health, a safe environment, social harmony and economic prosperity. On the contrary, a non-resilient city is evidenced by ill-health, insecurity, an unsafe environment, conflict and deprivation.

ARUP further proceeded to identify twelve factors in the six cities under study regarded as critical in achieving and sustaining urban resilience. Using each of the twelve factors, ARUP (2014) established indicators to determine a city's level of resilience. The outcome of the study was the City Resilience Index containing the four dimensions of urban resilience, the seven qualities of urban resilience as well as the twelve factors and their indicators. Table 4 provides the list of twelve factors and indicators used to measure urban resilience for cities extracted from ARUP's City Resilience Index. These twelve factors are closely linked with the five pillars and seven qualities of urban resilience discussed earlier on in the chapter.

Methodology

This chapter is informed by qualitative research. It is based on an extensive literature review on resilience and how the concept has been applied to urban planning – urban resilience. To gain understanding of the application of urban resilience in Harare, key informant interviews were conducted with experienced planners from the Department of Physical Planning in the Ministry of Local Government, Public Works and National Housing. The City of Harare as a planning authority has a fully-fledged Planning Department headed by a City Planner. Key informant interviews were also conducted with senior planners and engineers in the city. There are several Planning Consultancies who are engaged by the private sector, central government and local authorities including the City of Harare on planning issues. Experienced planners were also identified in these Planning Consultancies and key informant interviews were also conducted with them. The professional body for planners in Zimbabwe is the Zimbabwe Institute of Regional and

Urban Planners (ZIRUP). Senior members of the profession as well as the President of the Institute were also identified and interviewed regarding their perceptions on urban resilience in Zimbabwe using Harare as a case study.

Table 3: Building Blocks of Urban Resilience (ARUP, 2015; OECD, 2016)

Factor	Indicators
Minimum Vulnerability	• Safe and affordable housing • Adequate affordable energy supply • Inclusive access to safe drinking water • Effective sanitation • Sufficient affordable food supply
Diverse Livelihoods and Employment	• Inclusive labour policies • Relevant skills and training • Local business development and innovation • Supportive financing mechanisms • Diverse protection of livelihoods after experiencing a shock • Robust public health systems • Adequate access to quality health care facilities • Emergency medical care facilities • Effective emergency response services
Collective Identity and Mutual Support	• Local community support • Cohesive communities • Strong wide city wide identity and culture binding residents together • Actively engaged citizens
Comprehensive Security and Rule of Law	• Effective systems to prevent crime • Proactive corruption prevention • Competent policing • Accessible criminal and civil justice
Sustainable Economy	• Well-managed public finances

	• Comprehensive business continuity planning • Diverse economic base • Attractive business environment • Strong integration with regional and global economies
Reduced Exposure and Fragility	• Comprehensive hazard and exposure mapping • Appropriate codes, standards and enforcement • Effectively manged protection ecosystems • Robust protective infrastructure
Effective Provision of Critical Services	• Effective stewardship of ecosystems • Flexible infrastructure • Retained space capacity • Diligent maintenance and continuity • Adequate continuity for critical assets and services
Reliable Mobility and Communications	• Diverse and affordable transport networks • Effective transport operation and maintenance • Reliable communications technology • Secure technology networks
Effective Leadership and Management	• Appropriate government decision-making • Effective co-ordination with other government bodies • Pro-active multi-stakeholder collaboration • Comprehensive hazard monitoring and risk assessment • Comprehensive government emergency management
Empowered Stakeholders	• Adequate education for all • Widespread community awareness and preparedness

	Effective mechanisms to engage government
Integrated Development Planning	• Comprehensive city monitoring and data management
	• Consultative planning process
	• Appropriate land use and zoning
	• Robust planning approval process

Box 1 provides a summary urban resilience experiences in Oaxaca City in Mexico after the city experienced a hurricane which was caused by an El Nino condition in the 19990s with its devastating effects.

Box 1: Urban Resilience Case Study, Oaxaca City, Mexico (Yanez and Kernaghan, 2014)

Oaxaca city is the capital of the State of Oaxaca in Mexico. A hurricane induced by an El Nino hit Mexico in the 1990s affecting 83% of the land in Oaxaca translating to approximately 500 000 hectares which were severely eroded within the city and its hinterland. Consequently, access to fresh water and soil productivity declined after the hurricane. The frequency of droughts increased and food supplies became inadequate to feed the concentrated urban population in Oaxaca. Small scale agriculture was the worst affected as it became difficult to practice. This negatively food security for urban citizens in Oaxaca.

A horizontal network platform was established in response to the hurricane shock with key stakeholders from international non-profit organisations and civil associations. This platform engaged and facilitated the working together of all the key stakeholders against the effects of the hurricane and climate change. Such projects included organic farming, permaculture, composting, recycling of organic waste, capturing of water for irrigation, establishment of inter-cropping systems and water retention as well as development of new local seed systems resistant to negative effects of climate change.

The platform also critically analysed the current fragmented food security policies regarding accessibility to land, management of water, accessibility to local markets, seed production systems, health and nutrition. Consequently, an integrated food policy was formulated and this enhanced the lobbying capability from the grassroots and non-governmental organisations. The newly developed integrated food policy promoted food production from three sources: urban agriculture: urban agriculture, peri-urban and rural agriculture. This facilitated the storage of perishable food stocks within close proximity of the city while cereal production demanding larger farmland was undertaken on the periphery of the city.

It has been already been argued in this Chapter that resilience as an evolving process consists of three interconnected stages: coping, transitioning and transformation (Pelling, 2011). This model was applied to Oaxaca City. Hurricane which hit the city in 1990 had devastating effects including increased frequency of droughts, water shortages and inadequate food supplies. As a coping response to the shock, Oaxaca city developed a more flexible and wide ranging agricultural system with four levels of ecological practices: urban and peri-urban agriculture and proximate and remote rural areas (Yanez and Kernaghan, 2014).

As already highlighted, after Hurricane, a horizontal network platform of international non-governmental organisations and local non-profit organisations was created to finance collective projects as well as enhancing quicker sharing of knowledge. This marked the transitioning stage characterised by the evolution of an integrated food supply chain encompassing distribution, consumption and organic waste recycling.

Pelling's third stage on the evolution of urban resilience, the transforming stage was marked by the development of strong lobbying capability of the network platform described earlier on which questioned and queried the prevailing policies and government programmes. This resulted in the institutionalisation of the platform's best practices which eventually developed an integrated Oaxaca City food policy.

It can be observed that although Hurricane in 1990 hit Oaxaca as a challenging and devastating shock, by 2005, it had provided opportunities for change. Urban resilience was attained from collaboration efforts of diverse stakeholders concentrating their efforts across different scales and viewpoints. The city managed to adapt the hurricane shock, transformed it into opportunities and managed to satisfy the wellbeing of its citizens.

Urban Resilience in Harare, Zimbabwe

Harare is the capital city of Zimbabwe. It is an economic hub of both commerce and industry and houses the administrative headquarters of government, the private sector, non-governmental organisations and several diplomatic missions. According to the 2002 Census, the City of Harare had a population of 1 435 784 constituting 12.34% of the total population in Zimbabwe and 76% of Harare Province. The City of Harare has good transport and communication networks i.e. road, rail and air transport routes, telephone and satellite communication systems although the infrastructure has deteriorated due to lack of maintenance. It is situated in Zimbabwe's Natural Region Two with good climate in terms of rainfall and temperature. The city is surrounded by a hinterland with good agricultural soils for food security and this has attracted investment from agro-processing industries. Harare inherited a good administrative framework from its colonial past which has ensured proper land use planning with distinction and separation of different land uses although emerging informal settlements on its peripheral areas are not properly planned.

Harare is the largest city in the Greater Harare Metropolitan Area whose other settlements include Chitungwiza, Epworth, Norton and Ruwa. These are experiencing higher levels of population growth as shown in Table 5. It can be observed that over the years, Epworth, Ruwa and Norton have experienced phenomenal growth exceeding Harare's growth rate. The whole Harare Metropolitan area shares basic infrastructure services including a common water supply system sourced from dams owned by the Harare City Council. Thus the continued growth of these other satellite settlements has adversely affected the provision of basic infrastructure services in the whole Harare Metropolitan region as will be discussed later.

Table 5: Population of Greater Harare Metropolitan Area (thousands) (Central Statistics Office 1992, 2002 and 2012)

Year	Harare	Chitungwiza	Epworth	Ruwa	Norton	Total
1992	1 479	274	Na	Na	20	Na
2002	1 436	323	114	24	44	1 941
2012	1 469	354	162	56	58	2 099
Growth Rate pa (2002-2012)	0.2%	0.9%	3.6%	8.8%	2.8%	0.8%

Urban Economy and Society

The Fast Track Land Reform (FTLR) characterised by commercial farm invasions, described as *jambanja* in the vernacular language in Zimbabwe and undertaken by government in 2000 resulted in a significant economic decline during the years 2000-2008. This period was marked by hyperinflation which reached a peak of 231 150 888.87% as at 30 June 2008 (Zimbabwe Independent, 25 July 2008) and in January 2009, it was estimated to be ten times this official figure. All the key sectors of the economy namely agriculture and forestry, mining and quarrying, manufacturing, construction, real estate, distribution and hotels, transport and communication recorded poor performance. During this period of economic decline, the economy was characterised by the following:

- Acute shortages of foreign currency;
- Severe shortages of basic commodities due to poor agricultural performance and low capacity utilisation by the manufacturing sector;
- De-industrialisation
- Continued decline of the country's Gross Domestic Product (estimated at -12% for 2008);
- Intermittent supply of public utilities (electricity, water and sewage) resulting in an ailing public health system with a cholera outbreak that claimed more than 4 000 lives and infected 90 000 people in Zimbabwe in 2008 (Zimbabwe Multi Donor Trust, 2015);
- Severe price distortions due to multiple foreign exchange markets: (Old Mutual Implied Rate, official , cash, cheque and RTGS exchange rates);
- Serious brain drain as skilled people migrated the country seeking greener pastures in the region and overseas;
- Decline of foreign direct investment
- High levels of corruption in both the public and private sectors of the economy with Zimbabwe ranked 166 out of 180 countries by Transparency International Corruption Perception Index (Zimbabwe Independent, 25 July 2008).

Zimbabwe's national economy suffered a cumulative decline of 51% between 1999 and 2008 (Financial Gazette, 24 March 2016). The financial services sector was not spared by this economic quagmire. It was characterised by poor liquidity, low levels of confidence and high interest rates. The country failed to fulfil its financial obligations and accrued arrears with multi-lateral institutions including the World Bank, International Monetary Fund and the African Development Bank. In 2009, a government of National Unity was formed and the economy dollarised. There were signs of economic recovery since dollarisation when its growth averaged 10.6% between 2009 and 2012 but declined to 4.5% in 2013, 3.8% in 2014 and 1.5% in 2015 (Financial Gazette, 24 March 2016). The manufacturing sector employing a large proportion of the economically active was worst affected especially in Harare and other large cities. It declined from 188 600 employees to 93 100 in 2014 - a 50.6% decline while the mining sector declined from 43 000 employees to 38 400 - a 10.6% decline (The Herald, 13 April 2015). The Zimbabwe National Chamber of Commerce (ZNCC) forecasted a dwindling capacity utilisation of 31% in 2016, a decline of 3.3% from 34.3% reported in 2015 (Newsday 25 March 2016).

Harare as the capital city houses most of the manufacturing companies and consequently, most people who lost their jobs due to closure of companies engaged into the informal sector activities especially vending in the city centre. The implication of the economic decline for Harare is that most residents who are unemployed (unemployment estimated at 90%, Zimbabwe Independent, 12 August 2016) are increasingly finding it difficult to afford and pay for the basic urban services such as rates, water, sewage and refuse collection. The decline in collection of revenue in turn is negatively affecting the ability and capacity of Harare as an urban local authority to finance the supply and provision of most urban services. Urban residents are focusing on basic survival paying no attention to the payment of urban local authorities' service charges. Urban local authorities including Harare have experienced high default rates on the payment of these urban services. The performance of an economy is one of the major factors that determines the resilience and non-resilience of cities. It can be observed that where national economies fail to perform, the cities also follow suit as they are weighed down by their growing populations and poverty levels which all compromise the attributes of urban resilience.

Urban Planning, Growth and Development

Urban spatial growth brings about gradual change in land use from its natural state to a built environment form wherein the land is occupied by buildings, roads, storm water drains and physical features of the built environment. This change brings about transformation in the natural ecosystems, biodiversity and the natural equilibrium of the natural environment, the basic support system to human and urban development. Urban planning of a city is achieved through forward planning, research and development control/management. Key informant interviews with planners at the City of Harare revealed that the city is operating with outdated planning documents some of which were prepared during the colonial period. A number of operating town planning schemes in Harare were prepared prior to independence while the Harare Combination Master Plan was approved in 1992 and has not yet been reviewed despite the changes brought about by the ever-changing dynamic environment in which the city is operating.

Key interviews with planners at the City of Harare highlighted that the spatial growth of post- independence Harare can be broadly be divided into two broad phases namely pre- 2000 and the post year 2000. The pre-2000 growth occurred through properly laid down procedures of forward planning, land banking and estate development with the formal acquisition of rural agricultural land and its subsequent incorporation into the city for urban development. Subsequent to the acquisition, the land was carefully planned, zoned and serviced for urban development using resources from the City of Harare's Estate Development Account. However, the year 2000 marked the beginning of *jambanja* farm invasions, under the FTLRP – the beginning of chaotic unplanned and uncoordinated peri-urban settlements in Harare.

During the post 2000 period, no new infrastructure was developed to support the emerging peri-urban settlements in Harare. Their location has not been synchronised, linked and connected to the existing bulk infrastructure or sites for the development of additional bulk infrastructure. A few of these new developments that fall within the reach and catchment of existing infrastructure have been connected to the existing bulk infrastructure. However, the carrying capacity of this infrastructure and design lifespan have long been exceeded. Where the land falls outside the catchment of existing bulk infrastructure, development has proceeded without the prerequisite infrastructure such as water and sewage reticulation. Residents have resorted to digging deep wells and communal boreholes for water supply and pit latrines and septic tanks and soak ways for sewerage effluent disposal in the high density peri-urban settlements. The stand sizes for such settlements range from 200-300m^2 yet the City of Harare's standards for on-site treatment of sewage stipulate a stand size of 2 000m^2.

The prevalence of pit latrines in the peri-urban areas of Harare whose densities is unacceptably high for safe and sustainable underground water sources is a serious threat to the environment and domestic water consumption. The peri-urban stands are heavily contaminated with faecal matter due to percolation from the septic soakaways. Development management is totally lacking in these areas implying that most of the developments in these areas do not conform to basic standards and precepts of urban resilience. The process of development management encompasses a wide range of planning activities such as designing, analysing, influencing, promoting, engaging, negotiating, decision-making, co-ordinating, implementation, compliance and enforcement of planning standards and regulations. This ensures that development is in conformance with the planning framework as well as being sensitive to the fragile environment. The current peri-urban developments in Harare are thus at variance with principles of urban resilience.

The prevailing economic challenges have rendered enforcement of the city's bye laws almost impossible. Harare's city centre has been invaded by a large number of vendors occupying street pavements whom de Soto (2000:80) would describe as "....armies of vendors hawking their wares on the streets and countless crisscrossing minibus lines." These vendor come to Harare's CBD in desperation to sell their fruits, vegetables and other wares to the pedestrian traffic in the streets. The planners argued that the removal of vendors in Harare's CBD is a political issue highly dependent on the political will. Politicians are reluctant to remove them from the CBD as this move makes them unpopular resulting in loss of votes especially for the ruling party ZANU PF which has lost the urban electorate to the opposition party, MDC since its formation in 1999.

The planners also highlighted several challenges emanating from failure to enforce the city's bye laws in Harare's CBD. These include accumulation of large heaps of waste from uncollected garbage and increased insecurity due to the prevalence of increased theft cases, traffic congestion and inadequate parking. These problems in the CBD coupled with the downsizing of companies as well as company closures have resulted in increased building void levels in the CBD with average market void levels reported at 50% which far exceeds the real estate industry accepted level of 10%. High void levels in the CBD imply that property owners in Harare's CBD are incapacitated to pay rates to the municipality adversely affecting its revenue inflows and its ability to provide basic services and to maintain the city's infrastructure.

Infrastructure Capacity and Basic Services

The City of Harare's infrastructure consists of roads, water, sewerage, storm water drainage, public street lighting and traffic signals. This section discusses the road network, water and sewage infrastructure while storm water drainage and refuse collection will be discusses under urban disaster management. Key informant interviews with engineers in the City of Harare revealed that the city has a well-designed road network of approximately 6 000 kilometres all surfaced with tarmac except for the emerging peri-urban settlements such as Caledonia, Harare North and Harare South. However, most of the existing roads have outlived their design life hence the main challenge is to maintain them. It has been difficult for the city to undertake regular maintenance of the road infrastructure due to restrictive budgetary constraints and prohibitive costs hence most roads are in a deplorable state with potholes.

Harare's sewage infrastructure consists of two distinct but complementary units, the reticulation network and the treatment plants. The pipes of the sewage reticulation system experience frequent burst outs due to age and overloading. There are five major

79

sewerage treatment plants which include Crowborough, Firle, Hatcliffe, Mabvuku and Marlborough. The city has both the modern biological nutrient remover plant as well as the old conventional treatment ponds. Firle treatment works are the biggest modern sewerage treatment works in Sub-Sahara outside South Africa and Crowborough treatment works with both the modern and conventional plants are situated west of Kuwadzana and Mufakose suburbs. Hatcliffe works consist of a modern BNR plant catering for Hatcliffe. Marlborough works are traditional conventional ponds as well as the Donnybrook ponds which service Mabvuku and Tafara.

Key informant interviews with the City of Harare's engineers revealed that the sewage treatment works are currently overloaded. Their original design capacity in respect of the volume of sewage they receive on a daily basis has been exceeded as shown in Table 6. The implication of overloaded sewage is partial treatment resulting in discharging of raw effluent polluting water supply dams.

Table 6: The Capacity of Harare's Sewerage Treatment Works (Harare Water and Sanitation, 2015)

Sewage Treatment Plant	Design Capacity (Mega litres)	Estimated Current Load (Mega litres)
Firle	144	160
Crowborough	54	120
Hatcliffe	4	4.5
Marlborough	4.5	7
Donnybrook	7	10

Harare is located at the headwaters between the Manyame catchment to the South and West and the Mazowe catchment to the north. The engineers at the City of Harare highlighted that the city obtains raw water for treatment from four dams on the Manyame River: Harava and Seke Dams which supply Prince Edward (Seke) Water Treatment Works and Chivero and Manyame Dams which supply Morton Jaffray (Manyame) Water Treatment works. Harare's water infrastructure consists of the water reticulation system and water treatment works. Morton Jaffray Water Works in Norton, the major water treatment works in Harare have a capacity to process

600 mega litres per day while the treatment plant at the Prince Edward Dam has a capacity to process 70 mega litres per day giving a total of 670 mega litres.

The City of Harare's engineers reported that as in the case of sewage reticulation, 40-50% of the pipes in the water reticulation system are old and leak resulting in the loss of treated water. Harare's water demand currently stands at 800 mega litres to 900 mega litres per day. The City of Harare also supplies water to the other towns in the Harare Metropolitan area giving a combined water demand of 1 400 mega litres which far exceeds the treatment capacity of approximately 670 mega litres per day. This means there is a current deficit of at least 730 mega litres per day. To address these water shortages, the City Of Harare introduced water shedding from 24 hours in 2005 to over 72 hours in 2014 (Manzungu et al. 2016).

Lake Chivero located in Norton 40 kilometres from Harare suffers a myriad of challenges including heavy pollution from domestic and industrial effluent originating from both Harare and Chitungwiza. This presents treatment challenges especially procurement of water treatment chemicals. The engineers at the City of Harare highlighted that the quality of Harare's raw water has been deteriorating over the years due to agricultural, domestic and industrial activities in Chitungwiza, Norton and Ruwa. Sewage works in all these towns as well as Harare itself are dysfunctional. This results in raw sewage flowing into the water supply dams especially Lake Manyame and Lake Chivero thereby heavily polluting them. The consequence of this pollution has been an increasing demand for treatment chemicals. The engineers reported that due to heavy pollution, the city now uses 8 (eight) chemicals to effectively treat the impurities incurring monthly expenditure of US$3 000 000.00 (three million dollars). The engineers also pointed out that another treatment challenge has been reduced productivity of treated water as filters at the Morton Jaffray Works are frequently chocked and have to be backwashed. The current backwashing frequency is now every 8 (eight) hours resulting in water losses of 105 mega litres compared to the standard backwashing of once every forty eight (48 hours) where only 17.5 mega litres would be lost.

It can be observed that the City of Harare is situated on its water catchment area which has resulted in heavy pollution of its water supply dams (Zimbabwe Multi Donor Trust Fund, 2015). The construction of the proposed Kunzvi Dam has been on the cards for years but has not materialised due to financial constraints. It has been argued that the cholera outbreak in Harare was largely explained by pumping of partially treated water from Morton Jaffray Treatment Works to Harare residents. In addition to inadequate water, there are distribution challenges of the purified water for example due to the erratic nature of electricity supply system, there is inconsistency in the water supply. The acute shortage of foreign currency has also made it difficult to procure adequate treatment chemicals for processing the raw water.

Urban Governance

The formation of the major opposition party in Zimbabwe, Movement of Democratic Change (MDC) in 1999 marked a new political beginning in Zimbabwe. The *jambanja* land invasions occurred a year after the formation of MDC. Urban areas are assumed to be politically affiliated to the MDC formation (Chirisa, Gaza and Bandauko, 2014). On the contrary, to counter loss of political support in urban areas after formation of the opposition party, the ruling party, Zimbabwe African National Union Patriotic Front (ZANU PF), allocated peri-urban land from the *jambanja* invaded farms to housing co-operatives. This is evidenced by a resident in Caledonia, a peri-urban settlement in Harare who argued that had it not been for ZANU PF, which empowered them by allocating them stands for building houses, no one else could have given them the subject land (Chirisa et al. 2014: 41).

The allocation of land to housing co-operatives by ZANU PF was followed by uncoordinated land subdivision and/or parcelling for housing development without the pre-requisite infrastructure as provided for in the Harare Combination Master Plan or local development plans. Consequently, this has resulted in the emergence of informal settlements on the periphery of the city including settlements such as Caledonia, Harare South and Harare North without pre-requisite infrastructure. In 2015, central government appointed the Urban Development Corporation to regularise these settlements but very little progress has been made regarding installation of basic infrastructure services.

It has been observed that since 2002, local government elections have been won by the MDC. On the contrary, the ruling ZANU PF party has always won national elections thereby forming the central government. To maintain a grip on the running of the City of Harare, the ruling party has always interfered with the City of Harare's administration as shown by the major unfolding governance events of the city after attainment of independence as shown in Table 7. It has also been alleged that between 2006 and 2014, the City of Harare was headed by a town clerk described as a 'blued eyed boy' of the then Minister of Local Government and National Housing, Dr. Ignatius Chombo (Standard, 2015). His administration was characterised by controversies: involvement in land scandals, failure to implement Council's resolutions, creating an unsustainable salary bill, complete defiance of instructions issued by MDC Councillors and taking instructions from the Minister of Local Government, Public, Works and National Housing instead of the City of Harare's Mayor and his Council. In 2015, the MDC Mayor finally fired this town clerk but since then, the City of Harare has failed to conclude the appointment of a substantive town clerk to head the city's administration. The Local Government Board controlled by central government has always turned down candidates recommended by the MDC led Mayor and Council.

The ruling ZANU PF through central government ministries has always interfered in the running of urban local authorities and this has had negative consequential effects. For example in 2005, the management of water and sanitation was moved away from urban local authorities to the Zimbabwe National Water Authority (ZINWA) including for the City of Harare. The transfer of the management of water and sewerage from City of Harare worsened service delivery due to ZINWA's lack of adequate financial resources, inadequate usable assets and spares unskilled management which did not have the capacity and institutional memory on the management of water and sewer infrastructure, inability to charge economic rates due to political interference resulting in heavy unrecoverable subsidies for water tariffs and poor strategic business planning for the parastatal. On realising its mistake, central government returned water and sanitation management to the City of Harare in 2009.

Furthermore, vehicle licensing which had been the responsibility of local authorities was moved to the Zimbabwe National Road Authority, a parastatal created by government in 2001 tasked with the responsibility of enhancing the road network system in the country.

Table 7: Major Urban Governance Events in Harare after the Attainment of Independence in 1980 (Manzungu et al. 2016)

Time Period	Major Unfolding Governance Issues in Harare
1980-1995	City of Harare led by a Council dominated by the ruling ZANU PF with good relations with central government
1996-2008	City of Harare led by an Executive mayor after the amendment of the Urban Councils Act but there were problems with the new system resulting in the suspension of the then Executive Mayor, the late Solomon Tavengwa.
1999-2002	City of Harare led by a government appointed Commission (The Chanakira Commission)
2002-2005	Election of an MDC Mayor (Mudzuri) and Council but dismissed. Deployment of another government appointed commission (The Makwavarara Commission)
2008-2013	Winning of elections by the MDC opposition party and appointment of a Mayor by the opposition (Mayor Muchadei Masunda)
2013	Opposition MDC wins Council elections and appoints and MDC Mayor (Manyenyeni)
2015	Suspension and dismissal of the government appointed Town Clerk by the MDC Mayor and Council, Tendai Mahachi. The City of Harare to date (2018) runs without a substantive town clerk due to central government interference in filling up the post.

In 2013 prior to the harmonised national and local government elections, the then Minister of Local Government, Public Works and National Housing directed urban local authorities to write off debts on services they were owed by residents-a move seen as to lure urban residents to vote for the ruling party. The transfer of collection of vehicle licensing fees from local authorities and the failed water and sanitation transfer from local authorities to ZINWA were both perceived as central government's desperate efforts to widen its resource base by displacing local authorities from their traditional revenue collecting activities.

Urban Disaster Risk Management

As already indicated in the chapter, cities are exposed to diverse shocks and stresses including flooding, storms, heat waves, rising sea levels, droughts, soil erosion, food insecurity and water scarcity (ARUP, 2012). A well-developed infrastructure is critical in risk management and absorbing stresses and shocks. The engineers at the City of Harare reported that Harare's public street lighting system has deteriorated over the years due to non-replacement of poles knocked down during accidents and acts of vandalism. The City of Harare has been experiencing dwindling revenue levels due to non-payment of rates and other service charges by residents. This has negatively affected its capacity to maintain the public lighting system. Most emerging peri-urban settlements do not have public street lighting because the city has not been levying an electricity installation levy to housing co-operatives which spearheaded development in these areas. A significant number of traffic signals in the central business district of Harare have not been functioning well either because they do not have heads or they simply broke down. The situation has been worsened by the frequent breakdown of the computer system controlling the traffic signals in the central business district of Harare which has been poorly maintained.

Refuse collection in Harare's Central Business District and residential suburbs has been on an intermittent basis. This has resulted in garbage piling up in the city as shown in Plate 1 creating fertile background for disease outbreaks. The City of Harare's engineers acknowledge that storm water drains have not been timeously cleaned prior to the commencement of the rain season. After a heavy rainfall downpour, the city's central district business area experiences floods as shown in Plate 2. This flooding has threatened to submerge parked vehicles and damaged some properties.

Plate 1: Poor refuse Collection in the City of Harare
(http://263chat.com/harare-city-acquires-20-refuse-collection-trucks/)

Plate 2: City Floods Due to Failure of Storm Water Drains (Herald, 18 January 2014)

The study of Harare also revealed that the City has run out of serviced land for real estate development within the city's existing boundaries. Consequently, development pressure has been exerted on wet lands and land reserved for public open space and recreation. In executing its mandate to ensure sustainable utilisation of natural resources and protection of the environment as well as preparation of plans to prevent pollution and environmental degradation, the

Environmental Management Authority (EMA) promulgated General Notice 313/2012 which demarcated Harare's Wetlands accompanied by a Wetlands Map of Harare shown in Figure 3.

The purpose of General Notice 313/2012 of the Harare Scheduled Wetlands and accompanying maps was to protect the wetlands. However, developers objected to the preparation process of this map and argued that EMA did not consult them. In a land mark ruling, in the case of Augur Investments versus The Minister of Water and Climate and EMA referred to as HC 1017/14, the High Court nullified Harare's Scheduled Wetlands as contained in General Notice 313/2012. The Court argued that EMA did not give all parties likely to be affected by the decision a reasonable opportunity to make representations. The Wetlands Schedule was prepared ultra vires the provisions of the Environmental Management Act (Chapter 20:27) which requires EMA to engage diverse stakeholders during plan preparation.

Figure 3: Wetland Map of Harare (Environmental Management Authority, 2014)

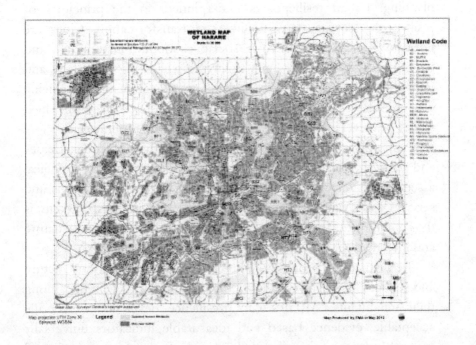

This ruling weakened EMA in its efforts to protect wetlands. After the ruling, Augur Investments proceeded to implement its proposed real estate development project on a vlei area in Borrowdale West. The Monavale Wetland in Harare is also under serious threats from residential real estate development projects. The Long Chen Plazza real estate project was constructed on a wetland in Belvedere adjacent to the Harare National Sports Stadium. The City of Harare planners reported that although the land is owned by the city, they were not consulted on the proposed commercial development. The Ministry of Local Government, public Works and National Housing allocated the land to a Chinese developer. The City of Harare planners were not aware of whether the Environmental Impact Assessment had been undertaken for the project.

Discussion

The concept of resilience has gained significant prominence over the last two decades in response to challenges arising from climate change, disaster events and rapid urbanisation. It originated from natural sciences but is now applied to social sciences including urban planning. Urban resilience is underpinned on the principles of resilience – coping, transitioning and transformation. Cities are intricate systems tying diverse social, economic, institutional and environmental threads which affect the well-being of society and individual citizens. They exist in dynamic environment experiencing chronic stresses and acute shocks including flooding, storms, heat waves, sea level increases, droughts, soil erosion, food insecurity and water shortage. In order to be able to cope with the chronic stresses and acute shocks, cities require key infrastructure and technological assets which facilitate efficient movement, exchange of goods and services and dynamic relationships among stakeholders. The city is thus a complex system of interconnected institutions, infrastructure and information.

Resilient cities promote equitable access to basic infrastructure and services as well as equality in the distribution of benefits among their inhabitants. ARUP's City Resilience developed universally acceptable, evidence based and measurable indicators universally applicable across cities of the globe with diverse backgrounds and physical locations to assess the ability of cities to persist and transform after experiencing shocks and stresses. The City Resilience Index could be a very useful tool for urban local authorities to assess their resilience capacity in the event of experiencing severe shocks and chronic stress.

Zimbabwe experienced significant economic decline after the year 2000 when government embarked on the FTLRP. National economic growth was severely curtailed. The period 2000 to 2009 has often been described as Zimbabwe's 'lost' decade. The decline of the national economy cascaded down to the cities including the City of Harare. The discussion on urban resilience in Harare has illustrated that city's infrastructure does not support or facilitate urban resilience. Political interference negatively affects smooth operations of the city which in turn incapacitate it to attain urban resilience. This is not only affecting the quality of life of Harare's residents but also threatening all the aspects of the urban environment in the city.

Conclusion Policy Options and Practical Recommendations

The chapter concludes that urban resilience of cities in Zimbabwe including the City of Harare hinges on the national economic recovery. It has been observed that Zimbabwe's economic recovery can be achieved if there is political will due to the following: Zimbabwe's good infrastructure (roads and railways), high literacy rate (89.41% of people aged 15 years and above), diversified economy as Zimbabwe is endowed with many natural resources, hardworking culture among the Zimbabwean people, possible investment flow from the UK and the Commonwealth due to colonial historical links and a significant number of Zimbabwean professionals in the diaspora eager to return home when economic recovery happens. National economic recovery will cascade down to local economies in cities. As soon as the cities begin to experience economic growth, they must prioritise the development of bulk urban infrastructure, a key foundation to resilient urban centres that reduces the environmental externalities of negative urban growth. Urban planning needs to take a central role in the structuring and management of the growth of cities being cognisant and sensitive of the central role that urban centres play in development as well as the environmental threats that they pose if not well planned, managed and supported by the necessary infrastructure. Political tolerance and harmony will facilitate creation of urban local governance structures which are autonomous and independent but working in harmony with central government.

References

ARUP International Development (2012) Visions of a Resilient City: Resilient Cities Scoping Study. ARUP and Engineers without Boarders-UK. London, UK.

— (2015) City Resilience Framework: Understanding City Resilience. ARUP International Development and Rockefeller Foundation. Retrieved from https://assets.rockefellerfoundation.org/app/uploads/20140410162455/City-Resilience-Framework-2015. Pdf. Accessed on 14/8/16.

Bogunovich, D. (2009) From planning sustainable cities to designing resilient urban regions. *Sustainable Development and Planning* IV, Vol. 1: 87-95.

Chelleri, L. (2012) From the Resilient City to Urban Resilience: A review essay on understanding and integrating the resilience perspective for urban systems. *Documents d'Anàlisi Geogràfica* Volume 58 (2): 287-306.

Chronicle, The. (2015). Cost of living up: CCZ. 10 November 2015 available at www.chronicle.co.zw/cost-of-living-up-ccz/ accessed on 1/08/2016.

da Silva, J, Kernaghan, S. and Luque, A. (2012) A system approach to meeting the challenges of urban climate change. International Journal of Urban Sustainable Development 4(2) 125-143.

Davoudi, S, Shaw, K, Haider, L. J. , Quinlan, A.E, Peterson, G. D, Wilkinson, C, Fünfgeld, H, McEvoy, D, Porter, L. and Davoudi, S. (2012) Resilience: A Bridging Concept or a Dead End? "Reframing" Resilience: Challenges for Planning Theory and Practice Interacting Traps: Resilience Assessment of a Pasture Management System in Northern Afghanistan Urban Resilience: What Does it Mean in Planning Practice? Resilience as a Useful Concept for Climate Change Adaptation? The Politics of

Resilience for Planning: A Cautionary Note, Planning Theory and Practice, 13:2, 299-333, DOI: 10.1080/14649357.2012.677124.

De Soto, H. The Mystery of Capital. Bantam Press, London. UK.

DFID (UK Aid) (2015) Urban infrastructure in Sub-Saharan Africa – Harnessing Land Values, Housing And Transport, Report on Harare Case Study Report No 1.9.

DiMSUR (2013) The City Resilient Action Planning Tool. DiMSUR and UN Habitat. Maputo, Mozambique.

Drobiank, A. (2012) The Urban Resilience: Economic Perspective. Journal of Economics and Management Volume 10. University of Katowice.

Environmental Management Authority (2014) Harare Wetlands Map. https://www.ema.co.zw/index.php/2014-06-12-03-51-59/2014-06-12-12-03-26/maps/60-harare-wetlands-map.html Accessed on 28/01/2018.

Folke, C, Carpenter, S. Elmqvist, T. Gunderson, L. Holling, C.S. and Walker, B. (2002) Resilience and Sustainable Development: Building Adaptive Capacity in a World of Transformations. *Ambio*, 31(5): 437- 440.

Godschalk, D. R. (2003) Urban Hazard Mitigation: Creating Resilient Cities. *Natural Hazards Review* 4(3): 136-143.

González, M. J. and De Lázaro, M. L. (2011) Urban Development and Sustainability. *European Journal of Geography* 1. Available at http://www.eurogeographyjournal.eu/articles/2_4_URBAN%20DEVELOPMENT%20%20AND%20SUSTAINABILITY_GONZ.pd. Accessed on 17/8/17.

Gunderson, L. H. and Holling C. S. (eds). (2002) Panarchy: Understanding Transformations in Systems of Humans and Nature. Island Press, Washington DC.

Financial Gazette, The. (2016) Zimbabwe's economic crisis depends. 24 March 2016. Available at www.financial gazette.co.zw/zimbabwes-economic-crisi-deepens/. Accessed on 1/08/16.

Harpham, T. Boateng, K. A. (1997) Urban Governance in relation to the operation of urban services in developing countries. *Habitat International*, Issue 1: 65-77.

Herald The. (2014) City floods after drain failure. 14 November 2014. http://www.herald.co.zw/city-floods-after-storm-drain-failure/ Accessed on 28/01/2018

Herald, The. (2015) Zim'o unemployment level up 11.3%. 13 April 2015. Available at www.herald.co.zw/zims-unemployment-level-up/. Accessed on 1/08/2016.

Harare Water and Sanitation (2015) Interviews Conducted with Officials from Harare and Water Sanitation, July 2015.

Holling, C. S. (1973) Resilience and stability of ecological systems. *Annual Review of Ecology and Systematics* 4: 1-23.

— (1996). Engineering Resilience versus Ecological Resilience». In: Schulze, P.C.

(1996). *Engineering within ecological constraints.* National Academy of Engineering

Press, 31-44.

Jabaree, Y. (2012) Planning the Resilient City: Concepts and Strategies for coping with Climate change and Environmental risk. Faculty of Architecture and Town Planning Technicon – Israel Institute of Technology, Haifa 32 000 Israel.

Klein, R. J. T, Nicholls, R. J. and Thomalla, F. (2003). Resilience to natural hazards: How useful is this concept? Environmental Hazards, 5(1), 35–45.

http://dx.doi.org/10.1016/j.hazards.2004.02.001Lamond

Lafferty, W.M. (Ed.) (2001) Sustainable Communities in Europe, Earthscan. London, U.K.

Lang, T. (2010) Urban Resilience and New Institutionary Theory – A happy couple for Urban and Regional Studies. *German Annual of Spatial Research and Policy.* 15-24. Available at http://www.springer.com/cda/content/document/cda_downl oaddocument/ Accessed on 17/8/17.

Manzungu, E, Mudenda-Damba, M, Madyiwa, S, Dzingirai, V. and Musoni, S. (2016) Bulk Water Supplies in the city of Harare-An endogenous form of privatisation of urban domestic water services in Zimbabwe? *Water Alternatives* 9 (1): 56-80.

Meerow, S. Newell, J. P and Stults, M. (2016) Defining Urban Resilience: A Review. *Landscape and Urban Planning.* Volume 147: 38-49. http://263chat.com/harare-city-acquires-20-refuse-collection-trucks/ Accessed on 28/01/18.

Mutongwizo, L. Harare City Council Acquires 20 Refuse Collection Trucks. 7 march 2017.

Musekiwa, A. (1993) Low-Income Housing Development in Harare: A Historical Perspective. In (Eds) Zinyama L.M, Tevera, D.S. and Cumming, S. D. Harare, The Growth and Problems of the City. Harare, University of Zimbabwe Publications.

Newsday (2016) Capacity utilisation to decline: ZNCC. 25 March 2016. Available at www.newsday.co.zw/2016/03/25/capacity - utilisation-decline-zncc/. Accessed on 1/08/16

OECD (2016) Draft Resilient Cities Report. Retrieved from http://www.oecd.org/cfe/regional-policy/resilient-cities.htm. Accessed on 31/12/17.

Pelling, M. (2011) Adapting to Climate Change. From Resilience to Adaptation. Routledge, New York, USA.

Rakodi, C. and Withers, P. (1993) Land, Housing and Urban Development in Zimbabwe: Markets and Policy in Harare and Gweru. University of Wales College of Cardiff, Department of City and Regional Planning.

Resilience Alliance (2007) Assessing and managing resilience in social-ecological systems: A practitioner's workbook. Retrieved from http://www.resalliance.org/576.php. Accessed on 13/8/17.

Romero, P, Lankao, Guatz, D. M. and Wilhelm, O. and Haylow, M. (2016) Urban Sustainability and Resilience: From Theory to Practice. *Sustainability* 2016, 8, 1224.

Scheffer, M, Carpenter, S, Foley, J. A, Folke, C and Walker, B. (2001) Catastrophic shifts in ecosystems. *Nature* 413:591-596.

Seeliger, L. and Turok, I. (2013) Towards Sustainable Cities: Extending Resilience with Insights from Vulnerability and Transition Theory. *Sustainability* Volume 5: 2108-2128.

Standard, The. (2015) Mahachi: The blue 'eyed boy' in hot soup. https://www.thestandard.co.zw/2015/08/31/mahachi-the-blue-eyed-boy-in-hot-soup/. Accessed on 3 January 2018.

Walker, B, Holling, C.S, Carpenter, S. R. and Kinzig, A. (2004). Adaptability and Transformability in Social-Ecological Systems. *Ecology and Society* 9(2).

World Bank (2012) Managing the Risks of Disasters in East Asia and the Pacific. Building Urban Resilience: Principles, Tools and Practice. The World Bank Group. USA, Washington DC.

— (2015) Investing in Urban Resilience: Protecting and Promoting Development in a Changing World. The World Bank, Washington DC.

USAID (2006) Concepts and practices of resilience compilation from various secondary sources. http://pdf.usaid.gov/pdf_docs/pnady190.pdf . Accessed on 14/08/17

United Nations (2010) World Urbanisation Prospects: The 2009 Revision. United Nations, Department of Economic and Social Affairs. Population Division. USA, New York.

UN-HABITAT (2009) Planning Sustainable Cities: Global Report on Human Settlements. United Kingdom, Earthscan.

Yanez, K. and Kernaghan, S. (2014) Briefing: Visions of a Resilient City. Proceedings of the Institution of Civil Engineers. Urban Design and Planning 167(3):95-101.

Zimbabwe Independent, The. (2008) Zimbabwe's Economic Revival Hangs in the Balance. 25 July 2008. https://www.theindependent.co.zw/2008/07/25/zimbabwes-economic-revival-hangs-in-the-balance/ Accessed on 16/8/2016

Zimbabwe Independent, The. (2016) Unemployment Levels in Zim a disaster in waiting. 12 August 2016. https://www.theindependent.co.zw/2016/08/12/unemployment-levels-zim-disaster-waiting/ Accessed on 31/08/16.

Zimbabwe Multi Donor Trust Fund (2015) Technical Assistance to the City of Harare for the Greater Harare Water and Sanitation Strategic Plan. Harare, Zimbabwe.

ZIMSTAT (Zimbabwe National Statistics Agency) (1992) National Census Report, Harare, ZIMSTAT.

— (2002) National Census Report, Harare, ZIMSTAT.

— (2012) National Census Report, Harare, ZIMSTAT.

Chapter 5

Resilience:
An Account of the Survival and Lifestyles of Street Children in Harare

Samson Mhizha & Patrick Chiroro

Introduction

The phenomenon of street children punctuating the cityscape of many urban areas is global, disquieting and escalating (Drane, 2010; Mhizha, 2010). Though the exact numbers of street children are elusive (Benitez, 2011) and impossible to quantify (UNICEF, 2005; Benitez, 2011), the figure almost certainly runs into tens of millions globally (UNICEF, 2005). It is indubitable that youth challenges in the twenty-first century are more chronic in Africa than elsewhere (Biaya, 2005; De Boeck and Honwana, 2005). The picture is strikingly grim with regards to the street children who have 'invaded' the public space of the streets of African expanding towns (Biaya, 2005) and have demonstrated tremendous creativity in making a living for themselves (De Boeck and Honwana, 2005). There seems to be an agreement that the challenge of youths in the twenty-first century is more acute in Africa than elsewhere (De Boeck and Honwana, 2005). The picture seems strikingly grim regarding the street children who have 'invaded' the public space of the streets of African expanding towns (Biaya, 2005). They have also demonstrated tremendous creativity in making a living for themselves (De Boeck and Honwana, 2005). This street children phenomenon is a trend characterising urban areas in developing countries all over the world (Strehl, 2010) and even the developed ones (Ennew, 203).

It is acknowledged that street children have elicited emotive public concern, received notable media coverage and have become a matter of priority global and national organisations for child welfare Both welfare and academic literature has stressed the dire scale of the global challenge, street children. It has endeavoured to analyse the background causes of this institution and enumerated the unique street children characteristics worldwide. It has also revealed the sheer outcomes of lifestyle in the streets on the children's development and health (Panter-Brick, 2002).

One of the assets the urban poor rely on is urban public space. As a place of trade and interaction, urban public space is key for the urban poor. Other than being key to urban poor's physical capital, it is key to their economic and social capital as well (Schernthaner, 2011). Therefore, having access to public space becomes a question of survival (Brown and Lloyd-Jones 2002). However, public space is subject to extensive regulation and control. It is contested and bound up with power relations existing between different groups (Brown and Lloyd-Jones 2002). In the last three decades of work and research on children and youth on the streets a shift of paradigms has taken place. The focus has recently been placed onto young people's agency and resiliency, seeing them as competent actors and agents of their own lives. Therefore, despite their limited opportunities and marginalization, young people on the streets still manage to assert resilience and agency over their lives and develop complex coping strategies to sustain their livelihoods. Hence, the children are not perceived as a problem – either as helpless victims or perpetrators of crimes – but as resilient competent social actors who interact with various environments (Ennew, 2003).

It is observed that street children around the world find themselves with no choice but to make a living for their own survival. They often emulate livelihood of their families, by it assuming roles traditionally played by their parents. It is imperative to pay particular attention to the economic livelihood of these vulnerable children. Past experiences have taught the international development community that various developmental needs of children and youth are interdependent and that dealing with one need in isolation from others is not effective (Kobayashi, 2004). In reality, for example, an economic livelihood is often inseparable from access to safety and physical health. It is also true for children and youths that their current welfare is a critical determinant of future welfare.

In Zimbabwe, the media and scholars alike have lamented the increase in population and menace of street children seen as 'uncouth' for their antisocial tendencies (Mhizha, 2010; Muchini,

2001; Ruparanganda, 2008). The upsurge in street children populace globally and particularly in Zimbabwe is a cause for concern. Street children are increasingly becoming a permanent mark in the morphology of Zimbabwean cities and growth points (Ruparanganda, 2008; Muchini, 2001). A warning has been heralded that street children are likely to even emerge in growth points and rural villages in Zimbabwe (Ruparanganda, 2008).

Arguably, the street children phenomenon in Zimbabwe has frequently been researched, but inadequately analysed by psychology researchers. It is revealed that a scrutiny of street children literature in Zimbabwe shows an outstanding lack of in-depth research on the lives and experiences of street children. The available literature on street children has paid significant attention to understanding street life experiences and aetiology (Ruparanganda, 2008). Nevertheless there is an astonishing lack of attention on the street children's career patterns (Karabanow, 2004). Studies have analysed the aetiology and outcomes of street childhood. These include abuse and trauma, poverty, family dysfunction, exploitation and alienation, addiction, child welfare inadequacies and mental health. However, the studies gave slight attention on how some of these street children complete the street career and shift away from street childhood (Karabanow, 2004). For Tyler (2008), street children are exposed invariably to early maltreatment which may lead them to engage in high-risk behaviour on the streets. Tyler goes on to say that the lifestyles and daily routines of homeless youth expose them to dangerous people and places, which creates the potential for crime opportunities and increased sexual victimisation. It is arguable that the lifestyles and lived experiences of homeless children further estrange them from their home families.

Purpose of the Study

The major aim was to explore the economic activities and lifestyles for the street children in the street of Harare.

Research Objectives
• To explore the economic activities engaged in by the streets children

97

- To explore the lifestyles that underlie the economic activities for the street children.

Research Questions

- What are the economic activities engaged in by street children?
- What lifestyles underlie the economic activities for the street children?

Operational Definitions and Terms

The current research adopts the widely-used definition of street children. The International Non-Governmental Organisation [Inter-NGO] (1983) defined street children as children yet to reach adulthood, for whom the street has become their habitat and source survival. This also include insufficient supervision, direction or protection by concerned adults (Mhizha, 2010). It is argued that this definition is all-encompassing but, it ignores diversity among the street children and the factors why they are the streets (Muchini, 2001). It is disaggregated between "children of the street" and "children on the street." The former entail street-living children who work and live in the streets while the latter entail street-working who work in the streets and live at home (UNICEF, 2003). These definitions have been useful and functional yet fraught with several challenges. Apparently, there is no clear distinction between those two categories hence its very tough identify the children who are street-working and those who are street-living (Muchini, 1994, 2001). Nonetheless, the categories are too narrow to cater for complexities of the phenomenon of street children. Lifestyles are the behavioural tendencies for a particular individual as they meet the challenges they face in life (Gaetz, 2004).

Theoretical Framework

To explain the resilience of the reunified former street children who are in schools, the researchers employed the Ecological Theory of Resilience by Ungar (2004, 2008, 2011). It has been found out that the Ecological Theory on Resilience better explain at-risk children's adaption to stresses in their lives (Malindi and Theron, 2010, 2015). The theory explains how individuals and environmental factors interact to result in resilience. Ecological theories focus on resilience as a reciprocal process between the individual and their social ecology in ways that enable the individual to access resources within their environment to cope (Ungar, 2011). To explain the phenomenon of resilience which influence the contextual development of resilience and our understanding of the manifestations of resilience in different cultures advanced four principles. These are principles of decentrality, complexity, atypical and cultural relativity (Ungar, 2011). The principles of atypicality and cultural relativity are key when it comes to street children's resilience (Malindi and Theron, 2010; Ungar, 2008, 2011; Theron and Malindi, 2010).

Principle 1: Decentrality

The principle of decentrality emphasises dominance of the environment over individual factors in determining resilience (Ungar, 2008, 2011). Therefore emphasis on resilience outcomes should be decentred from the individual to the environment (Ungar, 2011, 2013). Resilience presents more when there are facilitative environments and structures. It is also noted that scholars focus more on the resilience outcomes neglecting the processes leading to the resilience outcomes. The outcomes naturally focus on individuals neglecting the environment yet it is the environment that causes changes in the individuals. The environment cannot assume a secondary role. In resilience research, by focusing principally on individual factors, individuals are then blamed for not showing resilience even when the environment is toxic, a notion which several scholars have critiqued (Ungar, 2005, 2011).

Principle 2: Complexity

It is advanced that resilience is a multifaceted phenomenon that comprises various processes (Ungar, 2011). Scholars seem to focus only on protective factors and some desired outcomes neglecting rich information that can be generated by resilience studies. This information can enrich the body of knowledge on child development (Barton, 2005; Ungar, 2011). Indeed, a child cannot be resilient all the times and circumstances as shown by longitudinal studies on resilience (Phelps et al. 2007; Werner and Smith, 1982). The complexity in resilience studies arise from several processes that need to be considered when studying the resilience phenomenon. Scholars need to consider child's strengths, ecological factors and transactional patterns between the two and changes happening in the individual and in the child's environment. Protective variables that promote resilience also have differential effect on different people in diverse time and contexts.

Principle 3: Atypicality

The protective factors that promote resilience must not be classified as good or bad. The reason being the contextual ecologies in which protective processes emerge are not similar. A factor that can be regarded as dysfunctional in one setting can act as protective in another (Ungar, 2011). For instance, in a study on protective factors among African American children living in underprivileged neighbourhoods. It is shown that dropping out of school though viewed as dysfunctional was a protective variable for the children (Dei et al. 1997). Therefore, it is advanced the atypicality concept to warn people against using biased lens when assessing resilience variables in cultures or settings that are different from theirs. This is called hidden resilience (Ungar, 2008, 2011). Similarly, working on street children's stresses and coping strategies in Bombay, revealed that risky lifestyles and socially inappropriate behaviours by the children were indeed pathways to resilience (Kombarakaran, 2004). And street children were commonly labelled as at-risk (Kombarakaran, 2004:869). Therefore for many at-risk children, the deviant behaviours are indeed healthy adaptations that enable them to cope and survive unhealthy situations (Ungar, 2004). Indeed, it depends on who defines what constitutes protective resources, because the coping strategies can be unconventional yet do promote resilience to the youth at-risk (Ungar, 2004). Therefore, resilience is then conceptualised as a process and outcome which is context and culturally specific (Ungar, 2006:55). The children understand and explain their circumstances and behaviours greatly different ways than what is done by health professionals and society (Ungar, 2007).

The concept of hidden resilience was introduced and explained the principle of atypicality. It is believed to better explain street children's resilience (Ungar, 2004, 2008, 2011). Street children exhibit clear signs of resilience, albeit hidden (Malindi and Theron, 2010; Theron and Malindi, 2010; Malindi (2014). 'Hidden resilience' is a relatively novel concept. It refers to patterns of living that may not always fit in with mainstream psychological theories, or community conceptualisation, of socially appropriate behaviour, but that nevertheless encourage youth to bounce back from hardship (Ungar, 2004). Hidden resilience involves atypical behaviours bringing a sense of purpose, meaning and chances for participation in social activities. It brings a sense of attachment and belonging, financial stability, recreation, social and personal power, food, shelter and social support (Ungar, 2004). Resistance, deviance and other socially inappropriate behaviours displayed by the children are often pathways towards resilience though such actions explicitly oppose established norms and rules in a given setting (Bottrell, 2007). Examples of children withdrawing from school are given as an atypical coping mechanism that could affect normal developmental trajectories but understood by the child as protective despite the negative consequences. These are described as functional but culturally non-normative substitute adaptations hidden resilience (Ungar, 2004, 2008).

Principle 4: Cultural Relativity

The ecological theory of resilience depicts the coping strategies as entrenched in cultural systems (Ungar's, 2008, 2011). Culture refers to shared norms and values that guide a people's life patterns and while resilience expresses itself in culturally relevant ways. Custodians of culture in a certain setting normally guide people in that setting the guidance on how resilience can be expressed in that culture. It is critical to consider cultural variations in resilience studies while cultural lens have to be employed to appreciate the process of resilience. The atypical facet of resilience explained in discussed in principle 3 is closely related to the cultural relativity principle. This is because resilience tends to manifest differently depending on the existing ecologies and ways of life. People negotiate and navigate for resilience-promote resources in ways determined by culture (Ungar,

2011). Hidden resilience holds a key facet on the perspective of street children. It is the observation that street children are frequently supported ecologically towards resilience by kind strangers, social workers, strangers and NGOs (D'Abreu, Mullis and Cook, 1999; Kombarakaran, 2004). Earlier studies noted intrinsic assets that encouraged resilience in street youth that include ingenuity, tenacity and humour (Evans, 2002). However, recent studies have found other factors such as religiosity, stoicism and feistiness (Malindi and Theron, 2010; Theron and Malindi, 2010). The role of ecological protective resources in buffering the potentially harmful effects of risk processes is recognised (Armstrong, et al. 2005; Masten and Reed, 2005; Ward, Martin, Theron and Distiller, 2007). In other words, resilience involves the use the individual's physical and social ecologies to provide resilience-promoting resources and to negotiate culturally meaningful ways to share resilience resources (Ungar, 2008). In a study on resilience among street children in South Africa, it was reported that many traditions involve or include religious practices. Other cultural strategies for the street children included beliefs in ancestors (though contested), prayers and faith (Malindi and Theron, 2010; Theron and Malindi, 2010; Theron et al. 2011; Ungar, 2011; Oppong Asante, 2015). Faith or belief in a deity is a developmental and protective asset for children (Oliver, 2007:29). Involvement in church or religious activities and having a strong faith enabled resilient street children to have a sense of meaning in life (Theron and Malindi, 2007). It has been revealed that some black scholars were enabled by cultural practices involving ancestral worship as the students felt that they are not alone and were looked after (Dass-Brailsford, 2005).

Literature Review

It has been asserted the main reason street children are in the streets is to find food. The street children obtain food from bins or from scavenging through discarded food thrown away by supermarkets, restaurants and hotels (Makope, 2006). Street children sometimes cook their own food when they fail obtain adequate food from food outlets. The children put money together and buy relish and mealie-meal, cook and eat the food together. The relish is normally meat and vegetables. Additionally, street children use cardboard boxes and paper as plates for eating the food (Ruparanganda, 2008). The street children in Harare appeared to know all places where supermarkets, restaurants and takeaways drop their bins (Makope, 2006). Other children got food from drop-in centres (Muchini, 2001) while others were fed lunch by some churches and businesspeople (Mhizha, 2010). Some employees from hotels and takeaways throw filthy washing soap or dead rats into the bins that the food would not taste (Makope, 2006).

Street childhood has regularly been perceived as a vocation for the children's survival (Lankenaua et al. 2005). Indeed, these children are in the streets to eke a living. It is observed that the streets are an important source of the livelihood of the children. These children earned money through various piece jobs. These include cleaning the backyards of supermarkets, loading and off-loading commodities from vehicles, tending cattle for some business directors and cutting hedge and grass at the homes of many company directors (Muchini, 2001; Ruparanganda, 2008). Other economic activities for the street children include vending, begging, guarding cars, car-washing, taxi-touting and escorting blind parents (Muchini, 2001). Other economic activities for these street children included selling drugs, petty crimes, drug peddling and transactional sex (Makope, 2006). The drugs sold included marijuana and glue. These street children get too little money from the economic activities they engage in (UNICEF, 2003). The earned money is spent in paying school feels for siblings, procuring clothes and food (Muchini, 2001). Studies have indicated that economic activities have detrimental effects of child work on the physical and psychological development of children (Ennew, 2003). More so, the work done by some children; for example, unloading and loading vehicles, put great demand on their little calorific reserves (Muchini, 1994). This, together with poor nutrition and substance use, weakens their immunity to illnesses (Muchini, 1994).

One can reason that some types of work done by street children can certainly improve their psychological and physical health (Muchini, 1994, 2001). More, so families with street children can sometimes benefit in terms of earnings and remittances and can meet basic needs as the children contribute their earnings (Muchini, 2001). Additionally, some of the work done by the children can improve their physical strength hence improving their immunity to certain illnesses. Working and living in streets may nonetheless intellectual and academic progress as it affords them only little if any time for schooling at all (Muchini, 2001). Nevertheless, it is argued that street children work can be vital for their socialisation and also affords them necessary skills for potential jobs in the future. This can apply for the children who accompany and work with their vending parents (Muchini, 2001). Furthermore, schooling can limit their informal employment prospects as unemployment rates skyrocket in Zimbabwe. Studies also show that relationships with family members improve once the children start working on the streets (Muchini, 2001).

A study was conducted on street capital using a sample of American street children. It was found out that children acquire street capital which is latent knowhow and skill developed through experiences and observations within the streets. However, this street capital is linked to sexual activity, drug use and criminal behaviour which enables the street youths to acquire the skills on how to survive in the streets (Lankenaua et al. 2005). It is further identified that street children acquire competencies to survive in the streets which are concrete skills. The actions emerging from the acquisition of street capital, include trading in drugs, shop lifting and commodifying sexual activity. These authors argue that the street competencies enable the street children to eke a living in the street economy and develop cohesion in the social connections (street-living and non-street living) in the streets. Through these skills, the street children acquire street vocations linked with street economy, such as drug trade (Lankenaua et al. 2005). Similarly, it is observed that street children acquire street credit, which he defined as the status or credibility one acquires by performing illegal, violent and or bold behaviours acts. For instance, the male street children show street credit to the public by beating up female street children. Female street children got money and food through transactional sex with many (Flynn, 2008).

It is maintained that the lifestyles adopted by street children in the streets serve many purposes. The purposes enabling their survival and victimising the children further. It is concluded that risky lifestyles adopted by street children worsen their wellbeing and their chances of getting out of the streets. It is acculturation to the street economy and the streets with the time one spends in the streets with fellow street peers has been demonstrated. Without social service intervention, there is an increased likelihood of repeated exposure to trauma and victimisation (Gaetz, 2004). In a study of street children in America, it was found that street children acquire engage in certain lifestyles which involve acquisition of street capital. The lifestyles include sexual activity, drug use, drug peddling, violence, mobility, shoplifting and criminal behaviour which enables the children to develop survival strategies within the street economy (Lankenaua et al. 2005).

Studies on street children have shifted from their vulnerability and unhealthy environment to their rights to work in the streets and their resourcefulness and enterprise (Panter-Brick, 2002; O'Kane, 2003). These studies have shown, the children at times juggle several activities in a day as they respond to shifting demands (Thomas de Benitez, 2008). They also exploit seasonal opportunities, tourist resorts and cultural carnivals (Bordonaro, 2010) or even acquiring cunning survival strategies like blagging which involves inducing people to give them money or food (Smeaton, 2009). The children develop street careers (Lankenaua et al. 2005) as the children display agency involving survival strategies restricted and challenging street situations where there are a few viable options (Bordonaro, 2010). While street work involves agency, there is no resilience. This include even when fleeing from abuse at home, adversity or parental death at home since street living is not a successful outcome from the perspective of child development. Street work can have different experiences and meanings for different children. These differences include survival, forced labour, coping strategy, career and opportunity and to different individual street children. The differences also depend on the children's unique variables such as sex, age, individual aspirations, local conditions and their street situations. Use of psychoactive substances can also be interpreted as a coping strategy which is a form of positive agency involving assessing risks (O'Kane, 2003).

The current study which focuses on the economic activities and survival strategies for street children in Harare employs the Street Capital Theory by Bourdieu (1977; 1990) Bourdieu developed his

105

theory on street capital to explain the behaviours of people who lived and worked in the streets. This also encompass the developed social capital which they employed as they sought to make a living in the streets. The street capital includes cultural capital and social capital. Cultural capital involves the knowledge, competence, skills and objects given value in a street culture. These include violence, drug abuse and peddling, territoriality, violence, substance use, lying, entrepreneurship skills, streetism (being dirt to beg and using infants and young children. The concept street capital was developed by the researcher Pierre Bourdieu (see, for instance, Bourdieu 1977; 1985; 1990). Street capital is: The concept is used to capture the 'cultural capital' of a violent street culture. In a study of street children in America, it was found that street children acquire street capital which is latent knowledge developed through experiences and observations in the streets (Lankenaua et al. 2005). Street capital is tied to sexual activity, drug use, drug peddling, shoplifting, housing contingencies and criminal behaviour that enable the children to develop survival strategies within the street economy (Lankenaua et al. 2005). These street competencies which also include commodifying sex is acquired through street social networks. Social capital involves how the street youths become embedded in criminal communities and 'recapitalise' their diminished social capital through social networks among themselves and with non-street people". A study conducted in Moscow on street children showed that street children develop social capital in the streets which helps them to adjust to life. It argued that the street children gradually acquire the social capital that is useful there such as criminal ways (Stephenson, 2001). The underworld community provides protection in some sense and possibilities to cope with without the services of the larger society.

Resilience, a difficult term to define (Theron and Dunn, 2010), has attracted much research focus in recent years. It has stimulated researchers to define and study it (Liebenberg and Ungar, 2009; Malindi, 2014; Malindi and Theron, 2010; Masten, 2014; Theron and Malindi, 2010, Theron, 2009; Ungar, 2004, 2008, 2011). Itself related to positive psychology's emerging emphasis of the necessity to reconceptualise risk, resilience has even received more focus in recent years (Theron, 2012). Still disputed though, resilience is described as adaptive behaviour in the face of adverse situations whether chronic or acute, denoting one's ability to overcome adversity (Masten, 2001; Theron, 2008). Conventionally, street children are not perceived as resilient. Rather, as vulnerable, deviant and maladaptive youth who suffer from various psychological disorders (Malindi, 2014; Swart-Kruger, 1994; Guernina, 2004). Their lifestyles and risk are regarded as virtually synonymous. Besides the complex social and familial risks that compel street children to choose life on the streets, they are vulnerable to all types of added risks. These include careless motorists, lack of shelter, drugs, rude police officers, prostitute syndicates, criminality and abuse from fellow older street youth (Swart-Kruger, 1994; Human Rights Watch, 2003). It is argued that street children are perceived predominantly from medical perspective illuminating their vulnerabilities and the charity paradigm intending to save them from the adversities. These perspectives perceive street children to be psychosocially and physically vulnerable to development of psychopathology overlooking the strengths and assets that enable street children to cope resiliently amid adversity (Malindi, 2014). The vulnerabilities are believed to arise from their exclusion from shelter, families, health facilities and other facilities (Bourdillon, 2001; Kombarakaran, 2004; Theron, 2012). More lately, some developing literature has started to contest the view that street children as hapless and helpless (Cockburn, 2004; Donald et al. 2006; Bottrell, 2007; Conticini and Hulme, 2007). Researchers have since been conducted deploying resilience to explain adaptation to stresses in the lives of street children (Theron, 2012; Malindi; 2014; Malindi and Cekiso, 2014). They portrayed them as masterful children who grapple with the diversity anticipating to override pathology and maladjustment (Donald and Swart-Kruger 1994, Kombarakaran 2004; Theron, 2012).

Methodology

The current study being explorative employs a qualitative research approach as the research design. The current research employs qualitative methods approach to generate data on how the street children eked a living in the streets. The present study combines semi-structures interviews and key informant interviews with visual methods. Interviews remain emblematic of qualitative research. They afford participants the opportunity to talk more or less expansively about their lives (Ennew, 2003). This approach is qualitative and phenomenological. It involves detailed analysis of the lifeworld of the respondent and endeavours to explore personal and subjective experiences. It also focus on individual respondent's personal account and perception of any phenomenon different from attempts to give objective views of the phenomenon itself. One of the co-author's Doctor of Philosophy study led to this study.

There were 28 participants in the sample of the study, 14 street children and 11 key informant interviewees. The 11 key informant interviewees were adults' street dwellers, officials from a drop-in centre for street children, social welfare officers and community services officers from Harare City Council. The researchers felt that they would exhaust the various categories and dimensions in the current study after interviewing 28 participants. The study employed purposive sampling in recruiting the participants for the current study. Purposive sampling is influenced by multiple dimensions, such as time or availability (Strauss and Corbin, 1998). It is also influenced by nature of the topic, scope of the study, or amount of useful information obtained from each participant (Morse, 1994). The 28 participants were a size that ensured theoretical sampling was reached (Charmaz, 2014).

The current research, since it is qualitative hybrid method approach, employs a number of data collection methods to collect valid data. Semi-structured interviews and key informant interviews. The researchers sought to analyse in detail how participants perceive and make sense of their lives. Therefore, it requires a flexible data collection instrument. Use of semi-structured interviews is justified by their regard as primary means by which make sense of the world and their inhabitation. . For example, it is argued that narratives or stories can be described as a sense-making tool, as they have the ability to depict our experience of this world and us within this world (Morse, 1994). Therefore, the act of narrating is an act of meaning, as people struggle to make sense and show the different choices they made and how they dealt with them (Strauss and Corbin, 1998). This understanding of narrative relates to the study's aim to explore how people construct meaning in their perspectives on their everyday economic activities.

Consent was sought from gatekeepers of the street children who include the Ministry of Social Welfare, the Harare City Council and drop-in centre officials. Informed consent from the participants was obtained from the respondents and involved assuring them that they could terminate the interview at any time. Researchers also clearly spelt out and adhered to confidentiality and anonymity.

The study used Interpretive Phenomenological Analysis as the data analysis method. In this method, the researchers learnt about the respondent's psychological world in the form of constructs and beliefs that were provided by the participants (Smith, 1996). The data analysis focused upon the generation of explanation and common themes that arose from the transcripts. Codes were assigned to the themes which reflected the shared perceptions among respondents of the investigated phenomena (in this case, the economic activities and lifestyles among the street children).

Results

The analysis of the data revealed various themes which are presented in the present section. The data was analysed and hereby presented in line with the research objectives which are to explore the economic activities engaged in by the streets children and to explore the lifestyles that underlie the economic activities for the street children. Essentially the results revealed that the street children develop resilience to survive on the streets.

Picking food from the bins was a predominant economic activity for the streets children. Key informants revealed that poverty and drought drive some children into the streets as they source food on their own. One 55 year-old key informant interviewee narrated that how someone may want to buy food worth 50 cents but may not be able to as the cheapest costs $1. Therefore, they buy the food for a $1 but eat a portion worth the 50cents and discards the rest. In the streets, there are not dogs which eat left overs while some people do not chew bones.

Therefore the street children find food through picking it from the bins. One social worker working with the children on reunifying them said that when taking them sometimes they hear these children saying that they have money on them. She recalled one child saying the she had about $7 in a drain near the Joina City.

It emerged from the current study that some street children earned money through transactional sex. This was a predominant economic activity for female street children. Some of them revealed that they patronized night clubs and beer halls where they got clients while others claimed that they loitered at strategic points where clients came looking for them. The area around the Railway station especially inside the unused railway cabins. The girls also engage in sex work in the streets. Prominent business people lure the children to shoot videos and can be paid about $20 yet the videos can cost $1000. A 50-year old key informant interviewee noted that most female street children are 'night angels' who can have sex with all men from all walks of life and earn a living from that.

It also emerged that some children engaged in street vending selling various commodities in the streets. The commodities included cigarettes, food stuffs such as eggs, drugs like marijuana and cocaine. It was revealed that drug dealers used some male street children knowing that they would be suspected to be peddling in drugs. It emerged, the children sometimes peddle cocaine with a single line of cocaine 10cm long going for $60. It further emerged that drug traders prefer these young children knowing that people cannot suspect them of drug peddling and still they can be convicted of the behaviour if arrested because of their age.

Begging was also a predominant economic activity for street children. This involved asking for money from those passing by and motorists at strategic areas such as busy streets, road intersections and traffic lights. For those who begged, company of little children enticed more sympathy. It was revealed that beggars hired the little children from other street parents for a fee. Therefore, begging was lucrative for the younger ones or for parents who moved around with younger children. The respondents revealed that younger children were regarded as cash cows because they earned more money through begging since they elicit more sympathy from well-wishers. They maintained a dirty appearance to appear genuine street children and more pathetic. A 55-year old key informant interviewee revealed that it is possible for children from food insecure families to run to the streets and pick discarded food from the bins. They can beg for that food while one is about to discard it or worse, they can ask for it while they are still eating. Some just give such children.

Many male street eked a living though parking, washing and guarding cars. This was a predominant economic activity for male children. The children fought over parking bays which they claimed to own though all parking bays in Harare city centre were owned either by the city council or owners of the building close by. The children also made money from washing cars, kombis and buses in the city centre and in Mbare Bus terminus. Finally, the children also earned money through guarding cars especially at night and even during the day as they parked the cars. It was revealed, the children guard cars at night clubs getting a $1 per car the whole night. If a child guards 10 cars they get $10 dollars a night.

The street children also engaged in many piece jobs in and around the city centre. The piece jobs included loading and unloading trucks at wholesale and retail shops around the city centre. They also carried luggage from shops to bus termini, from one terminus to another, or to baggage owners' cars. Occasionally, street children would be hired to work in fields of some residents around the Central Business District even though it was an unpopular economic activity among them. In relation was the practice of renting-out children. It was revealed that some youths who had children in the streets hired them out for a fee of about $1 per day. Hence, more children, more money by renting them out. Related to this was the concept of demanding fees from street children living or working at their base. Also 'married' or 'cohabiting' ale children would send their partners to engage in transactional sex and bring the money to them.

Some children engaged in stealing. This involves snatching money and food from fellow and younger street children. The street children also stole items from members of the public and these items included mobile phones, food, money clothes such as hats and other items like umbrellas. The stolen items were used, or resold particularly to thieves in the city centre. Some street children were connected to underground activities in the city and would sell the stolen loot to some thieves. It also emerged that street children who were sent to schools in rural areas such as Mazowe and Chiredzi even stole crops and small livestock from communities who lived close to those schools. Such children were even earned nicknames 'goat thieves' after having been found stealing goats in such communities.

The children maintained networks with both street living and non-street living people. Children in the streets had groups or bands who stayed and worked collectively. These bands secured their own living and working bases. The children from the same band or base helped each other in buying food, dissemination of information, training on street behaviours and self-defence. Data showed, a new entrant into the streets is initially confused by the life but later received assistance from fellow peer street children. A 55-year old key informant interviewee commented on a male child who fled from Buhera to live in the streets. He lamented that initially the child is confused as they wonder what they will eat and where they will sleep. Such a child can contemplate returning home. However, he said he soon met peers who stopped him from going back. They forbade him from going back home where he was going to herd cattle the whole day and be denied food. These taught him how to get food and even advised them about begging, picking food from bins and doing piece jobs in the nearby plots. He was told that was better than herding cattle for nothing.

The 50-year old key informant interviewee commented that the day one enters the streets they are welcomed by what he termed the 'Boko Haram' (the street delinquents or street gangs). After just two or three days, the children are initiated into street lifestyles and street survival habits. They have different members who can teach different skills.

In starting living in the streets, the children appropriate bases for sleeping, keeping their possessions and economic activities such as vending, begging or parking cars. This appropriation of bases goes with joining peer groups who would have been using such bases. Therefore the children are received by fellow children.

Street children have also been found to network with non-street urban communities. The children have been reported to relate with drug traders whose drugs they sell for commission. The children also sold worked for some adult businesspeople and vendors. They provided them with accommodation and hired them to sell their food items such as groundnuts, buns and other items for a 10 percent commission. One middle-aged woman who vend her commodities through these street children in Mbare was arrested. Some children knew certain shop owners, NGOs, churches and certain benevolent individuals they approached for assistance in form of money, food, bathing facilities and clothes. Some street children also reported networked with thieves, they would steal and sell their loot to these thieves. Street children know persons to approach when selling any commodity. Other children acquired drugs from drug peddlers and sold them on commission.

One survival strategy for children living and working in the streets involved lying. Lying involved telling lies when begging to elicit sympathy to be given donations. The children also invariably used wrong names to avoid identification or arrest. Some children engaged in blagging which involved lying to elicit sympathy when begging.

The data revealed that violence was employed as a survival strategy among the street children. The violence was exhibited to both fellow street children and members of the public. This violence has a utility value used when stealing from fellow street children. It has already been revealed that younger street children make more earnings through begging than their older peers. Therefore, older street children could snatch money and food from the younger ones who have more money. Even street children who make more earnings through vending could have their earnings snatched from them. The street children especially the males also snatch food, money and other items such umbrellas and necklaces for resale. Indeed, it was revealed that violence has a significant survival value for the older and male street children. These male street children especially those who were leaders of the working and sleeping bases would sometimes demands fees from the female or younger male street children for protection. The older male street children would also use violence to get fees from Female Street children they 'married' but would send or allow to engage in transactional sex and give them the money.

Related to lying was the preponderance of criminal behaviours among the streets children. Some of the children started criminal behaviours before getting to the streets. Delinquency was a significant reason some of the children left home to leave in the streets. The children's tendency to go against the law was important.

Living in the streets was illegal. The criminal behaviours committed by the streets children included stealing, sexual abuse of female children (rape) and younger male children (sodomy). Other crimes included substance use and drug peddling, shop lifting and physical assault. Some of these criminal behaviours helped the children earn incomes.

The street children also engaged also seemed to own and defend working and sleeping bases. These bases were acquired and defended using violence sometimes. Trespassing in these bases is not tolerated. In Harare the economic activities go with geographical areas. The working bases in at the periphery of the city centre were associated with begging, sniffing glue and stealing while those in uptown are associated with vending and drug peddling. Sleeping bases in the CBD are associated more with male street children who work and sleep there. Female street children are found in bases in Avondale, Kensington, Mukuvisi, next to the Railways Station and behind Vehicle Inspectorate Department (VID). Female children prefer secluded bases to access water for bathing and washing. The female street children chose the base leaders for protection from having sex with other male children at the base. For females, sometimes they build shacks for warmth and privacy.

The data revealed that substance use is a key element of street childhood. Both key informants and street children respondents revealed that children used substances to deal with worries and to be able to commit crimes such as stealing. The substances were also used to withstand adverse conditions such as cold weather and rain. Younger street children used substances such as glue. Older street children used tablets prescribed for mental health patients, popular local illicit brews such as *kachasu, zed, musombodia* (prepared using fertilizer and rotten fruits) and *zava zava* (prepared using onions). The other drugs they use include marijuana, hashish, different types of cough mixtures like *histalix* and *broncleer*. An ordinary person would only need just two teaspoons of these cough syrups and may sleep but the street children can drink two or three 500ml bottles of 500ml at once. Hard-core abusers of substances would mix those cough syrups with prescription drugs for mental disorders such as G5 and *maragadu*. The children also take hard liquor they refer to as blue diamond which has 60% alcohol content and they take it without dilution. The street children's need for drugs to manage the adversities of the street and gain the courage to steal is alarming. Most of them spent majority of their earnings on purchasing drugs. For the street children to steal they need to take those psychoactive substances which give them courage to steal.

Some attend courses such as carpentry and sewing. Some end getting jobs. Some children do attend informal lessons offered by NGOs in the streets, while others took up offers from the same NGOs to get training in vocational courses such as mechanics, sewing, farming and carpentry. Some did not complete those courses while others did not regularly attend. Other street children were enrolled into formal schools. Some of the street children completed their primary school and others secondary with such assistance. Notably, some street children some even passed their advanced level education. One student completed her advanced her advanced level with 15 points and enrolled for Accounting at one of the major universities in the country. One male street child got 12 points and enrolled for honours in Administration and has even started working at one of the NGOs that help the street children. One female enrolled for sewing course at one of the NGOs that help the street children. She completed the training and got employment during the course of fieldwork for this study.

Discussion

The findings revealed that street children engaged in many economic activities to eke a living in the streets. These economic activities included transactional sex, vending, begging, dug peddling, carrying luggage, picking food from bins and stealing. The study also identified that street children take responsibility of their food and accommodation as they lack adult guardianship. The economic activities tally with what literature indicated. It has been shown that street children engage in activities such as vending, begging, guarding cars, car-washing, taxi-touting and escorting blind parents (Muchini, 2001; Makope, 2006). Other economic activities for these street children included selling drugs, petty crimes, drug peddling and transactional sex (Makope, 2006). The lifestyles exhibited by street children in the streets enabled them to engage in various economic activities. The survival strategies that emerged from the current study included territoriality, maintaining social networks with street living peers and non-street living people, violence, substance abuse and lying. These behaviours may not provide them with food or money but made sure that they were better able to use economic activities effectively to get money and food. These lifestyles also resonate with literature.

The data from the current study revealed that street children indeed develop street capital. It is the competency and knowledge necessary to make a living in the streets with own subculture (Bourdieu, 1977, 1990). The data showed that street children acquire resources and survival strategies than enable them to survive the hardships in the streets where they have fend for themselves without parental or guardian assistance.

Conclusion and Recommendations

The study has shown that street children are resilient and resourceful in eking a living in the streets. Street children engage in various activities to sustain themselves since they lack adult guardianship. The children also engage in survival behaviours which also enable economic activities for them in the streets. These behaviours include violence, maintaining social networks, lying, stealing and maintaining territories. The study has shown that the children have developed resilience and agency to decide for themselves as they seek to sustain their lives. The limited context where the children's stay is not only prohibited but their economic activities are illegal worsens their vulnerability.

The following recommendations are suggested. There should be reform in the family systems in Zimbabwe which provide sustainable livelihoods at home. Parents and schools should be conscientised to avoid neglect, harsh punishment methods and abuse as that can force the children to develop resiliency and eke a living outside family systems. Schools should offer relevant education that guarantees future employment opportunities. Parents and school authorities should be trained on how to detect and help children who are at risk of becoming street children. It is also suggested that vocational and life skills should be taught to street children to provide them with opportunities for employment and resilience. The life and vocational schools should then impart on the children the adverse effects of certain economic activities and survival strategies they engage in. The life skills should teach the children knowledge and decision-making on sexuality, sexual rights, reproductive health, child rights and the related responsibilities, criminality, violence, child exploitation, psychopharmacology, critical thinking, self-awareness, coping with stress and interpersonal relations. The teaching should be imparted by sensitive and child-friendly teachers. The vocational training should open vocational pathways for the street children as they seem to be closed from the formal education and employment systems. Indeed, there should not be stigmatization for the street children that they must be absorbed by the employment systems in the country. Schools and vocational training centres must stop labelling and stigmatising the street children and should provide informal, unique and career-oriented education. The vocational skills to be taught should include farming, manual printing, sewing, candle-making, brickwork, carpentry, knitting, craftwork, computers literacy, sports, shoe manufacture, mechanics, welding, theatre arts and sporting activities to inculcate self-sustenance in the children. This social disaffiliation is further worsened by the street children's lack of access to health facilities in times of illness as well as leaving away from family or home. Indeed, school attendance is closely associated with access to health facilities and to home environments.

References

Biaya, T. (2005). Youth and Street Culture in Urban Africa. In Alcinda Honwana and Filip de Boeck (eds.) *Makers and Breakers. Children and Youth in Postcolonial Africa.* Oxford: James Currey.

Bourdieu, P. (1977): *Outline of a Theory of Practice.* Cambridge: Cambridge University Press.

Bourdieu P. (1985): *The genesis of the concepts of habitus and field.* Sociocriticism 2: 11– 24.

Bourdieu, P. (1990): *The Logic of Practice.* Stanford: Stanford University Press.

Bordonaro, L.I. (2010) 'From home to the street: Cape Verdean children street migration', in Evers, S.J.T.M, C. Notermans and E. van Ommering (eds) *African children in focus: A paradigm shift in methodology and theory?* Leiden: Netherlands African Studies Association and Brill Academic Publishers

Brown, A.M.B and Lloyd-Jones, Tony (2002). *Spatial planning, access and infrastructure. In*: Rakodi, C.I and Lloyd-Jones, T (Eds). Urban livelihoods: A people-centred approach to reducing *poverty*, London: Earthscan, pp. 188-204.

Charmaz, K. C. (2014). Constructing grounded theory (2nd ed.). Thousand Oaks, CA: Sage

Ennew, J. (2003). Difficult circumstances: Some reflections on 'street children' in Africa. *Children, Youth and Environments, 13* (1), 128-146.

Flynn, K.C. (2008). Street credit: The cultural politics of African street children's hunger. In C. Counihan and P. V. Esterik (Eds.), Food and culture: A reader (pp.554-571). New York, NY: Routledge.

Honwana, A and de Boeck, F (2005). *Makers and Breakers. Children and Youth in Postcolonial* Africa. Oxford: James Currey.

Thomas de Benitez, S. and Hiddleston, T. (2011). *Research paper on the promotion and protection of the rights of children working and/or living on the street: OHCHR 2011 Global Study.* Geneva: OHCHR

Drane, M. (2010) 'Street children as unaccompanied minors with specialized needs: deserving *recognition* as a particular social group', *New England Law Review*, Summer.

Karabanow, J. (2004). Being young and homeless: Understanding how youth enter and exit street life. New York: Peter Lang.

Kobayashi. Yoko. (Mar.2004). Economic Livelihoods for Street Children: A Review. HIV/AIDS Response Teams. Development Alternatives

Lankenau, S.E, Michael C. Clatts, D. Welle, Lloyd A. G and Marya, V.G. (2005). Street careers: homelessness, drug use and sex work among young men who have sex with men (YMSM).International Journal of Drug Policy no. 16 (1):10-18.

Liebenberg, L. and Ungar, M. (2009). Introduction: The challenges in researching resilience. In L. Liebenberg and M. Ungar (Eds.),

Researching Resilience (pp. 3-25). Toronto, Ontario, Canada: University of Toronto Press.

Liebenberg, L. and Ungar, M. (2014). A comparison of service use among youth involved with juvenile justice and mental health. *Children and Youth Services Review, 39*, 117-122.

Makope, V. (2006). A Zimbabwean street story. Harare: German Agro Action.

Malindi MJ. (2014) "Exploring the roots of resilience among female street-involved children in South Africa". *Journal of Psychology 5* (1), 35-45

Malindi MJ and Cekiso Madoda P. (2014) "Exploring the lived experiences of children-of-the-street in Mthatha". *Journal of Sociology and Social Anthropology (5* (3) 339-347

Malindi, M. J. and Theron, L. C. (2010). The Hidden Resilience of Street Youth. *South African Journal of Psychology, 40*, 318–326.

Mann, G. (2001). Networks of Support: A Literature Review of Care Issues for Separated Children. Save the Children UK.

Masten, A. S. (2001). Ordinary Magic: Resilience Processes in Development. *American Psychologist, 56*, 227-238.

Masten, A. S. (2014). Global Perspectives on Resilience in Children and Youth. *Child Development, 85*, 6-20.

Mhizha, S. (2010*). The Self-image of adolescent street children in Harare.* Unpublished Masters Thesis, University of Zimbabwe, Harare, Zimbabwe.

Morse, J. M. (1994). Designing funded qualitative research. In N. K. Denzin and Y. S. Lincoln (Eds.), Handbook of qualitative research (pp. 220-235). Thousand Oaks, CA: Sage Publications

Muchini, B. (1994). Morality and Street Children in Harare. Thesis submitted in partial fulfilment of the requirements for the Master of Philosophy Degree Programme in Psychology at the University of Zimbabwe. March 1994 (Unpublished).

Muchini, B. (2001). *A Study on Street Children in Zimbabwe.* Retrieved February 6, 2007, from
http://www.unicef.org/evaldatabase/index_23256.html

O'Kane, C. (2003) Street and working children's participation in programming for their rights: conflicts arising from diverse perspectives and directions for convergence', *Children, Youth and Environments*, 13 (1), 167-183

Panter-Brick, C. (2002) "Street Children, Human Rights and Public Health: A Critique and Future Directions," Annual Review of Anthropology, No. 31, 147- 171.

Ruparanganda, W. (2008). *The tragedy of procrastinating? A case study of sexual behaviour patterns of street youth of Harare, Zimbabwe: In the era of HIV and AIDS Pandemic.* Unpublished doctoral thesis, University of Zimbabwe, Harare, Zimbabwe.

Schernthaner, M (2011). The struggle to belong. Dealing with diversity in 21st century urban settings. Coming of age the streets: An exploration of the livelihoods of street youth in Durban. Paper presented at the International RC21 conference 2011.

Smeaton E. (2009) *Off the radar: Children and young people on the streets in the UK,* Sandbach: Railway Children.

Smith, J. A. (1996). Beyond the divide between cognition and discourse: Using interpretative phenomenological analysis in health psychology. Psychology and Health, 11, 261-271

Stephenson, S (2001). "Street Children in Moscow: Using and Creating Social Capital." Sociological Review 49(4): 530-548

Strauss, A. and Corbin, J. (1998). Basics of qualitative research: Techniques and procedures for developing grounded theory. Thousand Oaks, CA: Sage Publications

Strehl, T. (2010) Street-Working and Street-Living Children in Peru: Conditions and Current Interventions. Leiden: IREWOC

Theron, L. C. (2008). Resilient Coping Strategies. In L. Wood (Ed.). *Dealing with HIV/AIDS in the Classroom* (pp. 88–107). Cape Town, South Africa: Juta.

Theron, L. C. (2009). Empowering Children and Adolescents with ADHD to be Resilient. In A. Decaires-Wagner and H. Picton (Eds.), *Teaching and ADHD in the Southern African Classroom* (pp. 178–184). Northlands, South Africa: Macmillan.

Theron, L. C. (2012). Resilience Research with South African Youth: Caveats and Ethical Complexities. *South African Journal of Psychology, 42,* 333–345.

Theron, L. C. and Dunn, N. (2010). Enabling White, Afrikaans-Speaking Adolescents towards Post-Divorce Resilience: Implications for Educators. *South African Journal of Education, 30,* 231–244.

Theron, L. C. and Malindi, M. J. (2010). Resilient Street Youth: A Qualitative South African Study. *Journal of Youth Studies, 13* (6), 717_736

Tyler, K. (2008). Social network characteristics and risky sexual and drug related behaviours among homeless young adults. Sociology Department, Faculty Publications. Paper 47.

Ungar, M. (2004). *Nurturing Hidden Resilience in Troubled Youth.* Toronto: University of Toronto Press.

Ungar, M. (2008). Resilience across Cultures. *British Journal of Social Work, 38*, 218-235.

Ungar, M. (2011). The Social Ecology of Resilience: Addressing Contextual and Cultural Ambiguity of a Nascent Construct. *American Journal of Orthopsychiatry, 81*(1), 1-17.

United Nations Children's Fund. (2003). *Hope never dries up: Facing the challenges. A situational assessment analysis of children in Zimbabwe 2002.* Harare: United Nations Children's Fund

UNICEF. (2005) State of the World's Children 2006: Excluded and Invisible. New York: UNICEF.

Chapter 6

Community Resilience and the Sustainable Development Goals in Zimbabwe

Joseph Kamuzhanje

Introduction

The Sustainable Development Goals[1] (SDGs), officially known as "Transforming our World: the 2030 Agenda for Sustainable Development", are an intergovernmental set of aspirational Goals with 169 targets. The SDGs act as the Post 2015 Development Agenda (successor to the Millennium Development Goals). On 19 July 2014, the UN General Assembly's Open Working Group on Sustainable Development Goals (SDGs) forwarded a proposal for the SDGs to the Assembly. The proposal contained 17 goals with 169 targets covering a broad range of sustainable development issues. This chapter discusses the potential challenges that should be considered as various stakeholders focus on building resilience using the Sustainable Development Goals (SDG) as the base.

The chapter's main argument is that potential resilience challenges are at different levels and should be contextualised in that regard. Communities should be central to the understanding and addressing of resilience challenges. The discussion emanates from the assessment done on implementation of the Millennium Development Goals (MDG), which are the predecessors of the SDGs. while the MDGs achieved much success, there is still a long way to go in reducing and eventually eradicating poverty. It is further argued that some of the failure of the MDGs can be attributed to poor understanding of challenges and factors that affected earlier interventions in their implementation (Sachs, 2012). Hence, the need to learn from the experiences of MDGs to increase the chances of success of SDGs. The chapter first briefly introduces SDGs and provides a conceptual if not analytical framework of resilience in

---

[1] The Sustainable Development Goals Report 2016, United Nations

SDGs context. It then discusses the resilience context in Zimbabwe dating back to the pre-independence period. The discussion sets the basis for potential barriers to the successful implementation of the SDGs. While there are several barriers, the chapter recognises the success stories. Three cases from different parts of Zimbabwe are presented before the chapter concludes with a discussion on emerging issues.

The Conceptual Framework

Resilience is the ability of countries, communities and households to manage change, by maintaining or transforming living standards in the face of shocks or stresses. These include earthquakes, drought or violent conflict - without compromising their long-term prospects (DFID, 2012). This definition is linked closely to the definition for sustainable development (Bruntland Commission, 1987). Sustainable development concentrates on development today without compromising the ability of future generations to benefit from the same resources.[2] Global Alliance for Resilience Initiative (AGIR), defines resilience as the capacity of vulnerable households, families and systems to face uncertainty and risk of shocks, to withstand and respond effectively to shocks, recover and adapt sustainably.[3] The common thread running through the three definitions is that they place the affected people at the centre of addressing the causes of their vulnerability. Therefore, realising affected communities withstand the worst of disasters, their need is to contribute to improvement of their preparedness. Second, an assumption exist that affected communities are aware of the causes of their vulnerability and more importantly their capacities to address them.

The resilience discussion focuses on addressing how the communities and other stakeholders can take advantage of the three capacities that are inherent at different levels: absorptive, adaptive and transformative. The three capacities are defined as follows:

---

[2] Report of the World Commission on Environment and Development: Our Common Future (1987)

[3] EU Resilience Compendium: Saving Lives and Livelihoods (2012)

- **Absorptive capacity**[4]: the ability to minimise exposure to shocks and stresses through preventive measures and appropriate coping strategies to avoid permanent, negative impacts. The absorptive capacity is what communities utilise to cope with a disaster in the short term. The coping strategies could be positive or negative. Mostly, the disasters result in life-and-death situations and the nature of the coping strategy is a secondary issue. However, sometimes, the coping strategies are negative and could very well exacerbate the vulnerability of communities. Regarding response, the humanitarian actions focus on the absorptive capacity of communities.

- **Adaptive capacity**[5]: combines assets, skills, technologies and confidence to make changes and adapt effectively to the challenges posed by long-term trends, such as climate change. Adaptive capacities ensure that affected communities can coexist with the prevailing conditions in their areas. During droughts, for example, communities will be encouraged to grow short season variety seeds, diversify into off-farm activities and practice conservation farming. Much has been done for example in developing climate smart agriculture as a response to the debilitating effects of climate change.

- **Transformative capacity**[6]: are the governance mechanisms, policies/regulations, infrastructure, community networks and formal and informal social protection mechanisms that constitute the enabling environment for systemic change. The transformative capacities are more about the institutional framework that allows local communities to actively participate in discussions and decisions that affect their responses to shocks and hazards.

---

[4] Transition from Relief to Development: Key Issues Related to Humanitarian and Recovery/Transition Programmes, United Nations (2006)

[5] Alejandra Kubitschek Bujones, A Framework for Resilience in Fragile and Conflict-Affected Situations, Columbia University SIPA 2013

[6] U.S. Government Global Food Security Strategy 2017-2021

Understanding the Resilience Context in Zimbabwe

The context of vulnerability in rural Zimbabwe should be understood through the cycles that the communal population went through since colonial period, before 1980. According to one scholar, the white-led colonial government put in place a deliberate mechanism that was supposed to promote the interests of the whites at the expense of those of the blacks (Herbst, 1990). During colonial era, the Government developed a system that ensured the locals would never enjoy the benefits of their country. From 1923 when the country got the self-governing arrangement, through the Land Husbandry Act of 1969, to the Unilateral Declaration of Independence in 1965. This was evident mainly in the land distribution and production patterns as shown in Table 1.

Table 1: Land and Production Indices at Independence in 1980[7]

Indicator	Large Scale Commercial Farms	Small Scale Commercial Farms[8]	Communal Lands
Average Farm Size (ha)	2,474	125	23
Value of Outputs ($[9] millions)	374	12	109
Per Capita Output ($)	214	117	31
Output per Hectare ($)	25	11	6

The resource allocation shown in Table 1 is a microcosm of the rest of the economy. Clearly, lack of control of factors of production by majority of the population increased their vulnerability.

At Independence, the Government embarked on a massive black empowerment programme which was designed to close the gap

---

[7] Ditto, page 39
[8] These were owned by black Africans
[9] This refers to Zimbabwe dollars

between the whites and the blacks. The foreign investment injected into the economy because of the Zimbabwe Conference on Reconstruction and Development (ZIMCORD)[10] hosted by the then Minister of Finance and Economic Development, Dr Bernard Chidzero in 1981. The donor conference resulted in many resources poured into the country. The period between 1980 and 1983 saw massive infrastructural development taking place throughout the country. However, successive droughts, poor prioritisation of programmes and the Bretton Woods driven Economic Structural and Adjustment Programme (ESAP) increased the vulnerability of poor communities.

Recently, the most often quoted period of vulnerability for rural households is from 2000 when the world responded to the Government Land and Agrarian Reform Programme. Combined with increasing drought frequencies, decline in the quality of service delivery, the poor performance of both micro and macro-economic fundamentals resulted in most households losing their capacities to respond and bounce back from shocks and stresses. The same period evidenced the influx of International Non-Governmental Organisations in efforts to address high levels of food insecurity and disease outbreaks which were exacerbated by the worsening political situation in the country. In 2002 alone, over 6 million households were in need of food aid and since then, the Government and the cooperating partners have provided food assistance to at least 1 million households every year.[11] At the same time, between 2007 and 2008, the country experienced a massive cholera and typhoid outbreak with a reported 100,000 positive cases and over 400 related deaths[12]. Therefore, the vulnerability context in Zimbabwe is shaped by different triggers. Political, economic, structural, cultural and social triggers. Intervention designed to respond must address as these triggers or at least realise their linkages.

---

[10] Herbst, J. State Politics in Zimbabwe, 1990
[11] Please refer to the various Zimbabwe Vulnerability Assessment Committee (ZIMVAC) reports as published
[12] The 2008 Cholera Epidemic in Zimbabwe: Experience of the ICDDR: Sirajuddin Ahmed, Pradip Kumar Bardhan, Anwarul Iqbal, Ramendra Nath Mazumder, Azharul Islam Khan, Md. Sirajul Islam, Abul Kasem Siddique and Alejandro Cravioto.

The Bottlenecks

This section identifies and discuss some of the potential bottlenecks to hinder the implementation and the impact of SDGs. Not discussed in order of importance, the following bottlenecks, are the most critical:

The Dependency Psyche of the Affected Communities

The period from 2000 has developed rural communities that depend too much on external assistance. Majority of the NGOs that came into Zimbabwe around 2002[13], were humanitarian in nature. Through no fault of their own, they created a situation where those affected by the drought or disease outbreaks received food and non-food items (NFI) free. The rise of opposition politics during the same period led to distribution of free agricultural and food handouts by the ruling government to maintain political support. Examples are the Presidential Well Wishers Agricultural Input Supply Programmes and the Basic Commodities Supply Side Intervention (BACOSSI) a facility established by government to counter the price increases in basic commodities. While these programmes are noble, they only entrenched the idea and notion in the people that Government and the NGOs will assist them in times of need. There have been anecdotal allegations that even community members capable of providing for themselves still wanted to benefit from the programmes because they could not forgo "free" things. While there now seems to be an understanding and agreement among the different stakeholders that free assistance is not sustainable for both the affected communities and those providing the support, it could take some time before the communities are completely free of this "disease".

Non-integration of Development Programmes

By their nature, humanitarian programmes focus on one specific issue. As the situation eases, other areas of concerned to be addressed. However, lack of adequate integration has been

---

[13] Chakawarika Bertha, Challenges faced by NGOs in the political harsh climate of Zimbabwe: Analysing the effects on sustainability and promotion of human rights.

recognised from experiences since 2002. A food security programme does not necessarily address other related issues such as nutrition, water and sanitation. As a result, the development interventions seem piecemeal. Other than programmatic and thematic non-integration, institutional non-integration exists where duplication of work by organisations in the same areas occur without collaboration in implementation of programmes. As a result, there is a lot of duplication or alternatively a lot of gaps are left. All this not only wastes resources but also reduces the impact of the interventions. Hence communities' resilience to one condition, they may not be to another condition, therefore perpetuating their vulnerability.

No Graduation from Humanitarian to Development Programming

In early phase of a disaster intervention, humanitarian response and focus on saving lives is acceptable. However, a clear plan should be outlined on graduating communities and institutional structures towards development. Lack of programme graduation is not necessarily a problem of communities since sometimes funding streams are uncertain. In Zimbabwe, there was a lot of humanitarian funding that came into the country between 2002 and 2010 mainly to deal with the food security crisis and the cholera outbreak. However, as the situation in the country stabilised, the donors developed a wait-and-see attitude as the Government of National Unity (GNU) came into being. So, a period existed when there was inadequate humanitarian or development funding. The unreliable funding had a net effect of maintaining vulnerabilities of the communities[14]. As a result, the disasters that struck the country after 2010 especially the 2014/2015 drought and the 2016/2017 floods created a lot of chaos in the country. Lack of communities' preparedness and incapacities to respond worsened the disasters' impact.

Short Term Nature of Development Interventions

The biggest hurdle to building sustainable community resilience is the short-term and project-based nature of development interventions. Building resilience cannot be a short-term target. It is

---

[14] Treda Mukuhlani Zimbabwe's Government of National Unity: Successes and Challenges in Restoring Peace and Order, Journal of Power, Politics & Governance, June 2014, Vol. 2.

a process which is sometimes iterative. Development literature defines communities as homogeneous, which is not always the case. The rate of adoption of innovations amongst the community members is quite different and if the strategy is to move with the early adopters (who are not many), then it means that the majority of the community members will be left behind. Some of the interventions that have the potential to build community resilience require more time. However, due to funding streams this is rarely the case. In agriculture for example, the impact of livestock programmes and interventions only start to show results after four or five years. Few donor programmes exist with such a long lifespan. Hence, implementing partners move out of the area during project closure at an average of three years. Given the short lifespan, neither the partners nor the communities have a full appreciation of the challenges, benefits and potential impact for the project.

Critical Stakeholders Are Left Out of Programme Design and Implementation

Resilience building is multifaceted and multi-stakeholder in nature. It follows a value chain approach where each stakeholder has a contribution to make at the relevant stage. Not going through all the steps and involving all the stakeholders' results in potential future challenges. The resilience framework for Zimbabwe depends significantly on the ability of vulnerable communities to generate income through different activities that they will be carrying out. Experience has demonstrated failure of most of these income generating activities. The failure is attributed to excluding private sector which is experienced in generating income and even making profit from the design. Other designs have not included an active role for Government structures yet they are the only structures that remain in the areas after the departure of external support.

Non-Functional Development Structures

Through the Prime Minister's Directive of 1984 and the attendant pieces of legislation, the Government of Zimbabwe established community development structures. These structures were supposed to lead in ensuring, development activities at the lower levels were participatory and addressed the needs and priorities of marginalized communities. They also sought to ensure communities took an active role in identifying their problems and challenges and devising strategies and mobilising resources to address them. The structures also sought to promote the ownership of development interventions and bridge between community aspirations and central government responsibilities. The Provincial Councils Act, the Rural District Councils Act, Statutory Instrument 15 of 2000 and, later the Traditional Leaders Act brought into being various grassroots structures. The village development committees (VIDCO) and village assemblies, the ward development committees (WADCO) and ward assemblies, Rural District Development Committees (RDDC), Provincial Development Committees (PDC) and Provincial Councils (PC). For a period, these structures served their purposes as communities, government and other stakeholders utilised these structures as entry points for all development interventions.[15] Several challenges were observed in the use of the structures. The increased political and social polarization as well as the economic upheavals the country experienced especially from 2000 brought the relevance of the grassroots structures to drive rural development into question. In most rural areas, the VIDCOs no longer exist. Where they exist, it could be just one or two people within a village, most likely from a political party, "driving" the development process. These are the structures that are supposed to support communities build and strengthen their resilience capacities.

A Constrictive Policy and Legal Framework

For transformative capacity to be effective, existence of an enabling policy and legal framework is important.[16] However, the framework is usually unavailable. Where the framework exists, usually affected communities are not adequately informed of its existence. There have also been cases where policies and legislation exist but contradict each other in both letter and spirit. The case of

---

[15] Kamuzhanje Joseph, Planning in Zimbabwe: The Case of Matebeleland South Province in Community Based Development Planning Approaches in Bulilima and Mangwe Districts of Matebeleland South Province edited by Melta Moyo and Themba Khombe (Kellogg Foundation, 2008)

[16] Alejandra Kubitschek Bujones, A Framework for Resilience in Fragile and Conflict-Affected Situations, Columbia University SIPA 2013

Zimbabwe, presents an interesting scenario. Policies are revised before understanding the implications or worse still, before the adequate implementation that enables the possibility of assessing their effectiveness.

"Words, No Action!"

One of the most common anecdotal observation made about Zimbabwe is its unimplemented best written and laid out plans in the world. The main reason for this is that policies have inadequate or lack the financial resources to support their implementation. Hence, policy failure is not mostly attributed to policy content by lack of funds for implementation. Funding challenges have become even more critical now as Zimbabwe's relations with Western donors are restrained and the government struggles to attract foreign direct investment.

No Learning

In Zimbabwe, lessons drawn from experiences of implementing development and resilience building programmes are not implemented in future designs. As a result, communities and stakeholders go through the same cycle and do not make significant progress in improving their well-being. For farmers, agricultural inputs are distributed way during the farming season, leading to farmers not taking advantage of the full season. Late agricultural inputs distribution has become a norm in agricultural support. While this compromises their food security, it also reduces the income they generate from the enterprises. Therefore, programme designs still focus on the same issues that proved ineffective in previous interventions.

Case Studies in Resilience Programming

The discussion above presupposes existence of several challenges to be overcome in order to build a resilient community in a futile exercise. Understanding the work involved in equipping vulnerable communities or households with the necessary resilience capacities is important. This section of the chapter gives cases of programming that has the potential to enhance the absorptive, adaptive and transformative capacities of vulnerable communities and the institutions that are meant to support such processes. All the names in the stories are being used with the express consent of the people mentioned here in line with the ethics of research.

Case Study 1 is an organisation that managed to work with communities, government, other NGOs and donors to completely turn around the fortunes of communities that were dependent on food assistance for over a decade.

Case Study 1: GOAL Zimbabwe's Experiences with Transitioning from Humanitarian to Recovery in Buhera District of Manicaland Province

GOAL[17] Zimbabwe started operating in Zimbabwe in 2002 as an implementing partner for the World Food Programme (WFP). GOAL was the implementing partner for Makoni, Buhera, Nyanga, Hurungwe, Makonde and Sanyati. Buhera has one of the highest levels of food insecurity in Manicaland Province. As shown in Table 2, compared with other districts in the province from 2010 to 2016, Buhera shows an average of 16 to 50% of the households being food insecure during the peak hunger period.

Table 2: Food Insecurity in Buhera District in Comparison with Other Districts in Manicaland

Year	Buhera	Makoni	Chipinge	Nyanga
2010	16	16	15	20
2011	25.1	12	14	2.2
2012	27.2	18	23	2
2013	23.3	26	28	26
2014	10	1.1	1.7	2.8
2015	37.8	9	13	9
2016	50	35	40	41

To reduce dependency on donors and the Government, in 2012, the WFP started implementing the Food/Cash for Assets (F/CFA)

---

[17] This is an Irish NGO that has been operating in Zimbabwe since 2002. GOAL is not an acronym but the actual name of the organisation

programmes. In these programmes, beneficiary households would work on productive assets in the district in return for cash or food. However, the programmes did not change much of the district's food insecurity.

During a strategy review in 2011 GOAL Zimbabwe undertook to transition from relief to development in all its programmes. As a result, GOAL Zimbabwe consulted communities and government stakeholders on what needed to be done to improve food security in the district. All the discussions pointed to the need to move away from crop to livestock based agriculture with emphasis on cattle and goats. GOAL Zimbabwe then partnered the Departments of Livestock Production and Development (LPD) and the Veterinary and Field Services to design a livestock programme. The programme was funded by the Office for Foreign Disaster Assistance (OFDA) and the European Union (through FAO). These two projects concentrated on animal husbandry and training community based animal health cadres referred to as "paravets".

In 2014, GOAL carried out a review of the livestock project with the communities and government stakeholders. In one of the meetings, one community member who had been a food aid beneficiary since 2002 "accused" GOAL of wasting time and resources giving and his family food. "If you had started with livestock interventions all that long, ago, I would have been a rich person by now", he said. The communities pointed out that while they now had knowledge on animal husbandry; their major challenge was the small size of stock caused by excessive inbreeding. As a response to this issue, GOAL Zimbabwe started working with two private sector companies, Makera Cattle Company and Cooper Zimbabwe on genetic improvement. Makera breeds pedigree bulls while Coopers focuses on animal health products and training on animal husbandry. As part of the genetic improvement, 39 Tuli bulls were introduced in 12 of the most food insecure wards in the district. At the same time, GOAL Zimbabwe got a grant from the Australian government and worked with 3,000 women to improve their economic wellbeing through goat production. The project introduced 73 Boer and Matabele goats in the same wards. Since 2014, over 700 improved calves and 3,500 kids have been dropped from the improved breeds. In order to provide a guaranteed market for the smallholder livestock farmers, GOAL engaged Surrey Meats to act as an off-taker for the farmers. Feed-loting for between 60 and 90 days would be used to improve the animals and Surrey Meats would pay the farmers a market price for their animals less the cost of feed and induction. By December 2016, the farmers had gone through four cycles of feed-loting and attested to the improved income from the enterprise. In addition to the cattle, the farmers had also started a poultry and gardening project to diversify their income streams.

In 2013, GOAL Zimbabwe took a strategic decision not to provide food assistance and there were no problems with the communities on this issue. In fact, there has been no food assistance programme targeting the 12 wards that GOAL implemented the livestock project in. The livestock project has become a model for other districts with similar programmes implemented in Chipinge by GOAL Zimbabwe and in Mount Darwin, Kwekwe, Shurugwi and Mutare by Coopers and Makera. The major lesson learnt is that it is possible to take communities off food aid if viable alternatives are available.

Case Study 2 presents a programme that is still a works-in-progress by the United Nations Development Programme in Zimbabwe funded by DFID and the EU. This programme, which is in the second phase of implementation has already shown the signs of potential to change the vulnerability map of Zimbabwe.

"Building Resilience in Zimbabwe"
Over the last decade, Zimbabwe has experienced several unprecedented economic, environmental and social shocks and stresses, many of which will have long-lasting impacts. Poverty, food insecurity, malnutrition and environmental degradation are serious challenges in Zimbabwe, particularly in rural areas and will continue to be challenging due to the effects of climate change. Resilience has emerged as a plausible framework particularly among humanitarian and development actors and government. It has emerged as a longer-term cost-effective strategy for substantially improving national and local capacity to withstand shocks and stresses, ultimately leading to a reduced need for humanitarian response and an improvement in people's well-being. To build resilience of households and

communities in rural Zimbabwe, the Government of Zimbabwe and its partners pursued various interventions. The interventions address the relations between hazards, poverty, livelihoods and food security, considering social aspects of health, nutrition, access to basic services and social practices. The overall aim of building resilience is to improve people's access to assets, resources, opportunities and choices which will allow them to withstand shocks and stresses and bounce back better once a shock occurs. Communities with capacity to prevent and manage shocks can better support households during times of hazards. This is essential for achieving sustainable economic development in Zimbabwe, as resilient households and communities can engage in society and contribute to economic growth.

Consultations supported by UNDP in Zimbabwe have brought together government departments and ministries, UN agencies, NGOs/CSOs, academia and donors to develop a Strategic Resilience Framework for Zimbabwe. The Framework seeks to improve practitioners' understanding of households and communities' response mechanism to shocks and stresses. It also identifies effects of shocks and stresses on livelihood outcomes and household well-being; and helps in identifying key leverage points to be used in developing a theory of change. During these consultations, stakeholders agreed on the following definition for resilience in Zimbabwe:

> "The ability of at risk individuals, households, communities and systems to anticipate, cushion, adapt, bounce back better and move on from the effects of shocks and hazards in a manner that protects livelihoods and recovery gains and supports sustainable transformation."

The Resilience Strategic Framework for Zimbabwe calls for long term strategies; multi sector and multi-level activities; context specific analysis and design; flexibility and strategic partnerships as part of the criteria. The Government of Zimbabwe and UNDP in collaboration with bilateral donors has responded by setting up a multi donor fund, the Zimbabwe Resilience Building Fund (ZRBF), to support resilience building in Zimbabwe. Multi donor funds have become an important funding mechanism in Zimbabwe. They channel and leverage resources in an effective and coordinated way in support of multi-sector, multi-partner, multi-level development efforts. The ZRBF is set-up as a direct application of the aid effectiveness agenda and UN reform initiatives in support of nationally determined and led development programmes. It incorporates the principles of national ownership and leadership which are key principles of the Paris Declaration on Aid Effectiveness, reconfirmed in the Accra Agenda and central to the UN operational activities for development.

Overall, the Zimbabwe Resilience Building Fund seeks to contribute to improvement of communities' capacities to protect development gains and achieve better well-being outcomes in the face of shocks and stresses. This will be achieved through three interlinked components:

a) Creating a body of evidence and building capacity for increased application of evidence-based policy-making;

b) Improving the absorptive, adaptive and transformative capacities of vulnerable communities; and,

c) Setting up a crisis modifier mechanism which will provide appropriate, predictable, coordinated and timely response to risk and shocks from a resilience perspective.[18]

Case Study 3 contains stories of most significant change from the Livelihoods and Food Security Programme (LFSP). Three consortiums of NGOs are responsible for implementing the programme in three provinces of Zimbabwe and DFID supports the project with funding. The three case studies come from the INSPIRE consortium in Manicaland.

Story 1: Chipendeke Farmers Reaping Where They Sowed

Farmers in Chipendeke irrigation scheme had lost hope in producing tomatoes because of disease infestations such as early and late blights. Poor crop management practices aggravated this problem. Lack of rotations, inadequate knowledge in proper use of chemicals especially fungicides and lack of a cooperative effort in the

---

[18] UNDP Call for Concept Notes for the Zimbabwe Resilience Building Fund, November 2015

general management of the irrigation scheme. Individuals planted without following the cropping system which resulted in the failure to maintain dead periods leading to the subsequent build-up of pests and diseases. This failure created a conducive environment for the development of strains that are capable of resisting chemicals. The irrigation scheme members got the encouragement to diversify into other horticultural crops such as sugar beans, tomatoes and peas. It led to a general resentment especially to produce tomatoes which they regarded as a non-starter. The INSPIRE project then intervened and supported the farmers through establishment of a sugar beans and tomato horticulture demonstration site at the scheme. The major themes for the demonstration were soil fertility management, fertiliser and pesticide management. The correct use of fungicides such as score and copper ox chloride and pesticides such as *imidachloprid* resulted in elimination of the earlier mentioned problem. Shining Rose, the group that played a major role in maintaining the demonstration site is now confident of growing tomatoes again. As at 29 March 2016, the group sold 22 boxes of good quality tomatoes to Sakubva Market at $20/box. Being the beginning of the sales, prospects for more harvest and sales from the 0.125 hectares' plot existed.

Story 2: Planting Small Grains Brings Heaps of Joy to Nhamo Kanyenze
Mr Nhamo Kanyenze is a farmer in ward 28, Chanakira village, under Headman Masasi. He is a member of Tanaka group which is into goat value chain as major value chain. As a group, they went through trainings facilitated and conducted by INSPIRE. The group is also into Internal Savings and Lending (ISAL) as a way of funding their field crops and the goat project. As a farmer in rural, hot, arid with and very low rainfall area. Mr Kanyenze took heed of the LFSP project which was advocating for planting small grains for food security. By the mid of October, Mr Kanyenze and the group members through their (ISAL) group joined others in their cluster to purchase seed from Matopo Research Station. In the same month INSPIRE coordinated a group competition on conservation agriculture (CA) land preparation. Tanaka as a group was amongst the first groups to complete land preparation in the fields of all their members. A knapsack sprayer and an herbicide motivated this group

138

to prepare land early. Tanaka had 5kgs seed and shared among its 11 members including Mr Nhamo Kanyenze. Upon receiving the seed as his field was already prepared waiting for planting, Mr Kanyenze and his hardworking wife planted on the 19 of November amid erratic rainfall patterns and scorching sun nevertheless. The crop emerged well and survived the harsh conditions of the area. Since the seed was not retained seed it did well. A field day was organised by cluster groups to honour and learn from Mr Nhamo Kanyenze, Tanaka group and family. During the field day Mr Kanyenze gave many thanks to the LFSP project and extension for the support in trainings. As many families struggle to bring food on the table, Mr Nhamo Kanyenze is now the talk of his area. Several farmers have learnt the importance of ISAL, group work, CA and above all, practising the initiatives by INSPIRE.

Story 3 "Growing Livestock Pays Off for Poor and Vulnerable Farmers
In 2013, a group of 13 farmers from Musandishowa Village, Ward 29 of Mutare district formed Dzidzai beef group. The group, which started as an Internal Savings and Lending (ISAL) scheme is made up of 6 males and 7 females. The group used to buy groceries in bulk quantities to benefit from reduced cost and share the groceries among themselves. Musandishowa Village is found in natural region 5 which receives little rains to sustain crop production but is suitable for livestock production. A consortium made up of GOAL Zimbabwe, Practical Action, Technoserve and Sustainable Agriculture Technology (SAT) is tackling food and nutrition security problems facing farmers in the Mutasa, Mutare and Makoni districts of Manicaland Province. The group Secretary, Chiedza Gadziwa had an opportunity to be trained as one of the Community Based Trainers. She then approached the chairperson Mr. Henry Maunga and shared the importance of having a certified constitution and record keeping and a well-established ISAL group. From the 2015 savings, the group managed to buy 13 beasts which were shared among the group members hence improving their livelihoods. Intensive trainings on cattle management, pen fattening and marketing were offered to group members by farmer peer leaders and INSPIRE officers. The provision of Veterinary Kits by INSPIRE and a field day held at their 3cross-sectional kraal in February 2016

transformed the group. They had an opportunity to meet their value chain off taker Molus' Meats who graced the occasion and boosted their desire to become commercial farmers. As a member of Kunzwana Beef Association, Dzidzai group is now into pen fattening with Molus Meats guaranteeing the market. The group secretary said," it's all because of INPSIRE trainings that we are who we are right now. We managed to open a group savings account with FBC Bank and have already applied for loan', to enlarge our business venture as we know that increased profits will come by an increase in scale of production".

Dzidzai Group aspire to sell high-quality beef and fetch higher prices. Hence, they now focus on feeding their cattle in the pen with the required drought pack they received at the field day as an outstanding beef group prize in their zone. Most Association group members and other groups in the zone have learnt from Dzidzai farmers and have since constructed 3-cross sectional pens in their homesteads.

Discussion

Through the conceptual framework and case studies, the chapter has shown the need for development interventions to focus on building the capacity of vulnerable and poor communities not only to bounce back after disasters in a sustainable manner. Experience has demonstrated that some of the interventions meant to achieve community resilience left communities worse off than before the disaster. This is a result of lack of deliberate effort to understand the underlying causes. More importantly, poor understanding of the potential barriers that can affect building of absorptive, adaptive and transformative capacities of the affected communities and the institutions responsible for assisting those communities. The three cases presented in this chapter show the possibility of designing programmes that cannot only change communities' lives but also build and strengthen their resilience capacities. This provides them with opportunities to effectively deal with future threats to their well-being. The SDGs have a time frame that last until 2030. Ideally, the impact on poor and vulnerable communities should stretch beyond the time frame. Reducing the impact of barriers to the implementation of SDGs will realise this resilience and sustainability of vulnerable communities.

Conclusion

This chapter has outlined some of potential barriers to the successful implementation of SDGs. These barriers are found at different levels. From individual to household level, communities and the institutional and legal structures responsible for assisting communities in resilience capacity building. There is need for commitment from all relevant stakeholders through effective community engagement, restructuring the institutions and working models as well as providing the requisite technical and financial support to the capacity building. The chapter has gone further indicating clearly the possibility of building community resilience and has cited several examples to show this. SGDs are critical for improving the wellbeing of individuals, communities and Zimbabwe, in general. Therefore, all stakeholders should support their implementation. The lessons learnt from Millennium Development Goals (MDGs) implementation should be considered during the design of programmes and projects meant to benefit communities. Zimbabwe has already shown the possibility to achieve the targets set. Therefore, it cannot allow the gains from MDGs to be lost.

References

Alejandra KB. (2013) A Framework for Resilience in Fragile and Conflict-Affected Situations, Columbia University SIPA

Chakawarika B (2011) Challenges faced by NGOs in the Political Harsh Climate of Zimbabwe: Analysing the Effects on Sustainability and Promotion of Human Rights

Government of the United Kingdom (2012) *Building Resilience in ARD: DFID's Approach*

Government of the United States (2016) Government Global Food Security Strategy 2017-2021

Herbst, J. (1990) State Politics in Zimbabwe, University of Zimbabwe Publications

Kamuzhanje J (2008) Planning in Zimbabwe: The Case of Matebeleland South Province in Community Based Development Planning Approaches in Bulilima and Mangwe Districts of Matebeleland South Province edited by Melta Moyo and Themba Khombe (Kellogg Foundation)

Mukuhlani T (2014) Zimbabwe's Government of National Unity: Successes and Challenges in Restoring Peace and Order, Journal of Power, Politics & Governance, Vol. 2

Sachs, J.D. (2012). From Millennium Development Goals to Sustainable Development Goals, The Lancet Vol 379 June 9

The European Union (2012), EU Resilience Compendium: Saving Lives and Livelihoods, Brussels, Belgium

Sirajuddin Ahmed et.al (2011), The 2008 Cholera Epidemic in Zimbabwe: Experience of the ICDDR: The Journal of Health, Population and Nutrition

United Nations (1987) Report of the World Commission on Environment and Development: Our Common Future United Nations, New York

United Nations (2006) Transition from Relief to Development: Key Issues Related to Humanitarian and Recovery/Transition Programmes, United Nations, Rome, Italy.

United Nations (2016) The Sustainable Development Goals Report, United Nations, New York, USA.

Chapter 7

Everyday Local Level Sources of Weather Forecasting in Rural Zimbabwe in the Face of Climate Change

Ignatius Gutsa

Introduction

This chapter examines the use of local stocks of knowledge for micro-level reading and forecasting of the weather and seasons. It focuses on elderly women heads of households in one rural village in Zimbabwe in the face of climate change. The study achieves this by examining the experiences of elderly female heads of households in Gutsa Village which is situated in Domboshava Communal Lands, Goromonzi District. This chapter's focus on micro-level reading and forecasting of the weather and seasons in Gutsa Village by elderly women is consistent with observations by Roncoli (2006). He observes that in the context of climate change, ethnographic research on local forecasting knowledge is important in highlighting the salient aspects of the climate (weather) and common indicators used to predict it. Therefore, it is important to reflect on Roncoli, Ingram and Kirshen's (2002, 413) observations that local environmental indicators are based on experience of those living in the immediate environment. Furthermore, anthropology as embodied in the ethnographic approach used in this study can serve as a form and activity of knowledge production (Einarsson, 2011). Barnes et al. (2013, 541) also stipulate on the existence of several factors that make anthropology important for the study of the weather and climate change. Most importantly is that the discipline draws attention to the cultural values and political relations that shape climate-related knowledge creation and interpretation which form the basis of responses to continuing environmental changes.

In climate change research, conventional science based on macro-level statistical modelling indicates evidence of climate change (Low, 2005; IPCC, 2007). On the other hand, indigenous (local) people show us that there are alternative ways of knowing about the environment (Smith, 2007, 212; Elia, Mutula and Stilwel, 2014). Local people draw on their close association and understanding of their weather and climate to forecast the coming rainy season using a wide range of local indicators such as flora and fauna. The Bonam in Burkina Faso for example, assess the favourability of the coming rainy season variably. They rely on fruit production of certain trees at the onset of the rainy season as well as temperatures during the dry season (Roncoli et al. 2002, 413). The importance of understanding and predicting the weather and climate is provided. It is argued that climate prediction is one among many sources of information that can be used by decision-makers to reduce risk and to optimise gains. This is particularly so in agriculture where production outcomes are closely linked to weather and climate information (Roncoli, 2006, 81).

Theoretical Framework

The theoretical approach used in this chapter draws substantially from a phenomenological approach. Phenomenological approaches have become increasingly important in anthropology as methods of investigating or inquiring into the meanings of our experiences as we live them. Such approaches have further contributed greatly to how anthropologists think of, among other issues, lived experience, communicative practices and subjectivity. This is important as human existence is structured temporarily to experience into the present, feeding forward to anticipate future horizons (Desjarlais and Jason, 2011, 89). In anthropology, such a theoretical approach is important as it flows naturally from prior work that socio-cultural anthropologists have done on small-scale societies or local communities where they tend to gather data on people's "emic" (insider) views (Baer and Reuter, 2015). Consequently, this chapter's focus is on the phenomenological or cultural reading and interpretation of the weather, seasons and climate change through the lens of social actors (elderly women) and their local knowledge. Therefore, this theoretical approach allows for the capturing of vernacular models of understanding the weather and climate as emphasised in this chapter.

Literature Review

Weather and climate information is available from two main sources, namely meteorological seasonal climate forecasts as well as indigenous knowledge-based seasonal forecasts (Ziervogel and Opere, 2010, 1). Local/indigenous people possess a wealth of traditional knowledge ranging from reading the weather and climate and making seasonal forecasts. This wealth of information has been achieved through maintenance of specific cultural systems and traditional values related to the weather and climate and natural resource management that has been transmitted over generations.

Indigenous/local knowledge systems are a term used to describe the knowledge systems developed by a community as opposed to the scientific knowledge that is generally referred to as modern knowledge. Indigenous knowledge encompasses the actual knowledge, skills and practices or methods of doing things based on local materials developed through various types of experimentation and practical experience overtime by the people of the place and adapted to the specific local context (Makwara, 2013, 3).

In this chapter the term local knowledge systems is used interchangeably with indigenous knowledge systems. Indigenous communities are known to observe local environmental indicators for early prediction of weather phenomenon variously. They use plant growth and flowering patterns, behaviour of animals to read and forecast the weather and its variations (Galloway and Burgess, 2009). In a study in Zaka, Zimbabwe it was also observed that local indicators of weather and seasonal forecasts were derived from flora and fauna observations as well as wind patterns (Makwara, 2013). Local knowledge based weather and climate information systems are more useful to the local communities. As such, stocks of knowledge can help local people to respond accordingly to the changes in the weather, climate and seasons (Ziervogel and Opere, 2010, 1). Furthermore, local people's actions are mediated by their experiences grounded on historical narratives/myths and local realities (Worby, 1992). This is important as scholars have observed that local understanding of the weather and climate by nomads appeared to contradict larger scale meteorological records in Mongolia. This is a result of the ability of local communities to gather finer environmental knowledge based on close association with their environment compared to the detached weather stations located further afield (Marin, 2010).

In focusing on elderly women and their knowledge of the weather in a specific socio-ecological system I appreciate the role they play in retaining and passing on biodiversity-related traditional knowledge to the next generation. Therefore, these elderly women can adequately be regarded as "living encyclopaedias" (Flintan, 2003). Here the knowledge of the elderly women related to long-term weather and local climate is grounded in the historical and contemporary understanding of their environment.

Methodology

Anthropologists typically conduct research over extended periods of time in a single community or set of communities. They gradually build relations of trust with respondents, closely observing people's everyday activities, interactions, conversations and conducting interviews (Barnes et al. 2013). This chapter evolves from my doctoral thesis where I was examining the impact of climate change on the livelihoods of elderly female headed households in Gutsa Village, Domboshava communal lands situated in Goromonzi district, Zimbabwe. I conducted close to nineteen months of ethnographic field research from the end of April 2014 to November 2015. I mainly relied on participant observation and Focus Group Discussions with a group of ten elderly female heads of households during fieldwork. These elderly women are: Mbuya Tarai, Mbuya Ku, Mbuya Gone, Mbuya Mizhu, Mai Njere, Mai Chota, Mbuya Tawira, Mbuya No, Amai Cha and Amai Reni. My methodological approach in this study is consistent with observations by Roncoli (2006). He asserts that in climate change research, ethnographic research on local forecasting knowledge can highlight salient aspects of climate change and common indicators used to predict it. As far as potential for bias exists, ethnography's strengths further derive from reliance on casual interactions and conversational interviews. These all serve

146

to enable a deeper insight into cultural meanings (Roncoli, 2006, 83). For readability and presentability, I allow the voices of the selected situated elderly women to be visible in the presentation and discussion of findings. These are mainly grounded in a historical perspective as well as the period I undertook fieldwork.

Results and Discussion

In Gutsa Village the impact of climate change is depicted in the changing behaviour patterns as well as sightings of both flora and fauna species. As I detail below, in the village fruiting patterns of some flora species have been used as predictors and markers of weather. For fauna, climate change has affected the migration, behaviour patterns as well as sightings of birds and insects which are seen during the rainy season. These range from the late sightings of birds such as *nyenga nyenga* (swallow), *shuramurove* (Abdim Stork) to the confirmed increasing challenge of *zvipfukuto* (weevils). Also, late sightings of insects which are considered delicacies in the village namely *ishwa* (flying termites), *dzambarafuta* (flying ants) and *mandere* (chafer beetles). The elderly women complained that increasing temperatures have contributed to the challenge of weevils in the village. When I first visited Mbuya Ku's homestead she was busy moving her maize from the grass thatched kitchen to the asbestos roofed bedroom. She complained, the kitchen was now a bit warmer due to the fire in the hearth as well as the gradually increasing temperatures of August. Therefore, she found a cooler bedroom as a better storage for maize. In addition, she planned to buy *Chirindamatura* (Actellic Super Dust) regarded as one of the best insecticides used by most villagers against weevils. Previously like most villagers she had stored her maize in an outside granary which was built on stilts. Unfortunately, as most villagers she stopped the practice of storing maize outside around early 1990s. This was due to increased risks of theft particularly from outside granaries.

Various birds are seen in the village as the rainy season approaches. The *haya* (yellow-breasted barbet known as a rain bird and is said to only drink water from tree trunks) which is usually heard singing as the rainy season approaches. *Dendera* (ground hornbill) which migrates and sings with the approach of the rainy

147

season. Also, *nyenga nyenga* is a bird only seen with approach of the rain season. *Shuramurove* is also seen in the village during the rainy season towards the beginning of *mubvumbi* (incessant rains). *Shuramurove* means (*shura*-harbinger) and (*murove*-moisture on the walls), *shuramurove* becomes the harbinger of moisture/incessant rains (Mararike, 1996). In the 2014-2015 farming season my first sighting of *shuramurove* was on the 13th of January as incessant rains were about to start. In the village, there is consensus that impact of climate change related to the late onset, distribution, quantity and cessation of the rains was affecting the migratory and behaviour patterns of these birds.

Birds which indicate the weather

Bird	Time seen	Meaning
Dendera (ground hornbill)	*Rainy season*	If you hear it crying/calling out *mubani* (veld) then you know the rains are very near
Haya (yellow-breasted barbet)	*Rainy season*	*Marks the onset of the rains.*
Nyenga Nyenga (swallow)	*Rainy season*	*The rainy season has commenced*
Shuramurove (Abdim Stork)	*Rainy season*	*Mubvumbi is about to commence*
Tsodzi (Yellow-bellied sunbird)	*Onset of the rain/Rain about to come*	*Its nest's mouth is always positioned away from direction of intense rain.*

Insect/Animals which indicate the weather

Animal/Insect	Time seen	Meaning
Dzvatsvatsva (sun spider)	*Rainy season*	*The rains are now near*
Zongororo (millipede)	*Rainy season*	*Only sighted during the rainy season*
Hamba (tortoise)	*Rainy season*	*Only sighted during the rainy season*

In addition, there are various signals in the village elderly women rely on to confirm seasonal changes. As pointed out by Mbuya Gone, the wind that characterises August which had not yet begun to be felt in September 2014 is an important marker. This August wind resulted in the month being named *Nyamavhuvhu* (the windy month).She references 2013 as the same case and August of 2015 being no different due to its stillness and calmness. Mbuya Tawira identified one of the markers to know a normal August was the blowing of all dead leaves off the trees "until the trees are just bare twigs".

Thereafter, when *munhondo* (*Julbernardia globiflora*) and *misasa* (*Brachystegia spiciformis*) have *pfumvudza* (the new and tender leaves) then you know the seasons have gone and the rainy season is now near. Mbuya Gone pointed out that it is first the *mikute* trees (*Syzygium cordatum*) that will begin to show green leaves before other trees.

In the village, some wild fruits are disappearing due to the impact of climate change. Also the rampant cutting down of fruit trees and the yearly veld fires, which affect the regeneration of the young trees, is also contributing. Mai Reni observed that partial disappearance and lack of *nhunguru* (Indian plum) in the forests was also a sign of climate change towards increased aridity. She noted that it indicated the decline of "*hunyoro*", "moisture" compared to previous season.

In the study village, villagers rely on observance of local multiple flora and fauna based sources of weather forecasting. These include reliance on the fruiting patterns of wild fruits such as *mazhanje* (*Uapaca kirkiana*) and *hacha* (*Parinari curatellifolia*) to forecast the favourability of the coming rain season. The existence of multiple coming rain season forecasting mechanisms in the village also appears consistent with conclusions that African farmers do not generally rely on a single forecasting indicator (Roncolli, 2006). Villagers also mainly rely on prophecy from Independent African Churches to predict the rains. As in Gutsa Village among the Mwingi in Kenya longer winters also indicate poor rainfall in the coming season (Mwadime, 1996). The rainy season forecast for the 2015-2016 season in The Herald edition on the 2nd of September 2015 showed normal to below normal rains. The forecast was on the main news bulletins of most radio channels and television station from the 3rd to the 4th of September 2015. The rains for the 2015-2016 season were forecasted normal to below normal. The Meteorological Services Department

(Met Department) advised farmers to plant short season crops, small grains and spread their planting while irrigating in areas with irrigation facilities. As villagers prepared and waited for the coming 2015-2016 rainy season, on the 2nd of November 2015 some areas close to the village received some very good rains. However, there was no rainfall in Gutsa Village specifically despite the presence of very promising clouds in the skies.

Mai Reni indicated that she sometimes listens to weather reports on the radio as well as forecasts for the rain season every year. Talking to her in September 2014, she pointed out that the weather reports on the radio had been saying that whenever the rains fell late in 2014 it was advisable to plant with those early rains. However, she said that she remembered one year when the radio people kept on guessing and guessing. Rain came when maize was about to be harvested, the crop rotted in the fields as the rains were not stopping".

The villagers commonly conclude that when *mazhanje* are abundant in the village it means the rainy season will be better, hence, the higher likelihood of a good harvest. Earlier studies indicate that fruiting patterns are a reliable indicator of the coming season's rains (Mararike, 1996; Mapeta, 2000; Mapara, 2009; Muguti and Maposa, 2011; Risiro et al. 2012; Ndiweni and Ndlovu, 2013). Inversely, lower availability of *mazhanje* indicates prospects for a poor rain season hence higher expectations for a poor harvest. It is suggested that an inverse relation between the abundance of fruit (especially *mazhanje*) and the abundance of rain (Mapara, 2009; Muguti and Maposa, 2011). However, just like in a study in Buhera, people in Gutsa Village believe that there is a direct (rather than inverse) correlation between fruiting patterns of *mazhanje* and rainfall (Mararike, 1996).

Abundance of *hacha* is believed to indicate a prospective bad rain season and inversely so when *hacha* is scarce. Between October and November 2014, the author observed that in Gutsa Village *mazhanje* were not in abundance as in other seasons. In fact, not a single fruit could be identified in the village's forest, few fruits could only be found from trees at people's homesteads.

On the radio, weather reports consistently forecasted favourable rains. The author assured himself that he had much time to observe the passage of the rainy season and check carefully for consistencies or inconsistencies. This was important as the weather reports on radio were contrasting with the local weather forecasts from the Met Department. Local people were providing their own reliable forecasts based on their understanding of the environment and their tried and tested predictors of rainfall patterns. The mango trees at homesteads in the village also had very poor signs of fruiting which was also seen as pointing to a poor rainy season ahead. Rainy season commenced and people planted their crops. As harvest time approached it was evident, the 2014-2015 rainy season had been a very poor one.

It became apparent, elderly women just as most people in Gutsa Village do not rely on the weather forecasts provided by the Met Department through various media outlets. The forecasts provided by the Met Department were never taken seriously in the village. As the elderly women pinpointed, for some years (e.g. 2012, 1997 and 1995) these forecasts had not been accurate. Just like scientific inquiry, local rainfall forecasts rely on observation and interpretation of specific phenomena in the surrounding landscape, including trees, animals and the sky, or they may be spiritually manifested in the form of divination, visions, or dreams (Roncoli et al. 2002: 413). Rather the forecasts are a laughing stock in the village due to their "unreliability". There have been perceptions of farmers to such forecasts in providing accurate forecasts for any coming rain season in south-eastern United States, Amazonia and Zimbabwe respectively (Patt et al.2005; Moran et al. 2006;Crane et al. 2010). Villagers are always saying that in there are they do not follow what the weather forecasters say. If it rains they simply plant.

The findings in the village in concerning the Meteorological Services Department are also consistent with Muguti and Risiro (2012) who demonstrated the conflict between science and tradition in rural Zimbabwe. They showed that weather forecasts from the Meteorological Services Department are not trusted by local people in comparison to their tried and tested local forecasts based on observations of behaviours of flora and fauna. Furthermore, as pointed out by FAO (2004) most rural farmers in Zimbabwe do not use information from the meteorological services for planning purposes. The lack of trust by communities towards the information from meteorological services due to its unreliability is the major reason communities do not use it (see Mwando, 2012, quoted in

Mudombi and Nhamo, 2014). Observations by Manatsa et al. (2012) in Chiredzi in Zimbabwe have also shown that since 1997 the local farmers have complained about misleading seasonal rainfall forecasts provided by the Met Department. For Manatsa et al. (2012) the seasonal forecasts provided by the Met Department are not useful due to high levels of climatic variability even at the micro-level of a single village. The usefulness of local farmer's forecasts which differ from scientific ones is important. They address a local rather than regional scale and crop-climate interactions rather than precipitation intrinsically (Roncoli, et al. 2002, 423). The existence of multiple coming rain season forecasting mechanisms in the village also appears consistent with conclusions that African farmers do not generally rely on a single forecasting indicator (Roncolli, 2006).

Prophesy from Independent African Churches also seems to be a method now used in the village by some elderly women to provide mainly forthcoming rainy season forecasts. As pointed by some scholars among the Bonam in Burkina Faso local rainfall forecasts also rely on spiritual manifestation in the form of visions (Roncoli et al. 2002, 413). This became evident during a conversation with one elderly woman, Mai Mizhu before the rains in October 2014. She indicated that since the year 2012 at the apostolic church she attends prophecy has now been used as a weather forecasting technique. This prophecy has mainly been used to predict the rains of the forthcoming farming season. Regarding the forecast for the 2013-2014 season she confidently said the Holy Spirit had said it was important to plant very early with the first rains. She indicated that she had confidence in their Holy Spirit's predictions for the 2014-2015 as at her church they accept it because since 2012 they had been hearing from the Holy Spirit. It tells them prospects of a good season with lots of rain as it also tells them prospects of a bad season marked by lack of rains.

The Holy Spirit had begun to prophesy precisely about what the coming rainy season would be like in 2012. In 2012, the Holy Spirit noted that the rains were not good and they were not. The following year, 2013 the Holy Spirit predicted fairly good rains and so they were. Subsequent year, 2014 was prophesied as another bad season and communities were advised to plant early as failure to do so would lead to hunger and that year proved to be a bad season. As I kept watch over the span of the rainy season, prophecy from Mai Mizhu's church proved correct as the rains were very poor, this was the common consensus in the village. Other apostolic church members in the village also concurred with the prophecies. They recounted that prophecy at their churches had predicted low rainfall receiving for three successive years starting in 2014. From the different apostolic churches, it appeared this prophecy on rain season forecasting had been a recent phenomenon which had started in the year 2010.

Mbuya Ku revealed, there are instances when humans could intervene and stop rain from falling in the village. These instances are namely when young boys are herding cattle or when villagers are at funerals and heavy rains appear imminent. She detailed, when young boys are herding cattle and heavy rains are about to fall, a bright orange rainy season flower called *nyamaradzo* can be burnt in a fire to stop the rains from falling. Furthermore, the approach of rain during a burial ceremony of a person can disturb the burial. To stop the rain during this ceremony, elders can place an axe into the fire; thereafter they will give ashes to the eldest child to place on the roof of a thatched kitchen. Alternatively, they can place the deceased's clothing item on the roof of a grass thatched kitchen and the rain will not come down until after the burial ceremony.

During *mubvumbi* (incessant rains), villagers could plead to the ancestors for a cessation of the rain for a day to allow people to weed their fields.

In the conversations with the elderly women, it became apparent that they are wary of giving definitive conclusions and predictions regarding the seasonal weather forecast. This is despite the accumulated tried and tested local knowledge. The weather forecasts provided by the elderly women in the study village appear to have a fifty-fifty chance. This relates to the Met Department weather forecasts as there is an element of probability. However, this is grounded on certainty derived from experiences. The elderly women regard definitiveness improper because you cannot judge for God regarding what the weather will be like. Concerning weather forecasting using local indicators that have been passed from generation to generation, Mbuya Ku pointed out the possibility of predicting the weather over a week or month long period. However, she cautioned on the limitedness of elderly women's use of vast stock of knowledge. She notes, God ultimately as having the final decision on what the weather would be like over a certain period of time.

The new weather prediction technique (specifically for coming rain season); from the Holy Spirit appear to be based on high levels of "certainty". This is compared to the Meteorological Services Department and local weather forecasting using flora and fauna as these appear to be based on "probability". For example, as pointed out by Mai Mizhu, the Holy Spirit predictions that she had been using since 2013 were not based on probability but absolute certainty as they were exact in fulfilment.

Conclusion

This chapter has examined the everyday sources of weather and rainfall forecasting by elderly women heads of households in rural Zimbabwe. It identified their use of local knowledge in the face of climate change as well as human beings' interventions to alter the weather. Evidence has shown that the elderly women and other community members use their stocks of local knowledge to understand the weather and climate change. Therefore their local knowledge provides local weather forecasts which are a critical aspect of their communal everyday life. The role of the Meteorological Services Department which represents scientific approaches to understanding climate and weather is increasingly being shunned for its reputation of inaccuracy. Increasingly elderly women are calling on a new weather and rain season forecast phenomenon in the form of prophecy from Independent African Churches in the village. Understanding the weather and climate is important as it can help in household level decision-making related to agro-based livelihoods for elderly women headed household.

References

Baer, H. A. and Reuter, T. (2015), Anthropological perspectives on climate change and sustainability: Implications for policy and action, *Brief for GSDR 2015*, Available at:

https://sustainabledevelopment.un.org/content/documents/58 34GSDR_brief_anthropology_SD_baer_reuter_rev.pdf.

Barnes, J, Dove, M. R, Lahsen, M, Mathews, A, McElwee, P, McIntosh, R, Moore, F, O'Reilly, J, Orlove, B, Puri, R, Weiss, H. and Yager, K. (2013). Contribution of Anthropology to the study of climate change. *Nature Climate Change* (3), 541-544.

Crane, T. A, Roncoli, C, Paz, J, Breuer, N, Broad, K, Ingram, K. T and Hoogenboom, G. (2010). Forecast skill and farmers' skills: seasonal climate forecasts and agricultural risk management in the Southeastern United States, *Weather, Climate and Society*, 2, 44-59.

Desjarlais, R & Jason, C. J. (2011). Phenomenological approaches in Anthropology, *Annual Review of Anthropology*, 40, 87-102.

Einarsson, N. (2011). Culture, conflict and crises in the Icelandic Fisheries: An Anthropological study of people, policy and marine resources in the North Atlantic Arctic, *Acta Universitatis Upsaliensis Uppsala Studies in Cultural Anthropology, 48*.

Elia, E. F, Mutula, S and Stilwell, C. (2014). Indigenous knowledge use in seasonal weather forecasting in Tanzania: the case of semi-arid central Tanzania, *South African Journal of Library and Information Science, 80* (1), 18-27.

FAO. (2004). Drought impact mitigation and prevention in the Limpopo River Basin: a situation analysis. *Land and water discussion paper 4*. Rome: Food and Agriculture Organisation of the United Nations.

Flintan, F. (2003). 'Engendering' Eden Volume III Women, gender and ICDPs in South and South-East Asia: Lessons learnt and experiences shared, *IIED Wildlife and Development Series, 18*.

Galloway, L. F. and Burgess, K. S. (2009). Manipulation of flowering time: phenomenological integration and maternal effects. *Ecology, 90*, 2139-2148.

IPCC. (2007). *Climate change: Impacts, adaptation and vulnerability. Contribution of Working Group II to the Fourth Assessment Report of the Intergovernmental Panel on Climate Change* (IPCC). Cambridge: Cambridge University Press.

Low, S. M. (2005). *Climate change and Africa.* Cambridge University Press: New York.

Makwara, C, E. (2013). Indigenous Knowledge Systems and modern weather forecasting: Exploring the linkages, *Journal of Agriculture and Sustainability*, 2. (1), 98-141.

Manatsa, D, Unganai, L, Gadzirai, C and Behera, S. K. (2012). An innovative tailored seasonal rainfall forecasting production in Zimbabwe, *Natural Hazards, 64*, 1187-1207.

Mapara, J. (2009). Indigenous knowledge systems in Zimbabwe: Juxtaposing postcolonial theory, *The Journal of Pan African Studies, 3* (1), 139-155.

Mapeta, R. (2000). *Drought mitigation and indigenous knowledge and practices: a rural farmer's perspective.* In Shumba, O (ed). (2000), Drought mitigation and Indigenous Knowledge Systems in Southern Africa: proceedings of the Southern Africa Regional Meeting, Harare, Zimbabwe, 19-20 November 1998. Harare: SAFIRE, 94-95.

Mararike, C. G. (1996). *The use of trees, birds and animal behaviour as measures of environmental change by the Shona People of Zimbabwe.* In Hambly, H & Angura, T. O (eds) (1996), Grassroots indicators for desertification experience and perspectives from eastern and southern Africa, Ottawa: IDRC, 120-128.

Moran, E. F, Adams, R, Bakoy´Ema, B, Fiorini T, S and Boucek, B. (2006). Human strategies for coping with El Nin˜O related drought in Amazonia, *Climatic Change (77)*, 343-361.

Mudombi, S and Nhamo, G. (2014), Access to weather forecasting and early warning information by communal farmers in Seke and Murewa Districts, Zimbabwe, *Journal of Human Ecology, 48* (3), 357-366.

Muguti, T & Maposa, R. S. (2011), Indigenous weather forecasting: A phenomenological study engaging the Shona of Zimbabwe, *The Journal of Pan African Studies, 4* (9), 102-112.

Mwadime, R. K. N. (1996). Changes in environmental conditions: Their potential as indicators for monitoring household food security, in Hambly, H & Angura, T. O (eds). (1996), Grassroots indicators for desertification experience and perspectives from Eastern and Southern Africa, Ottawa: IDRC, 85-94.

Ndiweni, J. A and Ndlovu, C. (2013). An exploration of the value of indigenous knowledge adaptation strategies in ensuring food security and livelihoods in Southern Zimbabwe, *Global Journal of*

Human Social Science, Geography, Geosciences, Environmental Disaster Management, 13 (7).

Patt, A, Suarez, P and Gwata, C. (2005). Effects of seasonal climate forecasts and participatory workshops among subsistence farmers in Zimbabwe, *Proceedings of the National Academy of Sciences, 102* (35), 12623-12628.

Reuter, T and Baer, H. (2015). Anthropological perspectives on climate change and sustainability: Implications for policy and action, *Global Sustainable Development Report* (3), 1-3.

Risiro, J, Mashoko, D, Tshuma, D. T, & Rurinda, E. (2012). Weather forecasting and indigenous knowledge systems in Chimanimani District of Manicaland, Zimbabwe, *Journal of Emerging Trends in Educational Research and Policy Studies,* 3 (4), 561-566.

Roncoli, C. (2006). Ethnographic and participatory approaches to research on farmers' responses to climate predictions, *Climate Research,* 33, 81-99.

Roncoli, C, Ingram, K and Kirshen, P. (2002). Reading the rains: Local knowledge and rainfall forecasting in Burkina Faso, *Society & Natural Resources,* 15 (5), 409-427.

Smith, H (2007). Disrupting the global discourse of climate change: The case of indigenous voices, in M, E. Pettenger (ed). (2007). The social construction of climate change: power, knowledge, norms, discourses, Hampshire: Ashgate.

Worby, E. (1992). *Remaking labour, reshaping identity: cotton, commoditization and the culture of modernity in northwestern Zimbabwe.* PhD Thesis, McGill University.

Ziervogel, G. and Opere, A. (Eds). (2010). *Integrating meteorological and indigenous knowledge-based seasonal climate forecasts in the agricultural sector.* Ottawa: International Development Research Centre, Canada. Climate Change Adaptation in Africa learning paper series.

Chapter 8

Thwarting the Sword of Damocles: Community Resilience Challenges in the Age of the Anthropocene

Christopher Mabeza

King Dionysius the Elder ruled over the ancient kingdom of Syracuse in 4th Century BC. Damocles was one of the courtiers in this kingdom and he spent most of his time flattering the King. Damocles believed that being a king was the easiest thing in the world. He thought the job involved eating good food, drinking good wine and in general having a wonderful time. In order to teach this courtier a lesson, King Dionysius invited him to a banquet. The food served was delicious and music played was lovely. Unfortunately, Damocles was unable to enjoy any of these things because unlike the other guests he found himself seated under a sword - a sword which was hanging by single horsehair. Damocles was afraid that the hair would snap at any time resulting in the sword falling on his head. This was the Dionysius' way of showing Damocles that although a king may be surrounded by luxury, he has little or no time to really enjoy them. The king's life is very precarious - as precarious as a man who has a sword hanging over his head*

- Philosopher Cicero in ancient Rome

Introduction

This chapter views climate change - a volatile tinderbox of our time – as an ever-present threat to rural communities' livelihoods. Disasters and shocks are occurring more frequently with chronic stresses lasting longer (Matthews, 2017). To that end, this chapter invokes a moral parable about the threat of a sword that hangs by a thread above Damocles' head. The moral of the story is about the ever-present threat to humanity engendered by perturbation. The parable about the sword of Damocles was made popular by philosopher Cicero in ancient Rome.

Therefore, it is the conviction of this chapter that building community resilience is an attempt to thwart the climate change sword of Damocles. This is, more so, as we enter the *terra incognita* of the Anthropocene. The Anthropocene is a new geological era in which the human footprint is the dominant force shaping planetary dynamics. Therefore, addressing this hyper-complex challenge requires new ways of thinking and doing things (Biggs, 2017). Humans are reshaping the world on a geological scale but at a far-faster-than-geological speed (*The Economist*, 2011). That humans have changed the way the world works, means they have to change the way they think about it, as well (*The Economist*, 2011). In the same vein, humans have to change the way they manage anthropogenic (human-induced) climate change so as to transition towards sustainable development goals (SDGs). In order to thwart the threat of the sword of Damocles (to manage the adverse effects of climate change), it is imperative to build resilience.

In the development arena, resilience is a flourishing buzzword that draws on an increasing concern with the impact of shocks and disasters on development progress and an awareness of the complex contexts in which development takes place (Daw, 2017). Climate variability impinges on livelihood activities across Africa. Therefore, it is exacerbating environmental threats such as water scarcity and land degradation, which negatively affect long and short-term livelihood prospects (Beckline, 2016). Resilience as a perspective plays a critical role in the analysis of human-environment systems that emphasise the need to comprehend and manage change, particularly unexpected change (Biggs et al. 2014). This chapter probes the concept of building resilience by smallholder farmers in rural Zimbabwe in the background of a changing climatic environment. The term resilience is probed together with the closely related terms – adaptation and vulnerability. Vulnerability is about the degree to which rural communities are exposed to the effects of climate change and other stressors.

Rural communities mainly practise rain-fed agriculture. Their livelihoods have become precarious due to increased extreme climatic events (ECEs) such as drought. The World Bank

Independent Evaluation Group has argued that "rain-fed agriculture is sensitive to climate variability – too little or too much rainfall this is especially true in the dry lands home to many of the poor and many dependent on agriculture" (Mabeza, 2015). The smallholders in rural Zimbabwe also have to contend with barriers and limits to successful adaptation such as poor extension services that are compounded by the country's economy. Soil fertility is in decline and smallholders do not have adequate financial resources to buy inorganic fertiliser. Smallholders face a new reality as already alluded to, the Anthropocene where disasters and shocks are occurring more frequently with increased intensity and duration. The challenge for smallholders is to use human ingenuity to conjure resilience initiatives in an age of ever increasing complexity.

In a bid to build resilience enterprising smallholder farmers have become innovative. Some harvest water as an adaptive mechanism. Zvishavane is home to many innovative smallholder farmers and some are not only surviving but thriving in a changing climatic environment (Mabeza, 2017). In a study in Charewa, in the Mutoko district of Zimbabwe, It is argued that the "process of adaptation is ostensibly not straightforward but complex. As it evolves, farmers find themselves facing numerous constraining structures and processes". In Mutoko smallholders are experiencing ECEs, mainly rainfall conditions that are significantly deviating from the conditions farmers are used to, thereby prompting heterogeneous responses. To illustrate the complexity of building resilience to climate change, ignoring contextual issues like economic, social and political can be disastrous. In effect, farmers do not live in a vacuum (Bhatasara, 2017).

The definition of community resilience is contested terrain. Community resilience means different things to different people. Community resilience is a measure of the sustained ability of a community to utilise available resources to respond to, withstand and recover from adverse situations (Patel et al. 2017). It is defined as the capacity of a community to sustain human well-being in the face of disturbance and change, by buffering shocks and adapting and transforming in response to change. On the other hand (Biggs, 2017), resilience as has been defined as "a fundamental concept in complex social ecological systems thinking and refers to the situation where social ecological systems, households or communities are able to respond to shocks and stresses and, moreover, use this as an opportunity for innovation and adaptation" (Folke cited in Shackleton and Shackleton, 2012: 276).

This chapter will use the definition by Folke as it recognises the critical role of innovation in building resilience. Resilience is all about dealing with change in an age of complexity and adaptation and transforming in response to change in an innovative manner. It is argued that the future will be defined by three drivers: increasing complexity. Societies and ecosystems become more intertwined. This global interconnectivity speaks to "surprising surprises" (Matthews, 2017).

Theoretical Framework

In order to probe the concept of building resilience in the Anthropocene, this study develops a theoretical framework based on the challenges that emerge in the era of complexity. There is general acknowledgement that studying complex phenomena ushers a paradigm shift from classical (Newtonian) scientific strategies (Walby cited in Presier, 2014). Newtonian scientific strategies assume that theories and models capture reality in a neutral and objective manner, on the other hand, complex systems are such that they are never completely graspable by any model; models of them are incomplete (Presier, 2014). Therefore, complexity is a new vehicle meant to rectify the "simplifications and idealisations that have led to unrealistic models in the sciences" (Biggs, 2017).

Engagement with complexity is emerging in all realms of knowledge: physical, social, economic, political, health, culture and social-ecological systems thinking (Wells cited in Presier, 2014). Interactions in the socio-ecological systems are cross-scalar (i.e. move from global to local and across sectors without easy demarcation) and are characterised by nonlinear dynamics (Keys, 2017). A system is a unit organised by interaction between elements, actions, or individuals (Morin, 1992c). Therefore, this calls on interventions to be conceived differently.

Current resilience discourse is grounded within a complex systems theoretical framework. Building resilience in the Anthropocene should embrace complexity. The Anthropocene will be defined by the following drivers: increasing complexity, global interconnectivity and surprises or what O'Brien calls "surprising surprises" (Global Resilience Partnership, undated). Stable conditions and assumptions of linear, incremental change are history. Disasters and shocks are occurring more frequently with increased intensity and chronic stresses are lasting longer (as stated explained later in this chapter) (Global Resilience Partnership, undated). All this attests to a global environmental change in an age of complexity. O'Brien cited in Mabeza et al. notes the following features of complexity as illustrated in Table 8.1:

Table 8.1: Characteristics of Complexity in an Era of Global Environmental Change (O'Brien cited in Mabeza et al. forthcoming)

Characteristic	Outcomes
Nonlinearity	- Outcomes within complex systems are difficult to predict with certainty - Small changes can have large consequences.
Irreversibility	- Systems can be pushed towards outcomes that can no longer be reversed through changes in policies, new technologies or altered behaviours. - The climate system is already considered to be moving into a non-analogue state (*i.e.*, one without precedence in humanity's history) that may eventually stabilise at a new state, but is unlikely to return to what it was.
Surprises	- Complex systems do not always act in ways that are expected, despite human efforts to consider all types of contingencies. - Global environmental changes at the scale, rate and magnitude that they are now occurring, will lead to new and unexpected outcomes e.g. ocean acidification, unanticipated biological responses, novel extreme events. - Society has to prepare not only for environmental surprises, but also for potential social surprises – the unexpected, nonlinear social responses that may emerge in reaction to global environmental change.

Building resilience entails reducing vulnerability. Vulnerability in the Anthropocene results from networks of multiple interacting causes that cannot be individually distinguished; must not be addressed in a piecemeal way and they are such that small inputs may result in disproportionate effects (Presier, 2014). Due to its complexity, "the discourses on climate change have shifted toward 'adaptation' as a means of addressing climate-related vulnerabilities" (Ribot, 2013: 2). However, just addressing climate related vulnerabilities will not suffice. Reducing vulnerabilities ought to be done in the context of a multi-stressor environment, i.e., addressing interacting climatic and non-climatic issues. Vulnerability is "the degree to which an individual, group or system is susceptible to harm due to exposure to hazard or stress and the (in)ability to cope, recover or fundamentally adapt (become a new system or become extinct)" (Tompkins cited in Levina and Tirpark, 2006: 16).

Methodology

The research mainly focused on ethnographic data generating techniques. The research mainly used ethnography because a study of this nature requires a period engaging in participant observation so as to explore the 'invisible' and 'unspoken' aspects of practices to do with interventions by marginalised rural communities (Mabeza, 2015). Data generated was a result of revealing interviews with research participants and the author's eyewitness account of events as they unfolded in two villages in rural Zimbabwe.

The villages are Muunganirwa-Chakona members of an irrigation scheme and Matamba. The villages of Muunganirwa-Chakona are under Chief Musana in the Bindura District. The Musana communal areas fall under agro-ecological region two. Agro-ecological region two is suitable for intensive farming based on livestock and crop production and rainfall amounts range from 750-1000mm per year (Vincent and Thomas, 1960). Matamba Village is found in Shurugwi District which is in agro-ecological region four. Rainfall amounts range from 450 to 650mm per year. Rainfall is erratic with severe dry spells during the rainy season. Crop production is risky and the region is suitable for drought resistant crops (Vincent and Thomas, 1960).

Key informant and semi-structured interviews were conducted in the two villages. The author interviewed three extension workers operating in the Musana rural areas and sought their views about the changing weather patterns. In addition, the author sought to establish the adaptive strategies employed in the district. Traditional leaders also gave their views about interventions for managing climate variability and barriers to successful adaptation. The author engaged in participant observation in the villages. Smallholder farmers engaged in an irrigation scheme were interviewed about the interventions they have deployed to adapt to a changing climatic environment. Village elders in both villages were interviewed and they gave their opinions about the perennial food insecurity in the rural areas. Members of non-governmental organisations (NGOs) operating in the two districts were also interviewed about the efficacy of their interventions. Names of the NGOs will not be named for ethical reasons as they were not comfortable with their identities being revealed.

Three focus group discussions (FGDs) were held in the two villages. The author held only one interview with seven members of the irrigation scheme because the villages are in a province which is politically volatile. Therefore, gathering individuals can be misconstrued to be politicking. In Matamba Village, the author did two FGDs, one with youths and the other with adults. Both FGDs sought to identify basic needs, interventions and hurdles the research participants face as they grapple with increased rainfall variability. The FGDs were aimed at stimulating the research participants to open up about their access to agricultural inputs and the adaptive strategies they deploy. These discussions also aimed at getting to grips with socio-ecological changes that have taken place over the years. The author also sought to identify the cultural practices and belief systems in both villages. The study conducted life histories in the villages mentioned above. Through the life histories, the study sought to establish how the farmers over the years have successfully adapted to climate variability. The farmers also mentioned the hurdles they encountered *en route* to successful adaptation. Life histories privilege the narration of personal biographies and can be used to identify key moments in an individual's life (shocks, pivotal moments and transition points) and their coping strategies (Bhatasara, 2017).

This study relies on the interpretation of data through the lens of what has been referred to as "thick description" (Geertz, 1973: 6). It is argued that besides observing, recording and analysing, an ethnographer must make interpretations to gain meaning (Geertz, 1973). However, these methods may not fully grasp the nuances in climate change adaptation.

Results and Discussion

The chapter focuses on two villages which encapsulate community resilience to climate change. The farmers in the two villages face several hurdles to successful adaptation but their stories give hope. Some of the farmers are not only surviving but thriving in the midst of adversity. Below is an overview of the adaptive strategies that the farmers have put in place.

Muunganirwa-Chakona Village Irrigation Scheme

About 64 smallholder farmers in the Musana Communal areas, in Ward 14 launched the Muunganirwa-Chakona Village Irrigation Scheme in 2002. The scheme was partly sponsored by the European Union. Members of the scheme weighed in with 75% of the funding. The irrigation scheme is based on water harvesting. The farmers harvest water from the Nyamapinga stream flowing down the Nyandiya Mountain. The secretary of the cooperative, Mr C Mushonga bought a pipe about 1 500m long to carry water to the communal garden. The farmers engage in market gardening and sell their produce in the cities of Harare and Bindura. Smallholder farmers engage in intercropping and plant different crops often plant several different food crops "so that failure of any one crop will not have catastrophic impacts on food provision" (Constant, 2017).

The smallholders face a suite of challenges that include lack of transport to ferry the produce to the markets, depressed markets, accessing inputs and increased rainfall variability (Mabeza, 2016). In addition, they are also engaged in fish farming and the market is readily available in the villages. However, fish feeds are becoming more and more expensive to the detriment of the fish project.

Besides addressing the smallholders' needs, the project also empowers them. Farmers realise profits enough to send their children to school. Some of them have diversified from market gardening to growing tobacco, a strategy which has shown a lot of promise. The irrigation scheme is ample evidence of the smallholders' relentless experimentation, they experiment with various seed varieties and stagger planting dates (Plate 8.1).

Plate 8.1: A member of the irrigation scheme holding the hosepipe at the mountain water source

Matamba Village

In Matamba Village, smallholder farmers are engaged in conservation agriculture (CA). According to the Food and Agricultural Organisation (FAO), CA is a system of agriculture that aims at:

Producing high crop yields while reducing production costs, maintaining the soil fertility and conserving water. It is a way to achieve sustainable agriculture and improve livelihoods. CA has three basic principles:

- Disturb the soil as little as possible
- Keep the soil covered as much as possible (mulching)
- Mix and rotate crops (FAO, undated: 3)

Mulching ensured that as much water as possible was conserved. Farmers without access to draught power benefited because CA did not involve ploughing with an ox-drawn plough. CA also implied a reduced acreage of land under cultivation.

The research participants in the village included a group of ten farmers. The farmers are led by what is known in CA parlance as a lead farmer. The rest are called mentored farmers. The lead farmer was the only member who got seed and fertiliser inputs from the NGO sponsoring the CA programme while the rest had to fend for themselves. However, farmers who had inputs realised an increase in grain harvested. For example, the lead farmer and a host of other farmers have realised their grain production increasing. They realise enough grain to feed their families. These farmers have realised the importance of not only moderating harm but exploiting risk into opportunity (Plate 8.2).

Plate 8.2: The lead farmer stands next to his maize crop

Smallholder farmers pool their resources together. For example, four smallholder farmers with an ox each, combined their oxen to form a *chipani* (span oxen for ploughing). During *humwe* (work parties) farmers pool their ox-drawn cuts to help ferry manure to the fields.

Most of the young adults (mostly male) engage in *chikorokoza* (gold panning) and some who have licences from the Ministry of Mines engage in artisanal gold mining. Some gold panners buy cars from their proceeds and convert them into taxis. Some enterprising young women are making a living by selling food to the gold panners. Remittances play an important role in the rural economy. Some parents have children in the diaspora who send remittances on a regular basis. However, with the cash crisis in the country, the villagers queue for days on end to be able to access their money.

Smallholder farmers in rural Zimbabwe have adapted to the impact of climate change with varying degrees of success. Rural communities as shown in the two case studies build resilience to climate change by pooling their resources. Some preserve their vegetables by drying them and others diversify their livelihoods. However, in a bid to adapt, smallholders face multi-scale forces. Rural communities contend with a multi-stressor environment which includes increased climate variability, HIV/AIDS, infertile soils and an erosion of their adaptive capacity (Ribot, 2013).

Framing environmental problems as technical ultimately means the solutions will be viewed as technical. In other words, such framing of environmental problems (terministic screens) are inadequate because adaptation to climate change means much more than technology. It is suggested that such dominant narratives as the 'Green Revolution' premised on technical solutions. These have "fostered a way of conceiving of social life as a technical problem, as a matter for rational decision and management to be entrusted to the group of people – the development professionals – whose specialised knowledge allegedly qualifies them for that task" (Escobar, cited in Mabeza, 2015: 71).

Tragically, most interventions in the rural areas perceive smallholder farmer vulnerabilities as a technical problem. Technological or financial inputs intended to 'push' the rural poor out of a vicious cycle of poverty, have had successes, but have also failed with serious consequences that can be maladaptive thereby reinforcing poverty (Lade, 2017). Technology alone will not suffice, equally important are values and beliefs - critical components of culture, because they influence the way people build resilience to perturbations such as climate change.

Roncoli et al. concur:

> culture frames the way people perceive, understand, experience and respond to key elements of the worlds which they live in. This framing is grounded in systems of meanings and relationships that mediate human engagements with natural phenomena and processes. This framing is particularly relevant to the study of climate change, which entails movement away from a known past, through an altered present and toward an uncertain future, since what is recalled, recognised, or envisaged rests on cultural models and values (Roncoli et al. 2009: 87).

More often than not, organs of the state tasked with disaster risk management resemble the proverbial rabbit is the headlights. Dazzled by the beaming headlights, the rabbit becomes lethargic, at times with tragic consequences. Similarly, at times state actors are lethargic in responding to hazards. These hazards have negative impacts on rural communities and will ultimately affect their capacity to build resilience.

Building resilience means "stepping away from reductionist thinking and accepting that within a socio-ecological system, several connections are occurring at the same time on different levels". Further to that complexity thinking means accepting uncertainty and acknowledging a multi-approach perspective and this requires reimagining resilience-building – addressing the structural inequalities that entrench vulnerability (Daw, 2017).

However, at times, as noted causes of vulnerability are not always external as argued by post development critics. It is argued that failure of a project, the New Gato Water Project (NGWP) in Shurugwi rural was internal and mainly influenced by local level politics and conflict (Mangoma, 2011). In the same vein, the CA project in the Matamba village has run out of steam as seen by the number of farmers who have dropped out. Some of the drop-outs appeared to have been influenced by local leaders who view NGOs with suspicion. In some instances, there were muted voices of farmers who accused the lead farmers of "bribing" their subordinates for their own ends. While this research cannot authoritatively claim that the irrigation scheme in the Musana communal lands has been bedevilled by similar reasons as the ones that led to the collapse of NGWP, some members have withdrawn from the scheme for reasons this research could not establish. The section below considers policy recommendations.

Conclusion, Policy Options and Practical Recommendations

At times, rural development players remain true to their idiosyncratic responses to ECEs to the detriment of community resilience. In some instances, however, local level politics and power increases vulnerability of rural communities to a multi-stressor environment. But all is not doom and gloom as illustrated by the "good news stories" of successful farmers who have transformed risk into opportunity. It gives a sense of hope that some smallholder farmers are thriving in the midst of increased climate variability. The rural communities' livelihoods in the Anthropocene are precarious, as precarious as Damocles who has a sword hanging above his head by a thread. These are strange times, but with human ingenuity, a knack for building resilience, hope is never in short supply.

Community resilience should not only aim at potential impacts of rainfall variability but also recognise the importance of meeting a range of goals beyond those of adapting to climate change alone. Rural communities adapt to a range of stresses some of which are non-climatic. To that end, governments should develop strategies and institutions that address complexity in the Anthropocene. Building resilience is not only about the deployment of hardware and financial inputs. That technology will solve all of the rural communities' problems is inaccurate. Therefore, an excessive focus on technology and finance by both state and non-state actors, risks alienating endogenous poverty alleviation pathways (Lade et al. 2017). The effort channelled to the deployment of large hardware such as dams at the expense of tried and tested smallholder technologies may be misguided. Interventions should take cognisance of what Davies and Moore (2016) term "technologies of life". These are technologies that have been practised since time immemorial by rural communities and have helped them to survive the effects of climate variability.

This study supports the suggestion by Buchner-Marais (2017) that researchers transform themselves from being "extractors and curators of knowledge towards being facilitators of relations and curators of transformative spaces". Therefore, this study emphasises "co-exploration" between researchers and those who are on the frontline of the adverse effects of climate change. Similarly, players in the rural development discourse from are cautioned from what Robert Kay calls "adaptation by ribbon cutting" (Mabeza, forthcoming). Adaptation by ribbon cutting is defined as "a short-term decision frame in preference to long-term adaption decision-making. The motivation behind the short-term focus being the hope from those sponsoring the adaptation infrastructure works that they will personally be present to cut the ribbon within their term of office and thereby in the public spotlight to reflect the success of this good deed" (Kay, 2009:15). It is advised that, "If we are to identify effective adaptive solutions, we must be prepared to think outside the confines of self-interest and expediency" (Kay, 2009:15). Adaptation by ribbon cutting leads to maladaptation.

Although climate models and simulations by their nature are problematic, nevertheless information on seasonal forecasts could play a pivotal role in helping farmers plan for agricultural seasons. Additionally, there is a new school of thought that decadal timescale information could help assist farmers build resilience. It is argued that focus has mainly centred on seasonal timescale and less attention has been given to information on the decadal timescale, yet much policy, planning, decision-making in rural development take place within this timescale (Nyamwanza et al. 2017). Decadal climate projections can be helpful in facilitating vulnerable communities in effective anticipatory adaptation. If rural communities are to be assisted to build resilience, vulnerability assessments are critical towards achieving that goal. Vulnerability must address causality. It is argued that vulnerabilities do not fall from the sky and that their causes are diverse. During policy formulation when exploring who is vulnerable, it is equally important to explore why individuals are vulnerable (Ribot, 2013).

References

Beckline, M, Yujun, S, Ayonghe, S, Loveline Etta, O, Constantine, I. and Richard, T. (2016) *Adaptation of Women to Climate Variability in the Southern Slopes of the Rumpi Hills of Cameroon.* Agriculture, Forestry and Fisheries 5 (6): 272-279. DOI: 10.11648/j.aff.20160506.19

Bhatasara S. 2017. Towards a Sociology of Adaptation to Rainfall Variability in Rural Zimbabwe: The Case of Charewa in Mutoko. *Fudan Journal of the Humanities and Social Sciences.* DOI 10.1007/s40647-017-0177-8

Biggs R, M Schlüter and M L Schoon. 2014. The Resilience Approach: Sustaining Ecosystem Services in Social-Ecological Systems. In R Biggs, M Schlüter and M L Schoon (eds), *Principles for Building Resilience Sustaining ecosystem services in social-ecological systems.* UK: Cambridge University Press.

Biggs R. 2017. Tackling the Anthropocene Challenge: The Resilience Thinking approach. Resilience for Development Colloquium, Johannesburg, South Africa.

Biggs R. 2017. Social-ecological regime shifts. *Resilience for Development Colloquium,* Johannesburg, South Africa.

Buchner-Marais C. 2017. Creating transformative spaces. *Resilience for Development Colloquium,* Johannesburg, South Africa.

Constant N. 2017. Hierarchies of knowledge: Ethnobotical knowledge, practices and cosmology of the VhaVenda in South Africa.

Davies I J and H L Moore. 2016. Landscape, time and cultural resilience: a brief history of agriculture in Pokot and Marakwet, Kenya. Journal of Eastern African Studies, 10:1, 67-87.DOI: 10.1080/17531055.2015.113441.

Daw T. 2017. What insights can social-ecological resilience research offer the challenges of development in the Anthropocene? Resilience for Development Colloquium.

FAO. Undated. What is Conservation Agriculture? Available at: www.fao.org/ag/ca/AfricaTrainingManualCD/PDF%20Files/01INTRO.PDF. Accessed on 05/09/2017

Geertz C. 1973. *The interpretation of cultures: Selected topics.* New York: Basic Books.

Global Resilience Partnership. Undated. Building Resilience in Complexity Lessons Learned & Lessons Confirmed.

Keys P. 2017. Understanding Anthropocene risk. *Resilience for Development Colloquium*, Johannesburg, South Africa.

Lade S, L J Haider, G Engstrom and M Schluter. 2017. Resilience offers escape from trapped thinking on poverty alleviation. *Sci. Adv.* 3:e1603043.

Levina E and D Tirpark. 2006. *Adaptation to climate change: Key terms.* Paris: Organisation for Economic Cooperation and Development (OECD).

Mabeza C M, T Pesanayi and C Luphele. Forthcoming. Business unusual: Towards transformational adaptation.

Mabeza C M. Forthcoming. "Living with the Anthropocene blues": Adaptation to Climate Change in Zimbabwe. Climate Change Department, Ministry of Environment, Water and Climate Change, Zimbabwe.

Mabeza C M. 2014. *Marrying water and soil: Adaptation to climate by a smallholder farmer in Zvishavane, rural Zimbabwe.* PhD thesis, University of Cape Town, South Africa.

Mabeza C M. 2017. *Water and soil in holy matrimony? A smallholder farmer's innovative agricultural practices for adapting to climate in rural Zimbabwe.* Cameroon: Langaa

Matthews N. 2017. The Pitfalls and opportunities of building resilience with complexity: Insights from GRP. *Resilience Development Colloquium*, Johannesburg, South Africa.

Morin E. 1992c. Towards a Study of Humankind, Volume 1: the Nature of Nature. (transl. Roland Bélanger). New York & Paris: Peter Lang

Nyamwanza A et al. 2017. Contributions of decadal climate information in sub-Saharan African agricultural and food systems. *Climate*

Patel S S, M B Rogers, R Amlot and G J Rubin. 2017. What Do We Mean by 'Community Resilience'? A Systematic Literature Review of How It is Defined in the Literature. *Plos Current Disasters.* Accessed at:
http://currents.plos.org/disasters/article/what-do-we-mean-by-community-resilience-a-systematic-literature-review-of-how-it-is-defined-in-the-literature/

Preiser R. 2014. Introduction to Complexity. SAPECS Winter School, Nelson Mandela Metropolitan University, South Africa. 30 June to 4 July.

Resilience Alliance. 2010. *Assessing resilience in social-ecological systems: Workbook for practitioners.* Version 2.0. Online: http://www.resalliance.org/3871.php

Ribot J. 2013. Risk and Blame in the Anthropocene: Multi-scale Climate Change Analysis. *Food Sovereignty: A Critical Dialogue. International Conference, Yale University, September 14-15.* Conference Paper #7.

Shackleton S E and Shackleton C M. 2012. Linking poverty, HIV/AIDS and climate change to human and ecosystem vulnerability in southern Africa: consequences for livelihoods and sustainable ecosystem management. *International Journal of Sustainable Development & World Ecology*, 19:3, 275-286, DOI:10.1080/13504509.2011.641039

Simonsen S H, Biggs R, Schluter M. 2014. *Applying resilience thinking. Seven principles for building resilience in social-ecological systems.* Stockholm: Stockholm University.

The Economist. 2011. The geology of the planet: Welcome to the Anthropocene. Accessed at: http://www.economist.com/node/18744401

Vincent V and Thomas R G. 1960. An Agricultural Survey of Southern Rhodesia. Part 1: Agro-ecological Survey. Salisbury: Government Printers.

Sword of Damocles. Accessed at: http://www.english-for-students.com/Sword-Of-Damocles.html. Accessed on 05/09/2017

Chapter 9

The Politics of Community Resilience: A Closer Look into the Settlement Hierarchy of Zimbabwe

Charity Manyeruke & Archimedes Muzenda

Introduction

In the past few decades, community resilience has become a critical topic gaining increasing academic and programmatic attention (Skerratt, 2013; Skerratt and Steiner, 2013; Steiner and Markantoni, 2014). The departure from the 'predict and prevent' model (IFRC, 2012) in development discourse has led to attention given to uncertain disruptions that may impact communities. Concurrently, human settlements around the world are evolving in response to changing development trajectories. Settlements have become more complex communities of connectivity and interdependency. However, the complexity is explained by the vulnerability to disruptions that can turn highly functional settlements into dysfunction. In Zimbabwe, human settlements have evolved and proliferated from the traditional rural and urban settlements adding peri-urban and resettlement areas to the hierarchy. These settlements in their existence face disruption that destabilise their form and function. Human settlements evolution is also being associated with increasing occurrences of global risks, rendering increased volatility, uncertainty and ambiguity of societal environments. Community resilience is extensively research in perspectives of disasters and different types of communities. In human settlements, nevertheless, cross-sectional studies that compares resilience at different settlements hierarchy are minimal.

This chapter explores and assess community resilience in different settlements of Zimbabwe. It adopts a reductionist approach of understanding conceptual components of community resilience as they apply to the evolutionary process and functionality of different settlements. The chapter applies livelihoods framework to the four settlements; urban, peri-urban, rural resettlement and communal settlements. In its multidimensional variation, resilience is more direct and tangible at household level. The abstract and intangible nature that resilience takes extends to larger sphere (Wilson, 2012a). Therefore, at the community level, the chapter explores is an intersection of micro-individual or household resilience and macro-national level resilience leveraging its upscaling or downscaling.

The chapter first tracks the human settlements evolution in Zimbabwe distinguishing the resilience attributes among the four settlement types. After conceptualising community resilience, the chapter applies the livelihoods framework to explore and evaluate the differences, similarities, convergences and trends in resilience and vulnerability of the different settlements. Deriving from the differences, similarities and trends, the chapter discusses the conceptual components of community resilience as they relate to connectivity and interdependency. It explores the institutional frameworks govern the four types of settlements in their capacity building of community resilience. The chapter concludes by exploring the politics of assessing and programming resilience in different settlements by it suggesting strategies for integrated resilience programming.

Human Settlements Development in Zimbabwe

The human settlement hierarchy in Zimbabwe can be classified into four. The communal, resettlements and the peri-urban settlements. Of the four settlements, the communal and urban settlements have been the primary settlements that existed since the colonial era. Before the colonial era, distinct human settlements existed as centralised kingdoms spread across the country that represented states such as the Great Zimbabwe, Khami and Danangombe. The emergence of resettlement and peri-urban settlements is a manifestation of how settlements evolve and transform in response to a changing environment entailing, transformability in settlement evolution. Communal areas and rural resettlements in Zimbabwe are intrinsically interconnected. Communal areas have been subject to over population since they were earmarked primary habitat for native population by British settlers during colonial era 1890-1980 (Palmer, 2003). By independence (in 1980) white commercial farmers owned almost 40 percent of prime agricultural land. On the contrary, 7 million black smallholder farmers where confined to about 42 percent of mainly marginal land in tribal trust lands (Makamure and Gutto, 1986). In these landholding variations, the white owned farms were estimated to be 60 percent underutilised. In the communal areas, agricultural production declined, increasing population reduced fields' areas, quality of agricultural land declined and decline in local storage levels. Drought occurrences such as the 1991-92 El-Nino drought increased the vulnerability of communal communities. They lost livestock, an important form of wealth that is used for agricultural production and as a more liquid form of assets. Decline of agricultural productivity in communal areas contributed to resettlement programmes in the post-independence era as government seek to empower communal populace with more productive agricultural land.

Since 1980 to 2000, the resettlement scheme under the model "A" scheme led to resettlement of several households in the former white settler owned commercial farms. This program administered on the willing-buyer-willing-seller basis, it was a way of transforming peasant agriculture (Geza, 1986). Under this settlement scheme, livelihood was supposed to be derived exclusively from agricultural production. The proposition was enforced by three permits that settlers signed in the offer letter. The permit to reside stated "The holder shall not carry on or allow any other person to carry on any trading, commercial or industrial operations on the site" (Department of Rural Development, 1981: 9). The conditions meant to restrict off-farm activities in the resettlement areas in efforts to make settlers full time small-scale farmers. However, it is noted the three intense drought that occurred between 1981 and 1990 led to the proliferation of off-farm activities as agricultural production became less viable (Scoones, 1998). Following the droughts was the relaxation of the rule since early 1990s as farmers could temporarily leave their farms on condition that their farms remain productive.

The resettlement areas in Zimbabwe which was intensified by the Fast-Track Land Reform Programme in 2000 ballooned in effect making resettlement areas a critical settlement hierarchy of the country. However, a state-appointed commission of inquiry in 1994 identified tenure insecurity as a major challenge that posed uncertainty and risk at the expense of the livelihood of settlers (Government of Zimbabwe, 1994). Without title deeds to the allocated land and just offer letters, the settlers are uncertain of the duration they have to occupy such land. Resettlement areas have been characterised by planned and spontaneous settlements. Communal population that did not receive offer letters, opted to resettle spontaneously forming a mosaic of planned and spontaneous resettlements. The spontaneous settlers proliferated as the District Development Fund did not legal authority to evict them. The Rural Lands Act that govern the resettlement areas was administered by a line Ministry of Lands and Rural Development (District Development Fund, 1994). More so, the spontaneity carried political overtones, used as an indication of landlessness for better support of donor partners in the land reform process.

At the top of the settlement hierarchy in Zimbabwe are urban settlements. Urban settlements dates from the colonial era where most urban areas were developed by the British South African Pioneer Column (BSAPC) as military and administrative 'forts' (Wekwete, 2014). As most urban areas in Zimbabwe are inherited post-colonial cities, they underwent remarkable social-spatial and economic transformation particularly emanating from rural to urban migration that was restricted during the colonial period. Colonial urban settlements were characterised by social discontinuity formed by racial classes. White settlers had designated regions of urban areas while native population were designated to African townships. Post-colonial social classes in urban areas have continued but in income dimensions. Low-income earners occupy the high-density areas of the city while high-income earners the low-density areas. This social discontinuity influenced by land prices has intensified overtime and manifested into decay of inner urban areas. The urban poor combined with urban poverty have increased in the inner-city and are contributing to capital flight from the inner city. Urban settlements in Zimbabwe varies from metropolitan cities to towns. Critical to note in urban settlements is the migratory trend of rush to the capital, where primary cities experience the most urban population growth.

As urban areas face challenges of social discontinuity in their spatial transformation, the huge influx of urban population beyond the capacity of the urban boundary has led to peri urbanisation. Defining peri-urban is conceptually cumbersome. Defined as a geography, concept or a process, the three definitions have been regarded as the urban fringe. It entails movement of commodities between the rural and the urban as a process; and conceptually as an interface between rural and urban activities (Narain and Nischal, 2007). It is highlighted that urban sprawl without the essential infrastructure such as transport network has culminated to the proliferation of 'precarious' peri-urbanisation (Chirisa, 2013). The peri-urban is regarded as rural areas on the outskirts of urban areas becoming more urban in character (Webster, 2002). Population pressures from urban and rural areas without supportive infrastructure, they tend to be the unwanted child of the rural and the urban. Peri urban settlements are characterised by vulnerabilities of both rural and urban yet have different robustness and capacity to respond to a disruption.

The Concept of Community Resilience

Defining community resilience proves to be as elusive as the terms community and resilience are both contested. Community resilience, refers to the capacities and capabilities of a community to 'prevent, withstand, or mitigate' any event that negatively disrupts its form and function (Ahmed, 2004; Islam *et al.* 2014). These disruptions while predominantly derive from external shocks that include social, political or environmental changes (Adger, 2000). The disruptions can also come from the community's internal evolutionary actions of vulnerability (Wilson, 2012). Contrary to the hard systems resilience, which is a descriptive concept with precise definition, meaning and quantitative operationalisation, community resilience is resilience of soft systems. It can be ambiguous, malleable, intangible, difficult to quantitatively measure and is normative (Brand *et al.* 2007). As a normative concept, dealing with community resilience is difficult. It is also the case with defining and identifying resilient actions conceptually, modelling its behaviour in a single framework operationally and even empirically measuring, collecting

181

and analysing data on resilience of communities (IFRC, 2012). Emanating from the socio-ecological system resilience that fails to conceptualise the totality of the role of human agency factors in the resilience. Therefore, while traditionally, resilience theorists gave less focus on power relations, politics and culture (Adger *et al.* 2000; Wilson, 2012a), the social resilient theorists, emphasise the importance of governance and social construct.

Framework of Analysis

This study make use of the livelihoods approaches to assess the resilience of communities of different settlement hierarchies in Zimbabwe (Figure 9.1). The communal areas, the resettlement areas, the urban areas and the peri-urban areas. In tracking the politics of community resilience, the chapter applies the livelihoods framework in a reductionist approach to understand the various components of community resilience and how they relate in the political sphere of resilience.

Figure 9.1: A livelihoods framework of resilience analysis (Adapted from Ellis, 2000, 30)

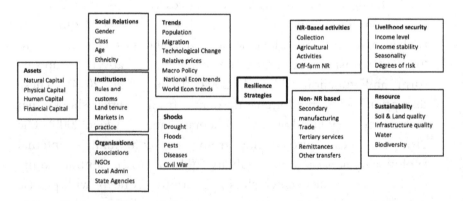

Resilience studies are generally multi-disciplinary that are best pursued through application of mixed methods (Ellis, 2000; Cumming *et al.* 2005). In this chapter, community resilience was explored focusing on understanding how nature and livelihoods of communities at various settlement hierarchy influence their resilience. It adopted a multi-method approach at two scales of community. At macro-level the analysis used policy archaeology to explore how components that make up the resilience of a community are enshrined in policy frameworks and their operationalisation in contemporary settlements. Micro-level analysis focused on policies and their application varies from settlement hierarchy and different regional of the country that are in a different context. Exploration of the "five capitals" provides a comprehensive understanding of community resilience strategies and vulnerabilities as they relate to power, access and control, unearthing the political dimensions of community resilience.

Findings and Discussion

The dynamic or static nature of settlements significantly influence community resilience. In Zimbabwe, resilience of communities in the four settlement hierarchies is more inherent than antecedent. Inherent resilience focuses on the community's being, by it reflects on the ontological definition of resilience by looking at a community to function well under normal times or non-crisis periods (McCrea *et al.* 2014). The gradual nature of social disruptions has led to the antecedent resilience of communities become less evident. In both inherent and antecedent form of resilience, the four-settlement hierarchy in Zimbabwe demonstrate different types of vulnerabilities, capacity to transform, tenacity levels. However, a deeper analysis on the differences shows that as settlements evolve their resilience differences becomes less different. Mirroring of resilience is attributed to their interconnectivity and increasing interdependency.

Communal areas present a peculiar case of vulnerabilities. Most communal areas in Zimbabwe faces the challenge of erratic rainfall, drought occurrences and loss of grazing pastures. This has led to on-farm activities becoming less reliable as single source of livelihood. Therefore, there has been increase in off-farm activities to supplement household income. To increase the income from off-farm activities, in resilience assessments, education featured as a prominent characteristic of resilience that ensure better off-farm activities and diversity of income within a household. After the occurrence of the 1991-92 El-Niño drought, the proliferation of cash-cropping particularly cotton increased in rural areas that are in drought prone areas. As a result, their food-crops production declined leading to their exposure to more external shocks such as global cotton price fluctuations and national food production fluctuations.

The variations in climatic regions in Zimbabwe significantly influence the vulnerabilities and coping strategies of different communal settlements. Communal areas in favourable climatic region that are region one, two and three regard access to agricultural markets and capital as important characteristics of a resilient community through improved agricultural productivity. On the contrary, communal areas in less favourable regions that include region four and five regard multiple income sources as a more important characteristic of a resilient community. The coping mechanisms of communal areas in less favourable climatic regions involve out-migration of able-bodied population to seek better off farm activities in nearby urban areas. Migration to resettlement areas is also another process these communal areas transform in period of instability. Such coping mechanism weakens the resilience capacity of the communities as it culminates into social discontinuity.

Nevertheless, the social construct of communal areas provides for better self-organisation which is critical for resource pooling and learning in periods of disruption. These include livelihood networks or livelihood cells where households share resources such as during peak demand for labour or during drought seasons. The strong civic engagement in communal areas still have strong civic engagement that spans from kinship and the importance of altruism in communal areas. As a result, at community level, they have better self-organisational capabilities to deal with the disruption. While these characteristics maybe shared in rural resettlements, they are not as strong as in communal areas where connectivity is higher compared to rural resettlements.

Resettlements areas in Zimbabwe, evolved from communal areas as a transformability process seeking to improve agricultural productivity under the government's land reform programme. As related to communal areas resettlement areas regard diversity of income and ownership of assets as common features of a resilient household and community. For resettlements households that have

184

not acquired more assets, multiple sources of income that combine traditional on-farm activities with off-farm activities is regarded a priority for community resilience. The frequent occurrences of drought and unreliability of rainfall for resettled farmers that do not use irrigation facilities off-farm activities act as supportive pillars in bad agricultural seasons. The need for off-farm activities to supplement income in resettled communities have made the communities vulnerable to be taken for labour by A1 commercial farmers. In balancing the off-farm activities and on-farm activities, the agricultural production tends to be overpowered, altering the normal function of the resettled communities as primarily on-farm production. The level of education among the community members is also regarded an attribute of resilient community. Higher education in resettled communities, enables households to undertake better off-farm activities that supplement their income.

Most of resettled communities are drier climatic regions of the country such as Masvingo. Therefore, larger land areas allocated without sufficient irrigation facilities, draught power, labour and agricultural inputs has led to low improvement in resilience of those communities. As agricultural practice under such conditions remain a risky business, off-farm activities become more critical to survival of these communities. Emphasis of multiple income sources in resettlement areas as resilience characteristic culminates to most settlers without notable assets opting to offer labour to nearby commercial farmers at the loss of their agricultural productivity. As highlighted earlier on how increased population pressures on land reduced fields and productivity in communal areas, the same challenge is now faced in resettlement areas. Official resettlement land was not meant to be subdivided based on the assumption that second generation will pursue non-agricultural activities on the settlements (Chimhowu and Hulme, 2006). Nevertheless, family farms have been subdivided to accommodate adult sons. Also, the regard of five hectares allocated to each household as vast, the popularisation of resettlement areas as 'minda mirefu' (long fields) has led to further in-migration from communal areas through spontaneous resettlement subdivision that is reducing farm sizes. It is also observed a similar land allocation trend in selected resettlement areas in Zimbabwe (Kinsey, 2004). Livelihoods strategies of resettlement communities are beginning to mirror that of communal areas. A study demonstrates the differences in resilience between resettlement areas and communal lands proves to be disappearing (Chimhowu and Holme, 2006). The observation is supported by a highlight that migration trends from communal to resettlement areas that include livestock migration and accompanying relatives has been strengthening the resilience capacity of resettlement areas since their establishment (Scoones, 2016).

While agricultural productivity in resettlement areas improved the livelihoods of settlers, community cohesion in resettlement areas is still in its infancy. The new inhabitants have not formed community bonds strong enough to shape the robustness of their communities. Inhibited by people of different cultural backgrounds, from different parts of the country, the sense of community is still minimum and mistrusts can cause conflicts over control of resources. Often these conflicts assume ethnic or political dimensions. Such social discontinuity is worsened by the tenure insecurity derived from lack of title deeds as settlers are discouraged to invest in the community socially and economically. The offer letters that settlers hold, do not promote a sense of permanence for settlers (District Development Fund, 1998). As settlers, do not build permanent structures, the sense of community that facilitate social enablers of resilience are minimal and investment in infrastructure is minimal. The temporary sentiments that prevails among resettled communities have led to most households maintain their ties with their communal homes as a fall-back plan since their future is uncertain. The act of balancing the resettled areas and their communal areas renders the social continuity of resettlement areas poorly established for them to be more resilient to external shocks as a community.

The resilience between the communal and resettlement areas regarding coping mechanism proves to be complex. Comparing to the former settlement hierarchy where commercial farmers held large tracks of land with almost 60 percent of it underutilised and producing agricultural commodities for export. The current resettlement structures where resettlement households export food to both urban and rural areas, presents a different case of reliance on local production and economies. It is highlighted that there are still more grey areas on the aspect given the unrecorded food production that circulate informally (Scoones, 2014). While some resettlement areas are located in productive agricultural regions some official and mostly spontaneous resettlements are in poor agricultural regions that were used for cattle ranching, wildlife preservation. Such regions present differences in vulnerabilities as the latter settlers are more vulnerable to seasonal raids by wild animals presenting a different case of vulnerability that is security.

Peri-urban settlements in Zimbabwe have become focal point of human settlements evolution as the urban population and rural population occupying the urban fringe are on the rise. Between 2002 and 2012 urban population in Zimbabwe declined from 35% to 33% (ActionAid, 2016). Such a decline amid urban population growth in the region presents a case of urban to peri urban migration for various reasons. Peri-urban areas, while they share resilience attributes related to those of urban areas, by virtue of their spatial configuration, peace and security is of critical concern to the resilience of their communities. A study undertaken by ActionAid found water, sanitation and hygiene (WASH) as a major hazard that disrupt urban areas followed by unemployment and food insecurity (ActionAid, 2016). Multiple income sources and security of tenure in peri urban areas is an important characteristic of resilience. Many peri-urban communities are made up of former farm residents whose farms were acquired for urban expansion particularly in major cities such as Harare and Bulawayo. Hence, livelihoods of most peri-urban dwellers are derived from informal activities such as informal agriculture, informal trading and informal crafts. The informality nature of livelihoods in per-urban settlements brings uncertainty to the stability of the communities on the fringe. More so, the lack of land rights and adequate infrastructure for urban service delivery, renders peri-urban dwellers more vulnerable to external shocks as their physical enablers are weak.

Urban Settlements, Resilience at the Centre

Urban settlements as complex systems, presents spatial dynamics that has diverse and multiple characteristic shaping the urban form and society. In the globalised world, urban areas are more vulnerable to external forces of economic globalisation, demographic changes and economic restructuring (Bourne, 1995). Urban space is not just a physical parameter of urban form, rather it reflects the socio-political organisation of urban societies in their times of stability and disruption. It is asserted that "space and political organisation of space express social relationships but also react upon them" (Soja, 1980:29). Delineating from this assertion, urban spatial change in Zimbabwe reflects social vulnerabilities that subsists in urban areas in their transformation.

It is iterated that social continuity plays a critical role in capacity building of a community to deal with disruptions and uncertainties through communication and organisation (Fleischhauer, 2008). The socio-spatial form of segregation in Zimbabwean urban settlements presents a vulnerability challenge that reduce cities' ability to deal with uncertainties. The socio-spatial segregation of urban areas in Zimbabwe emanates from colonial period where urban areas were spatially segregated by race. The white minority population occupied the inner city and most of the urban spaces while the black majority were restricted to the established African Townships. Socio-spatial segregation in post-colonial urban development continued nevertheless, taking form of income and social class based segregation. Different employment and education conditions, as well as income and property ownership have significantly reduced the interconnectedness and interdependencies among different social groups. This social discontinuity has culminated to poor support among the different segments of society and it has weakened the urban system and resilience of the urban areas in Zimbabwe. In times of both disruption and stability, the segregated nature of Zimbabwean urban areas has led to less chances of cooperation and coordination among the groups. The socio-spatial segregation particularly limits democratic participation towards common actions worsening the vulnerabilities of cities. This segregation nature negatively impacts the learning process of urban adaptation to uncertainties.

The resilience of urban settlements in Zimbabwe has been worsened by the inner-city decline which has increased the mobility of urban population to the urban periphery. The social discontinuity has emanated from emptying of some built-up areas and individual buildings in the decaying inner-cities and the occupation by new residents. The poor adaptive capacity to the urban in-migration has led to proliferation of urban informality in most urban areas through slum development, informal trading and informal transport systems. As asserted, the importance of flexibility for effectiveness of an adaptive management system during a disruption is still new to Zimbabwe's urban planning system (Gunderson, 1999). While mitigation and adaptation are relatively new to urban planning agenda (Davoudi, 2012), adaptation came later after mitigation has been around for the past two decades (inexplicitly). The late introduction of the two concepts in the urban planning agenda of urban settlements has weakened their resilience. The two concepts are critical for urban resilience for mitigation increase community robustness while adaptation increases the rapidity of recovery. Urban settlements heavily rely on secondary and tertiary sectors of the economy and are considerably integrated into the global economy. As a result, they are more vulnerable to external shocks that include commodity prices, national and global economic trends.

This chapter uses a reductionist approach to track the politics of community resilience in the four settlement hierarchies of Zimbabwe. Nevertheless, it does not ignore the complexity and elusiveness of community resilience as a concept. In simplifying the components as related to the political process of resilience, it identifies three 'enablers' that improves the resilience of a community. It illustrates the three forms of inputs into resilience of a community, characterised as physical, procedural and social enablers (McAslan, 2010). Physical enablers provide the *means* to survive and recover. Therefore, physical enablers entail infrastructure development, disaster warning systems, provision of basic needs such as secure shelter and food. Procedures, policies and plans provide *ideas* on how to survive and recover. Procedural enablers encompass development policies, strategies and plans; community innovation awareness raising; understanding and evaluation or threats and risks. This forms the mechanical process of resilience a critical component for flexibility. Social enablers as they provide the *will* to survive and recover encompass sharing of information and knowledge among communities, fostering of beliefs and values, promotion of local leadership and stewardship of the community. The three categories of enablers that determines the resilience outcomes of communities varies in the hierarchy of Zimbabwe's human settlements. Table 1 presents settlement types rankings against the three types of enablers.

Table 1: Ranking of settlement hierarchy against resilience enablers

Rank	Physical Enablers	Procedural Enablers	Social Enablers	Resilience Outcomes
1	Urban	Urban	Urban	Urban
2	Peri urban	Peri urban	Communal	Peri urban
3	Communal	Communal	Peri Urban	Communal
4	Resettlement	Resettlement	Resettlement	Resettlement

Looking at social enablers in communal areas, out-migration to urban areas, resettlement areas and to neighbouring countries has reduced the capacity of social enablers to overcome disruptions. The communal able-bodied population particularly men migrate to look for better opportunities and send remittances back home. While this trend enhances the physical enablers of communal areas they have trade off this with the social enablers of the communities and influence connectivity and interdependency of the communities.

There is a polarised debate on resilience of connected and highly connected communities. Some scholars argue that connectivity smoothen communication through information exchange, capital and good exchange between systems (Cumming *et al.* 2005). Other authors on the contrary, argue that isolated systems might be more protected from epidemic catastrophes, economic shocks and other systems (Davidson, 2010). Zimbabwe's urban and peri-urban settlements have more connectivity within their systems, among individuals, households and with organisations. Rural resettlements and communal areas on the contrary, have less connectivity particularly with organisations that support resilience of the communities. Their degree of isolation from each other reduces their vulnerability to epidemic disruptions, economic shocks as the isolation facilitate development of local capacity, diversity and innovation towards their local needs. The impacts of urban and peri-urban connectedness have been witnessed to how urban and peri urban areas were most affected by the global financial crisis of

190

2008/09 where their integration into the global economy, secondary and tertiary industrial dependency worsened. Impacts of internal connectivity was also witnessed by the impacts of 2008 cholera outbreak that mostly spread in urban and peri urban areas compared to the sparsely connected resettlement and rural areas.

Comparing the social organisation of communities across the settlements hierarchies, the urban setting finds itself in a precarious situation cause by its social organisation. The social cohesion in most of low-income residential areas is impacted by the temporary nature of most urban residents. The housing situation in urban areas where most urban residents are tenants that have no sense of permanence impact the deepening of social cohesion which is pivotal to development of community resilience. Social continuity has varied across urban areas emanating from social classes that shapes housing structure, a legacy of colonial racial segregation that culminated into segregation by income in the post-colonial era. Resettlement areas as highlighted earlier, face the challenge of social organisation in infancy hence not yet strong enough to make up a resilient community. They are often associated with conflicts and social discontinuity. The social organisation of settlements in Zimbabwe presents a political perspective of resilience that governance structures considers as political spaces that require intervention that lead to various outcomes.

Community resilience as promoted by the government in particularly rural and resettlement areas carries critical political overtones. Several scholars have engaged with different lines of political overtones associated with community resilience (Potapchuck *et al.* 1997; Coaffee and Rogers, 2008). Scepticism has been raised over the use of resilience as "bouncing back to the old state of affairs". It is argued that this as failure of a community to transform in addressing a disruption. Failure to transform entails maintenance of status quo, which purports to reproduce pre-existing vulnerabilities rendering maintenance of power by responsible authorities. Therefore, instead of regarding resilience as reconstruction of status quo ex ante, it is important to for a transformative form of resilience (Coaffee and Rogers, 2008). In designing resilience programmes and interventions, the notion of reverting to the old equilibrium proves to be retrogressive. In an increasingly uncertain environment, a system with multiple equilibria is critical to reduce structural vulnerabilities and increase flexibility of a community to shocks.

Resilience of communities critically depend on institutional frameworks that govern them. The frameworks and their operationalisation varies from one settlement to another. Communal areas have a hybrid institutional framework of customary and formal governance structures. Formal governance structures that include Village Development Committees (VIDCOs), Ward Development Committees (WADCOs) and Rural District Councils oversee the governance and capacity building of communal areas. As critical governance structures to build resilience capacities of communal settlements, inadequate fiscal and administrative decentralisation for the institutions to effective execute their duties have been identified (Manyena, 2006). Institutional frameworks in resettlement are a critical challenge. Community tensions that exist in resettlement areas are also worsened by the leadership structures that govern the areas. Given the need to control resources and protect personal interests. In resettlement areas, there is crisis for leadership and the quest for leadership positions creates deep divisions within the resettlements. Unlike communal areas governed by Village Development Committees (VIDCOs) and Ward Development Committees (WADCOs), resettlement areas are governed by Committee of Seven or Farm Committees, appointed elders that mostly exclude village heads from the committee. Emanating from the leadership crisis is the reduced capacity to cooperate in times of disruption.

Urban areas under the urban authorities that include city councils, town councils and local boards depending on the size of the urban settlement have related institutional structures with different capacity building leverage. Urban authorities unlike rural authorities, they have better fiscal, technical and administrative capacity to build resilience capacity of their communities. Nevertheless, the political overtones associated with the ability of urban areas to destabilise political regimes, have led to intense involvement of central government in urban authorities at the detriment of urban autonomy. As a result, localised interventions and coping mechanisms are significantly influenced by central government that seeks to maintain status quo and stability.

The involvement of organisational institutions in community resilience in Zimbabwe can fall under Handmer and Dovers' three-way generic classification of resilience. The *resistance and maintenance; change at the margins;* and *openness and adaptability* (Handmer and Dovers, 1996). *Resistance and maintenance,* is the most basic form of resilience. This is where a community tries to avoid change, denies existence of problem with intention of maintaining status quo and allocates resources without questioning the underlying assumptions or power asymmetries within a society. Because of its inflexibility, the community does not adjust to new situations leading to a collapse of a community rather than transformation. This form of resilience is related to the one that is preferred by societal elites that fear loss of their authority because of drastic change in the society. The second form of resilience, *change at the margins* is regarded as the standard approach to address community disruptions. A community that change at the margins admits existence of a problem, acknowledge its implications and the non-sustainability of the prevailing community setup. In response, *change at the margins* advocates for reforms to the extent that do not challenge the community basis or the regimes that govern the community. This resilience system addresses the symptoms of a disruption and not the underlying causes. The third form, *openness and adaptability* is the deepest form of resilience as it addresses the underlying causes of a community disruption. Openness and adaptability advocates major political and social shifts by transforming overarching political economy regimes and associated social notions on development, risk and security (Handmer and Dovers, 1996). While openness and adaptability is the most ideal resilience type, it is not applied in any of the settlements hierarchy in Zimbabwe. Resistance and maintenance and to some extend change at the margins have been the most adopted in programmes implemented. These types of resilience as they relate to governance structures, cascade into the politics of programming resilience particularly by government and/or development partners.

Measuring and programming resilience forms the core of community resilience politics. Assessing community resilience proves to be a complex process as it involves interactions of various actors and their environment at various levels. An exploration of a comprehensive model for assessing community resilience is beyond the scope of this chapter. Such model, will seldom be universal across the settlement hierarchy as communities in various settlement hierarchy face different threats and potential disruptive events (Hudson, 2010). One of the major challenge in the assessment of resilience of communities is the 'development assistance bias'. Interviewing communities across the settlements hierarchy particularly in less developed regions, households often understate their level of resilience or refuse to accept the designation of a resilient community. Accepting the designation, might lead their exclusion from peer support or from development interventions that target less resilient communities. As resilience assessment cascades to programming, interventions by the government and/or development partners may not always reflect the most prioritised threats to a community's stability. This can be attributed to the different scales that the stakeholders will be perceiving resilience and vulnerabilities. Where communities may have an individual/household perspective, government and development partners might take a community, regional or national perspective. For example, communal and resettlement communities may regard of primary and secondary education completion as a key characteristic of resilience while government and development partners may prioritise natural resources management.

Interventions into community vulnerabilities and capacity building is often either targeted or untargeted. Such interventions have been classified as specified resilience, "resilience of what to what?" and general resilience where a community develop a coping mechanism that improves the capacity of a community to all sorts of shocks (Folke *et al.* 2010). Most government and development partners' resilience programmes by their nature of being mostly protective or preventive they are coping mechanism that focus on specified threats. These social adaptation programme that include social transfers (food/cash), public works programmes, social pensions, livelihood diversification have been less effective in building adaptive capacity for a community to transform. As a result, coping mechanism can lead to other multitude of problems that further destabilise the community. The programming of resilience using reactive interventions of protect and prevent as coping mechanism are oriented towards an outcome approach. Reactive resilience is the resistance and maintenance that seeks constancy and stability. Its outcome-oriented approach makes use of command and controls that seek to retain status quo of the community presents the most basic form of resilience and change at the margins (Dovers and Handmer, 1992). Delineating from the shortcomings of outcome-oriented resilience which is reactive in intervention, an integrated resilience programming is fundamental. Such integration focuses on building the three capacities, the transformative, adaptive and absorptive capacity that strengthens a community's robustness, flexibility and transformability.

Conclusions

Two main conclusions emerge from this chapter. The different settlements in Zimbabwe, urban, peri-urban, resettlement and communal presents varying cases of resilience and vulnerabilities. The reductionist approach of physical, procedural and social resilience enablers finds urban areas ranking highest in overall resilience outcomes, followed by peri-urban, communal and resettlement areas ranking lowest in resilience outcomes. The ranking also, other than the peculiar resettlement areas, demonstrates the destinations of migration flows as population migrate from less resilient settlements to more resilience settlements. Therefore, this includes rural to urban and peri-urban migration. As a settlement in evolution resettlement areas excepting their agricultural productivity that is better than their communal counterpart, demonstrates the need for strengthening of all three enablers of resilience. In essence, high social vulnerability does not necessarily denote low level of resilience, as a settlement hierarchy with high social vulnerability might have high resilience compared to that with low vulnerability. The diversity of regions in the country, climatically, economically and socially entails differences in vulnerabilities and community coping mechanism even for communities that fall under the same settlement category. Deriving from the assessment of resilience, the chapter explored the politics involved in programming resilience in different settlement hierarchy. It identified the three resilience interventions as they apply to four settlement hierarchy. Often the most basic resistance and maintenance resilience is the most adopted form of intervention which seeks to maintain status quo and stability of the community. Change at the margins is adopted particularly in urban areas and merely in other settlements. Openness and adaptability as the most effective form of resilience that transform societies and reform political economy is rarely adopted at all for it destabilise the power balances in the society. This most communities have been relying on adaptive and absorptive capacity, but have low transformative capacity to have multiple equilibria. The chapter calls for multi-sectoral policy interventions in addressing the resilience capacity of critical communities paying special attention to context-proofing of resilience programmes for Zimbabwe is a heterogamous economy.

References

Adger, W.N. (2000) Social and Ecological Resilience: Are They Related? *Progress in Human Geography*. 24, 347–364.

Ahmed, R.; Seedat, M.; van Niekerk, A.; Bulbuli, S. (2004) Discerning community resilience in disadvantaged communities in the context of violence and injury prevention. *South African Journal of Psychology*. 34, 386–408

Andersson, E. (2006). Urban landscapes and sustainable cities. *Ecology and Society*, 11 (1), 34.

Bodin, P.; Wiman, B.L.B. (2004) Resilience and other stability concepts in ecology: Notes on their origin, validity and usefulness. *ESS Bull.* 2, 33–43

Brand, F.S.; Jax, K. (2007) Focusing the meaning(s) of resilience: Resilience as a descriptive concept and a boundary object. *Ecological Sociology* 12, 23.

Carpenter, S.; Walker, B.; Anderies, J.M.; Abel, N. (2001) From metaphor to measurement: Resilience of what to what? *Ecosystems*. 4, 765–781.

CCMT (2014) Challenges to Social Service Delivery in Zimbabwe's Resettlement Areas. Centre for Conflict Management and Transformation. Harare

Chimhowu A; and Hulme, D. (2006) Livelihood Dynamics in Planned and Spontaneous Resettlement in Zimbabwe: Converging and Vulnerable. *World Development* 34(4). 728–750

Chirisa I (2010) Peri-urban dynamics and regional planning in Africa: implications for building healthy cities. *Journal of African Studies and Development* 2(2):015–026

Chirisa I (2013) Politics in environmental stewardship in Zimbabwe: reflections on Ruwa and Epworth. *African Journal of History and Culture* 5(1):13–26

Coaffee and Rogers. ((2008) Rebordering the city for new security challenges: From Counter Terrorism to Community Resilience. *Space and Polity.* 12(2), p. 101-118.

Cumming, G.S.; Barnes, G.; Perz, S.; Schmink, M.; Sieving, K.E.; Southworth, J.; Binford, M.; Holt, R.D.; Stickler, C.; van Holt, T. (2005) An exploratory framework for the empirical measurement of resilience. *Ecosystems.* 8, 975–987.

Davidson, D.J. (2010) The Applicability of the Concept of Resilience to Social Systems: Some Sources of Optimism and Nagging Doubts. *Social and Natural Resources International Journal.* 23, 1135–1149.

Davoudi, S. (2012) Resilience: A bridging concept or a dead end? *Planning Theory and Practice.* 13, 299–307.

Department for Rural Development (1981). Nyamakate accelerated resettlement scheme. Unpublished Project Report. Ministry of Lands Agriculture and Rural Resettlement, Harare.

District Development Fund (1998). Squatters: The problems, causes and proposed solutions. Unpublished Project Report, Ministry of Lands Agriculture and Rural Resettlement, Harare.

Dovers, S.R.; Handmer, J.W. (1992) Uncertainty, sustainability and change. *Global Environmental Change.* 2, 262–276.

Ellis, F. (2000). *Rural livelihoods and diversity in developing countries.* Oxford: Oxford University Press.

Fleischhauer, M. (2008). The role of spatial planning in strengthening urban resilience. In H. J. Pasman & I. A. Kirillov (Eds.), *Resilience of cities to terrorist and other threats. Learning from 9/11 and further research issues* (pp. 273–298). Dordrecht: Springer

Folke, C.; Carpenter, S.R.; Walker, B.; Scheffer, M.; Chapin, T.; Rockstrom, J. (2010) Resilience thinking: Integrating resilience, adaptability and transformability. *Ecological Sociology*. 15, 20.

Geza, S. (1986). The role of resettlement in social development in Zimbabwe. *Journal of Social Development in Africa*, 1, 35–42.

Godschalk, D. R. (2003). Urban hazard mitigation: Creating resilient cities. *Natural Hazards Review*, 4 (3), 136–143.

Government of Zimbabwe (1994). *Report on the commission of inquiry into appropriate agricultural land tenure systems: Volume one, Main report.* Harare: Government Printers

Government of Zimbabwe (1998). *Land reform and resettlement programme phase 11 policy framework and project document 1998.* Harare: Ministry of Lands and Agriculture.

Gunderson, L. (1999). Resilience, flexibility and adaptive management – antidotes for spurious certitude? *Conservation Ecology*, 3 (1), 7

Handmer, J.W.; Dovers, S.R. (1996) A Typology of Resilience: Rethinking Institutions for Sustainable Development. *Indian Environmental Crisis Quarterly*. 9, 482–511.

Hudson, R. (2010). Resilient regions in an uncertain world: Wishful thinking or a practical reality? *Cambridge Journal of Regions, Economy and Society*, 3 (1), 11–25.

IFRC (2012) (International Federation of Red Cross and Red Crescent Societies). *Understanding Community Resilience and Program Factors that Strengthen Them: A Comprehensive Study of Red Cross Red Crescent Societies Tsunami Operation*; IFRC: Geneva, Switzerland.

Islam, M.S.; An, Q.R. (2014) Climate Change and Urban Resilience: The Singapore Story. In *Globalization, Development and Security in Asia* (Vol. IV); Li, J, Ed.; World Scientific Publishing: London, UK, 205–220.

Kinsey, B. H. (2004). Zimbabwe's land reform program: Under investment in post-conflict transformation. *World Development*, 32(10), 1669–1696.

Makamure, K. and Gutto, S. (1986). Spontaneous resettlement and squatting in Zimbabwe. In UNCHS (Ed.), *Spontaneous settlement formation in rural regions*. Nairobi: UNCHS.

Manyena, S.B. (2006) The concept of resilience revisited. *Disasters*. 30, 433–450.

McCrea, R.; Walton, A.; Leonard, R. (2014). A conceptual framework for investigating community wellbeing and resilience. *Rural Sociology.* 23, 270–282.

Norris Fran, H.; Stevens, S.P.; Pfefferbaum, B.; Wyche, K.F.; Pfefferbaum, R.L. (2008). Community resilience as a metaphor, theory, set of capacities and strategy for disaster readiness. *American Journal of Community Psychology.* 41, 127–150.

Palmer, R. (2003). Struggling to secure and defend the land rights of the poor in Africa. *Austrian Journal of Development Studies,* 19(1), 6–21.

Potapchuck, W, Crocker, J, Schechter, W, & Boogaard, D. (1997). *Building community: Exploring the role of social capital and local government.* Washington, DC: Program for Community Problem Solving.

Reid, R.; Botterill, L.C. (2013) The Multiple Meanings of 'Resilience': An Overview of the Literature. *Australian Journal of Public Administration.* 72, 31–40.

Rose, A. (2007) Economic resilience to natural and man-made disasters: Multidisciplinary origins and contextual dimensions. *Environmental Hazards.* 7, 383–398.

Roth, M, & Haase, D. (1998). Land tenure security and agricultural performance in southern Africa. Madison: University of Wisconsin LTC BASIS Working Paper, June 1998. Available from http://www.ies.wisc.edu/ltc/live/bassaf9806a.pdf.

S. Bernard Manyena (2006) "Rural local authorities and disaster resilience in Zimbabwe", Disaster Prevention and Management: *An International Journal,* Vol. 15 Issue: 5, pp.810-820

Scoones, I. (1998). Sustainable rural livelihoods: A framework for analysis. Institute of Development Studies Working Paper 72, Sussex.

Scoones, I (2016) Does land reform increase resilience to drought? Zimbabweland: 29 February

Shaw, K. 'Reframing' resilience: Challenges for planning theory and practice. *Planning Theory and Practice.* 2012, 13, 308–312.

Skerratt, S. (2013) Enhancing the analysis of rural community resilience: Evidence from community land ownership. *Journal of Rural Studies* 31, 36–46.

Skerratt, S.; Steiner, A. (2013) Working with communities-of-place: Complexities of empowerment. *Local Economy*. 28, 320–338.

Soja, E. (1980). The socio-spatial dialectic. *Annuals of the Association of Geographers*, 70 (2), 207–225

Steiner, A.; Markantoni, M. Unpacking community resilience through Capacity for Change. *Community Development Journal*. 2014, 49, 407–425.

Walker, B, & Salt, D. (2006). *Resilience thinking: Sustaining ecosystems and people in a changing world*. Washington, DC: Island Press.

Walker, B, Holling, C. S, Carpenter, S. R, & Kinzig, A. (2004). Resilience, adaptability and transformability in social-ecological systems. Ecology and Society, 9 (2)

Warner, M. (2001). Building social capital: The role of local government. *The Journal of Socio-Economics*, 30 (2), 187–192.

Webster D (2002) On the edge: shaping the future of Peri-Urban East Asia. Stanford University Press, Stanford

Wilson, G.A. Community Resilience and Environmental Transitions; Routledge: London, UK; New York, NY, USA, 2012.

Wilson, G.A. Community resilience, globalization and transitional pathways of decision-making. *Geoforum* 2012, 43, 1218–1231.

Chapter 10

Externally-Fostered Sorghum and Millets Production in Semi-Arid Regions of Zimbabwe

Julius Musevenzi

Introduction

This chapter brings out the adverse perceptions of climate change among rural small holder farmers. It bases on their experiences of externally fostered small grains production (sorghum and millets) as an adaptive strategy and response to the impact of climate change. It also brings out the emerging debates on small grains production in semi-arid regions of Zimbabwe. Smallholder farmers positively responded to the provisions of free small grain inputs from non-governmental organisations' that resulted in high sorghum output to deal with poverty and food insecurity. Smallholder farmers questioned climate change as a genuine challenge facing their communities or simply a marketing tool that NGOs are taking advantage of to foster a shift in the production of small grains varieties. Therefore, the chapter questions whether the promotion of small grains production in the districts under study is a solution or not regarding a response and new perceptions to climate change. Challenges are experienced in making smallholder farmers understand climate change and its impact compared to similar past crop production challenges they overcame without a shift in small grain varieties. These issues have generated a debate in the understanding of climate change vis-à-vis small grains as an adaptation strategy.

Background and Overview

It is concluded that greenhouse gas emissions are already beginning to change the global climate (Inter-governmental Panel on Climate Change (IPCC, 2012). However, Africa is also experiencing increased water stress, decreased yields from rain fed agriculture, increased food insecurity and malnutrition, sea level rise and an increase in arid land as a result of the process. The effects of the exposure to change in climate are exacerbated by the high sensitivity of the social and ecological systems in the region. They are also induced by the limited capacity of civil society, the private sector and government actors to respond positively and appropriately to these emerging threats (Chaguta, 2010). Similarly, it is acknowledges that Africa is one of the most vulnerable regions in the world due to widespread poverty, limited coping capacity and its highly variable climate. Zimbabwe is particularly vulnerable due to its high dependence on rain fed agriculture (Madzwamutse, 2010).

Climate change presents risks to lives and livelihoods at the individual household level and to the economy (Helmuth et al. 2007). Addressing challenges of climate change will ultimately require both reducing emissions in an effort to prevent irreversible changes to climate and limit its impacts to deal with changes that are expected to occur. But for Zimbabwe's rural communities in semi-arid regions adaptation strategies are the only options as other actions are beyond their control. As observed by some scholars, if climatic conditions continue to expand, traditional agricultural systems will become increasingly unsustainable. If there are no adaptation measures taken, yields from rain fed agriculture are expected to decrease by up to 50% by the year 2020. As maize the country's staple crop is particularly vulnerable due to its intolerance to drought the options of small grains was brought into the perspective (Kahinda et al. 2007). The chapter focuses on this as it interrogates its relevance as the solution and the resulting debates.

The reduction in rainfall amount had the expected negative impact on grain yield but not only in maize but also in some of the small grain varieties. However, increasing temperature has the most dramatic impact on crop grain yields leading a reduction of 16% for most cereals (Tadross et al. 2009). Therefore, climate change is regarded as likely to make matters worse with increases in rainfall variability being predicted for the semi-arid tropics. It is admitted on the reason conservation agriculture is promoted as a better response to climate change in rain-fed cropping systems. It's better management of the rainfall resources for crop production (Bwalya,

2008; Nyagumbo, 2008). Sorghum and millet have also been promoted for production under conservation agriculture to maximise yields. Given this background the chapter dissects the acceptability of small grains as a solution to climate change in semi-arid regions. Given that small grains production under external support new debates of climate change have emerged casting doubts over its existence and reality.

Theoretical Framework

This chapter is informed by two theoretical approaches, the actor-oriented analytical approach and the social structure – human actor debate. The actor-oriented approach is based on the simple recognition that even under similar conditions social life contains a variety of social and cultural forms (Haberecht, 2009). It contradicts structural models that explain social change and development as resulting from external forces, state interventions or development agencies.

It is noted that the actor-oriented approach is grounded in the structure-actor debate in social sciences in general and in rural development in particular (Chekole, 2006:17). It is also argued that the approach intends to bridge the gap and seek a way out of the theoretical discord between macro-level structural theories and voluntaristic models of micro-level interaction and decision-making (Arce and Long, 1994:12). The actor-oriented approach is concerned with how different individuals and social groups interact and develop strategies to deal with social change. It also concerns with how different social actors become involved in negotiations over resources, meanings and control, while attempting to create room to manoeuvre and pursue their own projects. At the same time the approach focuses on how individual choices and practices are influenced and shaped by other dimensions of social life and interaction (Long, 2001).

Throughout the history of rural development, researchers have been grappling with the relationship between social structure and human agency in various ways. The recent years have shown that the role played by this relationship in social change has become a pivotal issue in debates about development inquiry (Chouinard, 1996:386).

It is noted that the new Marxist conceptions of the 1970s treat both human agency and societal structure as mutual determinants of social outcome. Development practitioners with more humanist inclinations treat this outlook as inherently flawed by structural determinism and are deeply critical of its impoverished notion of human agency (Chekole. 2006:18).

This humanist critique, together with the rise of feminist research, reshaped the debate by including social relations – which were understood as constituents of the structure of society. It also reinterpreted the role of structural forces in social change without its deterministic angle (Unwin, 1992:167). For that matter, emphasis was placed on how social structure limits rather than directly determines social action and experience. In the 1980s the need to explore an approach that combines human agency within the structural perspective led British sociologist Anthony Giddens to develop a theory of structuration. Structuration saw structures as being both the outcome and the medium of agency. He held that structures were created and recreated through human agency (Unwin 1992: 172). Unlike most social theories it sees time-space relations as constitutive features of social systems (Bird, 1993). Structuration theory received considerable attention in social sciences and other disciplines. Despite this advance, several critiques emerged in the early 1990s. They emphasised a pressing need for further conceptual and empirical work on the precise ways in which social structures shape human actions and how people's practices help to perpetuate or challenge those structures (Chouinard, 1996).

The actor-oriented approach departs a little from the empirical and conceptual shortcomings of structuration theory. It is noted that the intention is to grapple conceptually with the flexibilities, ambiguities and socially constructed and self-transforming nature of social life. Therefore, required are conceptual frames for doing so, rather than promoting a full-fledged theory (Long, 2001).

Literature Review

A consensus among scientists, sociologists, economists, environmentalists and policymakers exists concerning climate change as a real and serious long term threat to the entire globe .(Hansen et al. 2007). Scientific evidence shows increase of mean temperature and the temperature is expected to increase further at a rate of 0.05 degrees Celsius per decade. Also, rainfall has been erratic, decreasing on average at a rate of 5 to 10% per annum with annual anomalies mostly below normal. It is rightfully shown that global temperatures are increasing largely attributed to the anthropogenic activities especially the global use of fossil fuels. The developing world are contributing less to the greenhouse gas emissions than any other region in the world held responsible for global warming, yet they are more vulnerable. The effects of exposures to changes in climate are worsened by high levels of sensitivity of the social and ecological systems in Southern Africa (Mawere, 2011). However, the limited response of government and private sector exacerbate the region's vulnerability.

The developing world's dependence on rain-fed agriculture and natural resources for livelihood worsens its vulnerability to climate change. Therefore, what is climate change, do all people of different walks of life understand its meaning and possible impact? Climate change is defined as a long-term process of global warming partly attributable to the greenhouse gasses, generated by human activity. It can also be considered as a long term significant change in the "average weather" that a given region experiences (Manyatsi, 2010).

For this study, the El Nino dry weather conditions that have affected the Southern African region including Zimbabwe cannot be ignored. The El Nino refers to the large-scale ocean-atmosphere climate interaction linked to a periodic warming in sea surface temperatures across the central and east central equatorial Pacific (Tadros et al. 2008). El Nino happens when ocean temperatures and rainfall from storms off South America warm up due to less upwelling of cold water from below to cool the surface. The clouds and rainstorms associated with the warm ocean waters shift toward the east. The warm water releases so much energy into the atmosphere that affects weather changes all over the planet.

The presence of El Nino can significantly influence weather patterns, ocean conditions and fisheries. The influence can span across large portions of the world and dry conditions and long dry spells particularly in Southern Africa. The impact of the El Nino which is considered part of climate change affects precipitations as

205

conditions tend towards drier than normal conditions. Temperatures run hotter than average and drought can be widespread affecting the whole of Southern Africa (Mayhews and Penny, 2008).

El Ninos occur every three to five years but may come as frequently as every two years or rarely as every seven years. Each El Nino lasts about twelve months and in the Americas they often begin to form in spring and reach peak strength between December and January and then decay by May of the following year. Different explanations show that the reason Southern Africa experiences long dry spells and erratic rainfall as currently experienced during the 2015/16 period (Mutekwa's, 2009). As a result, the region requires a strong policy response to reduce food insecurity particularly in semi-arid regions. Nevertheless, El Ninos are not similar, the atmosphere and ocean do not always follow similar patterns from one El Nino to another. There is also no one big cause which is one of the reasons why El Nino can't be predicted perfectly and this may also affect the adaptive strategies by small holder farmers (Slater et al. 2007). Based on this understanding of the El Nino dry conditions as part of climate change. Therefore, it is important to understand the extent it impacts on smallholder grain production in Chiredzi and Mwenezi districts and discuss the externally fostered adaptive strategies as well as the emerging perceptions thereof. The chapter also proffers what could be the most appropriate policy adaptation strategies by smallholder farmers in food production to reduce insecurity and rural poverty.

Small grains are considered traditional crops that produced in semi-arid regions over years. They are found in a wide range of types and varieties including sorghum, pearl millet and finger millet, among others. However, this chapter focuses on sorghum and millet. It is observed that sorghum and millet are major crops of the semi-arid tropics of Africa and Asia and are an important component in traditional farming systems. Unfortunately the potential of these small grain cereal crops has not been realised because of several draw backs that have kept its production at lower levels compared to other cereals (FAO, 2008). While maize is a major staple grown in southern Africa as a region, sorghum and millet were found to be important crops in driest regions where rural households have limited production capacity and lowest incomes.

Studies on small grains in southern Africa show that sorghum and millet are drought tolerant crops with a strong adaptive advantage. They also have lower risk of failure than other crops that makes them suitable for withstanding climate change and rainfall variability challenges (FAO, 2008). Similarly, it is pointed out that sorghum and millet are some of the most important crops for communal farmers affected droughts. THE small grains, particularly sorghum and millet, have the potential of stabilising household food security in drought prone areas (Leuschner and Manthe, 1996).

It is noted that sorghum and millet have been observed as staple food grains in many semi-arid areas. It is attributed to their good adaptation to hard environments and climate change and their potential for good yield (Dicko et al. 2005). Sorghum and millet have been described as generally the most drought tolerant cereal grain crops that require little input during growth and with decreasing rainfall annually. They can reduce the probability of zero yields even under minimal rainfall (Taylor et al. 2006). Therefore they can make a significant contribution to household food security in drought years and help mitigate and reduce the impact of climate change in semi-arid regions of Zimbabwe. It is suggested that there is enough evidence from literature showing that small grains particularly sorghum and millet can outperform maize in semi-arid areas both in yield and drought tolerance (FAO, 2006). However, small grains can only outperform maize if appropriate policy and institutional support framework are designed to promote their production (Rukuni, 2006). While all these arguments about the adaptability of sorghum and millet to drought and climate change are accepted, the major question remains. Why sorghum and millet adoption is very minimal and not widely considered as a climate change strategic crop in semi-arid regions of Zimbabwe.

It is posited that small grains particularly sorghum and millet remain the answer to chronic food shortages rural communities in semi-arid regions of sub-Saharan Africa (FAO, 2008). However, the levels of adoption in sub-Saharan Africa as a cropping strategy responding to climate change are not convincing. One scholar is of the view that in semi-arid regions of Africa, sorghum and millet are still very low because they are naturally low yielding varieties (Taylor, 2006). The failure of small grains wide adoption as a response to climate change is attributed to inadequate government failure to support and promote these small grains (Rukuni, 2006). In one earlier study of small grains in 2003, it was observed that research on small grains such as sorghum and millet has been lagging behind in Africa. This was attributed to the observation that the crops suffer something of an image problem and the often tendency to prefer maize as the premier crop (Taylor, 2003).

The same view is supported in that in Zimbabwe's drier areas where small grains can be produced economically and sustainably, maize remains the mainstay of household food security. Therefore, production of sorghum and millets is seen as another crop diversification strategy that can alleviate food security in Zimbabwe's semi-arid regions (Rukuni, 2006). One study shows that actually small grain production is on the decline in Southern Africa. In Zimbabwe in the 1980s the agricultural boom experienced saw maize outcompeting sorghum and millets as major staples of rural communal farmers in semi-arid regions. Hybrid maize varieties adoption as the premier staple crop ahead of sorghum and millets was because maize was suitable in many areas. Moreover, communities in the 1980s had access to credit and the government supported good maize prices and provided marketing subsidies (Eicher, 1995).

Since most communal households live in areas with less than 650mm of rainfall per year, the largest part of Zimbabwean population lives in natural regions four and five ((Rukuni et al. 2006). Therefore, this calls for an urgent need to review the competitiveness of sorghum and millets in Zimbabwe's semi-arid areas. The review and adoption can be achieved at the policy level. However, it is identified that lack of clear policy promoting small grain production amongst smallholder farmers in Zimbabwe's semi-arid areas where they are thought to have a comparative advantage over maize particularly regarding their research (Mudimu, 2003). Therefore, without the policy the full and wide adoption of small grains as a strategy and response to climate change in semi-arid regions, may remain a challenge.

Methodology

The participatory rural appraisal (PRA) methodology, which uses a variety of techniques or tools was used. Selected were ranking techniques such as preference ranking and scoring, pair-wise ranking. Time trends analysis were also used during the study particularly calendars such as seasonal and historical seasonal calendars.

Plenary presentations kick-started the process in all study areas where objectives of the process were explained to people, as well as how the process was going to be handled until the end. Plenary presentations were used for people to understand the process and for them to be involved and participating and that formed the basis for other methods that followed.

Participants began by identifying different livelihood activities they depended on in their specific community in no particular order of importance. This technique generated basic information about livelihood activities, sources of food for different people, income generated and available support services. It also sought to understand opportunities available for both women and men, how people allocate time for labour and ownership of property, both movable and immovable.

Pair wise ranking was used to rearrange the listed agricultural crops in order of importance. This technique reorganised crops according to their importance, with the most important at the top down to the least important at the bottom. Some of the crops were not even accorded a ranking, showing they were very peripheral to the rural livelihoods of people in that area.

Timelines were used to determine patterns and trends for each crop listed and prioritised by the community members throughout a ten-year period looked at. Participants easily remembered what happened in 2010 and 2011 by each season and month. The technique generated data on rainfall distribution patterns and how crops were affected; food availability. It focused on own production savings and food aid; agricultural production patterns; income generation by local people, health problems and human development.

Four FGDs were conducted each with an average of 16 people both men and women. This method assisted and triangulated data generated from the other previously mentioned methods on perceptions of preferred crops, small grains intervention and about climate change. It determined levels of understanding by participants on changing weather patterns, cropping systems.

Results

Generally the findings show that government support in all semi-arid areas in Zimbabwe is limited due to financial and human resource constraints. As a result the number of NGOs providing development support in semi-arid areas is high and they focus on both farm and non-farm livelihood support but the focus in this chapter is on agricultural support. Most interventions by different NGOs in all study areas are similar, with the largest component being agricultural support. The forthcoming paragraphs detail the specific findings on small grains interventions.

The findings show that small grain production is a general intervention in all study areas aimed at food security in response to the decline of maize production due to persistent droughts (Plate 10.1). As indicated by one study, the impact of persistent drought in the study period influenced a shift from maize to small grain production in Gwanda (Manyani, 2010). This is also found in Chiredzi and Mwenezi areas of this study, although they differ as the production is externally induced. Small grain crops grown are sorghum, millet, rapoko, cowpeas, groundnuts, sunflowers and open pollinated varieties of maize that are more drought and heat resistant. The Department of Agricultural Extension Services indicated that the promoting small grain varieties aimed to cushion smallholder farmers during drought years. However, the government lacks financial support for the programme a gap filled by NGOs.

Plate 10. 1: Sorghum and Millet crops under irrigation in Mwenezi district (Musevenzi, August 2016)

NGOs conducted research in semi-arid areas aimed at ascertaining appropriate crop varieties that would guarantee food security in these areas. The findings show that with technical support from the Department of Agricultural Extension Services, NGOs have introduced and promoted increased production of small grains (sorghum and millet) for food security since 2003. However, it is at the expense of cotton and maize. This became a reversal of a vigorous promotion of maize production in semi-arid areas undertaken since 1980, which did not consider the unsuitability of maize varieties in agro-ecological region four. Therefore, it created food shortages over the long term since independence, according to interviews with the Agricultural Extension Services Department. NGO officials in their study on food security identified that government's focus on increased cotton production as a cash crop over food crops worsened the food deficit show that based on their study on food security the food deficit in most semi-arid areas over the years was worsened by the government's focus on increased cotton production as a cash crop at the expense of cereal crops. This gap can only be occupied by small grains if the adoption rate in target communities increases.

The study by the NGO recommended an increased focus on small grains. However, the same study indicated that switching people from maize to small grain production was a challenge as smallholder farmers believe in maize production as a staple and food security crop for livelihoods. Brevets (1997) also found that

211

smallholder farmers in rural Zimbabwe stuck to maize production as a cultural activity that they are used to. Despite efforts to promote small grain production NGOs were also sceptical about the success associated with its production. This has casts doubt over the feasibility and adaptability of small grains as a perfect solution and response strategy to climate change in semi-arid areas.

Findings show that after five years of small grain intervention, each beneficiary household produced an average of 21 bags of white Macia sorghum for consumption. Based on World Food Programme calculations of 10kg of maize meal per person per month, such a harvest provides food security for a household of seven people for nine months. This leaves a deficit of three months in a year. Sorghum production in all study areas was promoted under conservation farming. Its production has also been increasing since 2006 with a household producing a minimum of 1, 5 tons per hectare. It was found out that before the intervention sorghum production levels were very low because not all smallholder farmers produced the crop. For those who produced it the average production was 0, 7 tons per hectare. The intervention increased small grain output by 60-100% per household.

Evidence shows that conservation farming technology has increased crop output in all study areas. The output of groundnuts and cowpeas increased from 0, 2 tons per hectare to 0, 8. Table 10.1 shows increased land under small grain cultivation in Mwenezi district compared to land under maize.

Table 10.1: Small Grain Production Hectarage: The Ten-Year Trend in Mwenezi District (World Vision, 2016)

Agricultural Season	Hectares Under Sorghum	Hectares Under Pearl Millet	Hectares under maize
2008-2009	Below 200	Below 100	Above 18 000
2009-2010	600	400	19 000
2010-2011	800	600	16 000
2011-2012	1 300	1000	14 000
2012-2013	14 151	1 700	10 000
2013-2014	11 954	2 500	7 000
2014-2015	20 000	3 083	5 000

The increase in sorghum and pearl millet production is attributed to small grain production advocacy by NGOs and increased free distribution of inputs. The increased number of hectares under small grains also indicates an increase in uptake by households in small grain production. The diversification has been a strategy against the uncertainties of maize production. The findings also show that NGOs mostly distributed more small grain inputs compared to maize in all study areas. This is reflected by a sharp increase of hectarage in 2012 due to drought predicted in 2011. It was also influenced by the expected political violence in the 2013 general elections predicted to likely affect the distribution of some of the inputs. Based on calculations for an average household of six people, 300kg of sorghum could last for about six months. For a household of eight people if it is consumed daily with no major alternatives it could last for about four months for.

Community level findings show that although there is an increase in small grain production, the harvesting and processing of small grains – particularly sorghum, millet and cowpeas – is very labour intensive. Hence, only households with economically active age groups performed better in terms of increased yield. This indicates that vulnerable groups such as widows, the elderly and orphans or child-headed households face challenges harvesting and processing small grains. These households gradually went back to maize production despite its limited output. This raises questions over the adaptability of small grains as a response strategy to climate change.

Despite an increase in small grain production, particularly white sorghum, the most promoted crop does not have a well-developed market in Zimbabwe. Although small grains were meant for food security, people's consumption levels of the product are very low in all study areas. The crop was widely adopted, but it has not filled the food security gap left by maize production. Rural people failed to consume small grains on a daily basis and as a result people remained with large stocks of white sorghum that could not be sustainably consumed. The option of selling the surplus for cash was not available as there was no market for it.

The failure of sorghum exposed the weaknesses of the recommendations of the food security research reports by NGOs in relation to consumption and marketing suitability. The effort put into the promotion of small grains did not equal the benefits, in other words it has not reduced food insecurity. The large reserves of white sorghum observed in semi-arid rural communities show that it was an ill-advised intervention that missed its intended objective. Small grains have failed to meet the requirements for improving rural livelihoods in semi-arid districts of Zimbabwe, despite their increased production.

Discussion

The increase in small grains production could be considered a successful switching of cropping systems activities but as discussed in the previous section this is not an unqualified success story. On the one hand, it was one of the most successful shifts from maize to small grains. It was – in theory anyway – sustainable in terms of productivity for food security signifying and good adaptive strategy to climate change. The rolling out of this strategy shows that NGOs and other players as external actors could easily influence the actions of local actors but without a deep understanding of climate change to some extent. Although people are actors in their own right, in some cases the external world influence them especially if their room to manoeuvre is limited. However, the failure to sustainably consume the small grains resulted in new conceptions of climate change as a myth used by those pushing for increased production.

As actors in their own right climate change is just a tool that NGOs are using to influence the adoption of their new varieties of small grains because the high production levels failed to cover the food insecurity gap. As more stocks of sorghum are still available and failing to fully cover the food insecurity gap smallholder farmers considered it an experiment that wasted their time rather than concentrating on maize production. In this regard there is evidence that the consumption patterns in semi-arid regions may lead to different perceptions regarding climate change particularly in situations where adaptive strategies fail to achieve the intended objectives.

The sharp increase in sorghum from 2011 to 2014 contributed to improved asset holding, particularly physical assets related to daily subsistence because people had increased quantities of small grains for food security. In spite of evidence for increased crop output, the contribution of small grains to food security and livelihood improvement was minimal. Production was sustainable but, although the crops are easy at the cropping stage they are difficult to harvest and process to get the final small grain. The last stages of production were too labour-intensive, as compared to maize, for households headed by children and the elderly to manage. Therefore, the initiative did not support such vulnerable households. This was despite the provision of free inputs. Only households that were already economically active anyway successfully produced the crop.

In addition, beneficiary households produced white sorghum in large quantities that resulted in a glut of the grain in all semi-arid communities and the consumption did not match production. It was not eaten as a daily staple as was maize and neither were there multiple uses for it as there were for maize, for example rural people eat homemade bread made from mixing white maize meal and wheat flour, but the same cannot be done with sorghum. Therefore, the contribution of sorghum to an improved quality of life for the rural poor was limited. This indicates that crop shifts to largely small grains does not always produce positive results. People reverted to maize production for multiple uses despite the challenges with climatic conditions and availability of inputs. The argument is that despite the significant success in production of small grains, its aim of improving food security and livelihoods as well as the quality of life of rural people was not realised. This resulted in new perceptions that climate change does not exist and it's not a reality but a marketing tool for NGOs to justify their relevance.

The big question is, had NGOs promoted maize production as a strategic response to climate change and were smallholder farmers going to come up with the same perceptions. This calls for sound policy options that should not only focus on production but on changing the smallholder farmer's mind-set. Therefore, it is important to also consider the social side of food security when coming up with appropriate adaptive strategies. The religious belief on maize despite its failures in semi-arid regions started as a policy option that was targeted at an agricultural boom. Now that climate change has taken its toll on this staple crop, new policy messages targeted at changing the existing thinking and mind set by smallholder farmers will help turn climate change into a reality. Therefore, with wrong perceptions on climate change adaptive strategies, it remains difficult to not only implement but to be adopted fully.

Pearl millet, another promoted small grain crop, also had low consumption levels but its production was complementary to other food crops and it was never intended as an alternative. Its production directly contributed to crop diversification and although its total hectarage was low it contributed to food availability and security. Fieldwork revealed that the crop can be consumed in different forms and this made it more acceptable to its target beneficiaries, although in general its adoption levels were low. One could argue that its limited adoption in rural communities was influenced by the advocacy programmes that focused more on sorghum production than pearl millet. However, its limited success story failed to change the smallholder farmers' mind-set about maize crop production and the reality of climate change. The nature of the interventions were not also sustainable in ensuring that the adoption of small grains becomes a fully adopted strategy. Farmers received free inputs from NGOs and the availability of small grains seed in the market is not supported by any policy and was never made a priority. Therefore, any strategic responses to climate change that are void of supporting policy tend to demean the reality of climate change particularly in semi-arid regions.

Conclusion, Policy Options and Recommendations

The chapter concludes that not all externally fostered interventions meant to adapt to climate change are successful. Whilst the focus on small grains production is supported by research as an appropriate staple crop for semi-arid regions, the failure to consider the social side and consumption patterns of the smallholder farmers affected the adoptability of this strategy to climate change. Wrong and inappropriate varieties were promoted but could not be consumed leading to emerging perceptions on climate change as just rhetoric. The chapter also concludes that the successful adoption of small grains production lacked the change of the mind set of smallholder farmers from maize to small grains as a good alternative.

The production also lacked supporting policy shift to small grains as seed houses continue to support maize production despite production failures in semi-arid regions. Whilst small grains research is largely focusing on production it has given a blind eye to the palatability of the small grains in different forms by smallholder farmers. Therefore, the promotion of small grains lacked adequate research information and ignored aspects related to consumption patterns that inevitably gave rise to new perceptions regarding climate change as a genuine threat to food security.

At the policy level, issues of climate change are still wide open to viable policy options that may proffer solutions not only in southern Africa but the whole globe. For specific semi-arid regions whilst small grains production were suggested to provide better cropping regimes in areas experiencing persistent droughts due to climate change, they need to be supported by a government policy that should enable a shift in cropping systems and consumption patterns.

Over years the government has been operating without a policy on climate change until 2016 when it was developed but finalised in 2017. The policy on climate change should enable funding on various and different research programmes on various crop varieties that should be adaptive to persistent droughts but producing a significant crop yield. This should be accompanied by research funds to enable research work to smoothly proceed to conclusion.

Research that seeks to promote crop production regimes that are highly adaptive to climate change should not only focus on production and increased output but also should focus on improved processing and consumption palatability. Whilst the NGO intervention was successful in small grains output production it completely failed in ensuring adoption as a staple crop and in shifting consumption patterns from maize to sorghum and others small grains.

Assessing the policy options required to enable a successful strategic response to climate change in semi-arid regions, it is imperative to come up with participatory programmes that enables the smallholder farmer to understand climate change and change the prevailing mind-set that that climate change is not a reality but a tool for marketing and promoting new small grain seed varieties.

Externally fostered interventions particularly on small grains should be guided by a policy that incorporates the socio-cultural production and consumption patterns of people in semi-arid regions of Zimbabwe. Ignoring consumptions patterns would result in more production without reducing food insecurity.

References

Alumira, J, Rusike J (2006) The Green Revolution in Zimbabwe. *Journal of Agricultural and Development Economics, 2(1):50-66*

Chekole, Z.F. (2006). "Controlling the Informal Sector: Solid waste Collection and the Addis Ababa City Administration, 2003-2005". Unpublished MPhil Thesis Submitted to the Department of Geography, Norwegian University of Science and Technology, Trondheim

Chenje, M et al. (1998). *The State of Zimbabwe's Environment in 1998,* Ministry of Mines, Environment and Tourism, GoZ, Harare

Chitiyo, T. (2000). "Land Violence and Compensation: Reconceptualising Zimbabwe's land and War Veterans Debate", *Track Two, Vol 9 (1)*

Chouinard, V. (1996). "Structure and Agency: Contested concepts of Human Geography" in Caralle, E, Kent, M and Martin, S.K (Eds) *Concepts in Human Geography*, 383-410 Rowan and Littlefield Savage

De Wit, M. (2006) The economic impacts of climate change on agriculture in Zimbabwe. Climate Change and African Agriculture, Policy Note No. 11, August 2006. CEEPA.

Drimie, S and Gillespie, S. (2010) Adaptation to Climate change in Southern Africa: factoring in AIDS, Environmental Science and Policy 13: 778-784.

Eicher, C K (1995) Zimbabwe's maize based Green Revolution: Preconditions for Replication. World Development, 23 (5):505-508

FAO (2005) Irrigation in Africa in figures, AQUASTAT Survey 2005, Food and Agriculture Organisation, Rome, pp. 1-74.

Food and Agriculture Organisation (FAO) (1995), Sorghum and Millets in Human Nutrition, Rome, Italy

Frost, P.G.H. (2001) "Zimbabwe and United Nations Framework Convention on Climate Change" ODI Working Paper.

Kahinda, J, M, Rockstrom, J, Taigbenn, A, E, Dimes, J (2007) rainwater harvesting to enhance water productivity and rain fed agriculture in semi-arid Zimbabwe. Physics and Chemistry of the earth, 32 (2007)

Leuschner, K, Manthe, C,S (1996), Drought Tolerant Crops for Southern Africa, Proceedings of the SADC/ICRISAT Regional Sorghum and Pearl Millet workshop, 25-29 July 1994, Gaborone, Botswana

Madzwamuse, M (2010) Climate Convergence in Africa: Adaptation strategies and institutions Hein rich Bill Stiff Tung (HBS)

Mudimu, G (2003) Zimbabwe food security issues paper Forum for Food Security in Sothern Africa, Department of Agricultural Economics, University of Zimbabwe

Rukuni, M. Tawonezvi, P. Eicher, C, Munyuki-Hungwe, M and Matondi, P (2006)Zimbabwe's Agricultural Revolution Revisited, University of Zimbabwe Publications, Harare.

Sukume, C, Mukudze, E. Mabeza-Chimedza, R and Zitsanza, N (2000) Comparative Economic Advantage of Crop production in Zimbabwe. Technical paper No.99, Department of Economics and Extension, University of Zimbabwe.

Taylor, J, R, N (2003) Overview importance of sorghum in Africa (Online) Available from http://www.sciencedirect.com/science?

Chapter 11

Havana (Cuba) and Harare (Zimbabwe) as Innovative Hubs of Resilient Systems in Urban Food Security

Innocent Chirisa & Elmond Bandauko

Introduction

Poor performance in economies especially in developing countries can be a driver towards innovative ways for survival and growth in food security among the urban residents. The statement 'necessity is the mother of invention' is a clear reflection, people's exposure to difficulty circumstances promote the devising of survival means and strategies when people are exposed to difficulty circumstances, they are poised to devise means and strategies to get out of them. This study seeks to explore how residents from Havana, Cuba and Harare, Zimbabwe have managed to survive under stressing economic circumstances. Both Harare and Havana 'fell victim' to 'sanctions' and trade embargoes. This chapter seeks to advance the argument that strenuous and little performing economies can be a breeding ground for innovative ways towards survival and growth in food security for urban residents.

Background and Context of the Study

The collapse of the Eastern Europe block and increased economic sanctions by the United States led to Cuba to lose more than 75 percent of its import and export capacity in the 1990s. As a result, it was forced to find new ways to provide food to its citizens. After 1990, reform was passed in Cuba called the National Alternative Agriculture Model (NAAM) (Altieri *et al.* 1999). After the collapse of the Soviet Union, Cuba became a chief example on urban agriculture as the main source of food production in cities. This marked the beginning of a new era in Cuba. Urban agriculture was no longer viewed as a sign of poverty and under development. The economic crisis and absolute need pushed people to create the urban gardening movement. Urban agriculture emerged as subsistence since the government could no longer provide food at very low prices (Altieri *et al.* 1999).

The Cuban government was forthcoming in promoting urban agriculture (Altieri et al. 1999). The Ministry of Agriculture (MINAGRI) created a specific Urban Agriculture Department in 1994, which was responsible for providing support services and material resources for the urban gardeners in Havana. Cuba has tropical climate and the country is endowed with red ferralitic soils, which are not of high-quality. Cuban soils have less than 1% organic matter due to excessive weathering which causes rapid oxidation of organic matter. In the context of Zimbabwe, a serious economic crisis started in the 1990s and intensified in 2000 (Murisa, 2010). The economic crisis eroded livelihood capacities of both urban and rural population. The crisis was worsened by government's economic mismanagement as well as structural constraints in the local economy. The economy of Zimbabwe shrunk by 20 % since 2000 (Moyo and Yeros, 2007). Urban employment in Zimbabwe also shrunk from 3, 6 million in 2003 to 480 000 in 2008. The other dimension of the crisis was the general collapse in social service delivery. The government of Zimbabwe has been arguing, economic sanctions imposed on the country by Western countries are also worsening the economic problems in the country. The problem of food insecurity in Zimbabwe used to be more prevalent in the rural areas than urban areas. However, the challenges in the socio economic and political environment have worsened food insecurity even in urban areas by it causing many urban households to opt for urban farming as a survival strategy. In addition, Zimbabwe has experienced a series of droughts since 2002. Against this background, this chapter seeks to examine how urban residents survive and innovate under such harsh economic conditions.

Literature Review

Survival strategies or survivalism, food security and innovations are the concepts underpinning this study. Urban agriculture is often believed to be a response to urban crises. It is regarded a survival strategy of migrants from rural areas who respond to lack of employment by turning into urban agriculture as a livelihood strategy (Phiri, 2000). The poor are not the only who produce food in cities and towns (Nugget, 1999). However, they are more dependent on it than their rich counterparts. Richer inhabitants practice urban agriculture for dietary diversity and a healthier food supply and entrepreneurs have created thriving agricultural businesses. Several local and national governments are promoting urban agriculture in response to poverty, food insecurity.

Survival strategies are specific stress responses, which include specific adaptive and maladaptive, biological, psychological and social constituents (Valent, 1998). Examples of survival strategies include rescuing, attaching, asserting, adapting, fighting, fleeing, competing and cooperating. Food security is not easy to define and explain. Measuring and defining food security is a difficult task (Ignowski, 2012). The concept and definition of food security have changed since its introduction in the early 1940s. In the 1970s, the definition of food security was developed from the perspective of food-supply to ensure that all people everywhere have enough food to eat (Clay, 2002; Pangaribowo *et al.* 2013). The current terminology in use, as adopted from the 1996 World Food Summit, emphasises the multidimensionality of food security. This conceptualisation states, food security exists when all people always have physical and economic access to sufficient, safe and nutritious food to meet their dietary needs and food preferences for an active and healthy life (FAO, 2000). This definition suggests that there are four critical pillars of food security; availability, accessibility, utilisation and stability (FAO, 2008).

Food security is understood as multidimensional function of three critical aspects:

(i) food availability, which is the amount of food available to a household (micro-level) or in the area of concern (macro) through all forms of domestic production, commercial imports, reserves and food aid,

(ii) food access, which is the physical (for example roads, networks, markets) and economical (for example own production, exchange, purchase and the ability of a household to acquire adequate amounts of food and

(iii) Food utilisation is the intra-household use of accessible food and the individual's ability to absorb and use of nutrients (for example, the function of health status).

It is argued that food security an inherently unobservable concept that has largely eluded precise and operational definition. Interesting perspectives are forwarded about the concept of food security which concur with what other sources such as the Food and Agricultural Organisation and the World Summit on Food Security have regarding food security. It is asserted that the most common definition of "food security" is "access by all people always to enough and appropriate food to provide the energy and nutrients needed for an active and healthy life". It is further argued that if food security involves access at all times to enough and appropriate foods, then "food insecurity" reflects uncertain access to enough and appropriate foods (Barrett, 2002:4). Therefore, food security is an inherently ex ante status with respect to nutrition and health.

Several innovations have been adopted to address the daunting agricultural challenges and towards boosting urban food security. Theoretically, it is argued that much has been learnt about policies to reduce hunger and increase food insecurity and there have been significant innovative developments in policy process and content (Scherr et al. 2010). Examples include:

- Decentralisation of many policies to the district level to enable locally tailored policies
- Systematic stakeholder consultations to determine policy priorities that facilitate regional smallholder agricultural market developments
- Civic mobilisation to advocate for policy action
- Public-private partnerships to mobilise and finance food security initiatives

The key innovations towards urban food security are summarised in Table 11.1.

Table 11.1. Innovations towards Urban Food Security (Adapted from Scherr *et al.*, 2010)

Type of Innovations	Description of Innovations
National Level Actions	• Decentralisation of many policies to the district level to enable locally tailored policies • Systematic stakeholder consultations to determine policy priorities to facilitate regional smallholder agricultural market developments • Civic mobilisation to advocate for policy action • Public-private partnerships to mobilise and finance food security initiatives
Community Actions	• Increase the agricultural productivity of food-insecure farmers • Improve nutrition for the chronically hungry and vulnerable • Reduce the vulnerability of the acutely hungry through productive safety nets. • Increase incomes and make markets work for the poor • Restore and conserve the natural resources essential for food security
Technical and Institutional Innovations	• Improved germplasm for an ever-broader group of crops, grasses, trees, • Improved soil management, with more effective fertilisers and organic management • Development of agroforestry systems • Improved water management, including rainwater harvesting at the field, farm and landscape scales • Farm diversification to supply micronutrients through gardens, fruit trees, domestication of wild foods and medicines • Horticulture

	• Capacity-building for smallholder farmer groups to access and get higher value from markets and link to supply chains into exports and national systems· • Mobile phones and other electronic communications applied to agricultural markets • New agricultural input distribution channels to facilitate smallholder access • Micro-watershed development, practice and organisation • Low-cost methods of land/resource health assessment for targeting interventions • Tools to facilitate community-based natural resource management • Rotational grazing management for rangeland restoration • Zero-grazing, fallow banks and fallow reserves • Rainwater harvest at plot, field and sub-catchment scales

Another critical dimension on innovations towards food security has been brought out. It is highlighted that the growing economic and physical scarcity of water calls for innovative approaches on supply and demand of water resources. Innovative measures of managing water supply include promotion of water harvesting, developing new sources of surface and ground water and regulated use of waster water in urban and peri-urban agriculture. Innovative water-demand management include policies and technologies that promote water and soil conservation (Innocencio *et al.* 2003). These innovative approaches are affected by factors such as limited amount of land and financial constraints. It is observed that in East and Southern Africa, the most common innovations fall under water harvesting, organic matter management and gully harnessing (Critchley, 2000). In Ethiopia, similar innovations have been observed in land improvement, soil fertility management and rainwater harvesting (Alemayehu, 2001). Another significant innovation in urban agriculture, multi-storey gardens have been implemented in Kenya and Ethiopia. These gardens involve growing vegetables in empty cereal bags and empty cans rather than growing them directly in the ground. The gardens use minimum land space, are water efficient and ideal for areas with contaminated and/or poor soil quality. Low input household gardens (LIG) can also promote innovative agricultural practices. They create environmentally and economically viable agriculture systems in which maximum reliance is placed on locally renewable resources and management of ecological and biological processes (Kutiwa *et al.* 2010).

Resilience has been defined as the capacity of a system to continually change and adapt yet remain within critical thresholds. It is the long-term capacity of a system to deal with change and continue to develop. Resilience of an ecosystem such as a forest, involve dealing with storms, fires and pollution (Stockholm Resilience Centre, 2007). For a society it isnvolves ability to deal with political uncertainty or natural disasters sustainably. Knowledge on strategies to strengthen resilience in society and nature is becoming increasingly important in coping with the stresses caused by climate change and other environmental impacts. Sometimes change is gradual and move forward in roughly continuous and predictable ways. At other times, change is sudden, disorganising and turbulent reflected in climate impacts, earth system science challenges and vulnerable regions. It is stated that resilience is the ability of a system, community or society exposed to hazards to resist, absorb, accommodate to and recover from the effects of a hazard in a timely and efficient manner (UNISDR, 2007), This includes through the preservation and restoration of the commmunity's essential basic structures and functions. Resilience means the ability to 'resile from' or 'spring back from' a shock. The resilience of a community to potential hazards is determined by availability of resources and capability of self orgrnisation as a community.

Research Design and Methodology

This study is a comparative case study. Comparative case studies emphasise comparison within and across contexts. Comparative case study was chosen for lack of feasibility to undertake an experimental design and there is a need to understand and explain how context influence the success urban food security innovations in Havana and Harare. Comparative case studies involve the analysis and synthesis of the similarities, differences and patterns across two or more cases that share a common focus or goal. In this chapter, Havana and Harare were compared regarding: climate, geography, population, practices of urban agriculture and innovations to substantiate the discussion of this chapter. This study was largely a desktop study where various research reports, publications and journal articles were reviewed to provide answers to research questions.

Results

This section presents the results from the reviews done on the issue of urban food security in Havana and Harare. The section starts by providing an outline of the urban food security in Havana. Under this heading, the socio-economic and environmental context of the city is presented, followed by an outline of the major urban agricultural practices and innovations. The narrative on Harare's urban food security is also given, reflecting on the major innovations and limits.

The Havana Narrative

The City of Havana was founded on Cuba's north-western coast in 1519 (Coyula and Hamberg, 2012). Havana is the largest city in the Caribbean and the home to 2.2 million people -500,000 to 600,000 families and roughly 20 % of Cuba's population (Murphy, 2010). By the end of the 20th century, Havana's population was nearly 2.19 million – around one-fifth of the country in an urbanised area of 360 square kilometers. The city's population grew slowly because of balanced development policies, Havana's low birth rate, its relatively high rate of emigration abroad and its low rate of domestic migration. In terms of the city's economy, it is diversified, with traditional sectors, such as manufacturing, construction, transport and communications and new or revived ones such as biotechnology and tourism. Havana's climate is sub-tropical, which is suitable for crops such as coffee, sugar, cocoa, fruits and vegetables (Cisneros, 2012).

Urban agriculture in Havana with immense government support has far surpassed the dimensions of conventional vegetable gardening. Gardening in Havana has shifted from being subsistence to producing food for other cities in Cuba (Companioni et al. 1997).

In fact, Cuban agricultural officials now perceive these programs as key components of the overall national food production strategy. Gardeners in efforts to pool resources and experience and facilitate information and technical knowledge dissemination among themselves, they organised themselves into groups. These groups share ideas and educate themselves on sustainable farming practices such as organic gardening. There are over 400 horticulture clubs registered with the MINAGRI in Havana alone. This city provides one of the best models so far of a comprehensive, successful urban food production strategy. It includes land reform, technical support and research and development, demonstrating both strong government and country support. Urban farmers in Havana have advanced in ecological systems of production where they plant on high raised beds while integrating organic methods of fertilisation and pest control. These methods have without doubt optimised the health and yields of crop plants. Unsanitary or unsightly areas, which were previously full of garbage and vacant lots, were transmuted into healthy and green productive environments. Cuba also experiences a dry season from November to April which a pauses a challenge on water available for irrigation. Water scarcity coupled with old and unreliable water pies and pumps have caused a serious challenge on irrigation water even on supply of drinking water. In response to this crisis, the Cuban government restricted the use of potable water for irrigation.

In Havana, there are various typologies of urban agriculture. These include intensive gardening, which is practiced on mixed state land and privately owned land. This type of farming is usually located in areas with adequate water supply and rich nutrient soils with good drainage. Intensive gardening covers approximately 1000-3000 m2 of Havana. The major objective is for commercialisation. The other type of urban agriculture is Organop´onicos. This type of farming shows great efforts in technological innovations. Gardeners in areas with poor soil incompatible with agriculture use this form of gardening. Seeds are cultivated in containers such as dishes or old car tyres and they make of use of rooftop space. They also use raised beds filled which are filled with highly nutrient organic matter and soil mix to improve the poor soil quality. To be precise, the urban agriculture types in Havana are summarised in Table 11.2.

The Urban Agriculture Department (UAD) advocated for changes in the city's laws to accommodate urban agriculture on all unused land in Havana. Any citizen could request the use rights to unused land if they wanted to establish a garden on it. Local delegates notified the legal owners to grant land use rights to aspiring local food producers. The Urban Agriculture Department worked on securing land use rights for all urban gardeners. Since the establishment of UADs locally, it entailed minimum bureaucracy by it speeding up the transfer process. Local authorities also eased difficulties in transportation by locating production near consumption. Decentralisation of state farming sector has been some of the innovative measures on food production in Havana. . The decentralisation included new organisational forms, distribution of idle land to encourage the production of different forms of crops as well as greater emphasis on local production among others (Cisneros, 2012). This helped to maintain a supply of fresh fruits and vegetables throughout the year and to cover for seasonal shortages. The UAD also relaxed laws on the sale of garden food items that consequently helped many gardeners to improve the family economy by selling any excess. Cuba is now able to produce for beyond its borders. Havana is now producing organically certified sugarcane, which is exported to Europe. By selling crops they grow, urban households in Havana generate income, used, amongst others, to purchase other food items. Therefore, they contribute to the households' members' dietary health, a crucial component of food security (Warwick, 2001).

Havana also benefit from the use of indigenous knowledge by utilising the knowledge and experience in agriculture of the rural migrants. The major aim was to reduce the environmental damage that can be accompanied by poor agricultural practices. In this regard, the UAD banned use of chemical fertilisers within the city boundaries. Extension officers encourage and educate farmers to rely on organic fertilisers, using minimal external inputs and applying principles of agroecology, which are low cost and most importantly environmentally sound and based on locally available resources. Urban farmers rely on locally available inputs such as recycled animal and industrial residues.

Table 11.2: Typologies of Urban Agriculture in Havana, Cuba
(Companioni et al. 1997)

Type of Urban Agriculture	Brief Description
Intensive Gardening	• Intensive gardening is practiced on mixed state land and privately owned land • Located in areas with adequate water supply
Organop´onicos	• This type of farming shows great efforts in technological innovations • Seeds are cultivated in containers and rooftop space is used
Suburban farms	• This type of urban agriculture is practiced on the urban fringe and the units exceed 2ha • Farmers use highly integrated systems of production
Popular gardens	• Users usually obtain private use rights from state or private landowners • Community clubs practice farming on vacant lots and the previously neglected dumpsites
Enterprise and factory gardens	• The plots are usually less than 1 hectare and are owned by the enterprise. • The gardens are located on or near the property of enterprises. • The produce is used to promote self-sufficiency by feeding factory workers and their families
Hydroponics	• This form of agriculture is the least practised because it is very expensive. • Artificial environments with rich nutrient solutions are created indoors.
Household gardens	• These usually cover less than 100m² and it is practised on one's residential plot. • This form of gardening is for household self-provision and it produces a variety of crop produce.

However, urban agriculture in Havana is not as perfect as it sounds. The major challenge is the provision of a more equitable access to locally available resources and low-input technologies required for food production (Altieri *et al.* 1999).The other problems include water challenges at times. The urban farmers adopt recycling of wastewater in order to deal with the problem of water.

The Harare Narrative

Harare (then Salisbury), was the first urban settlement to be established in Zimbabwe in the 1890s (Marumahoko and Fessha, 2011). Harare is the capital, the largest commercial centre and the seat of political and administrative power in Zimbabwe. The 2012 National Census indicates that the population of Harare is pegged at 2 098 199 (Zimstats, 2012). Urban agriculture in Harare is defined as the production of crops and/or livestock within the administrative boundaries of the city. Harare has several conditions favourable to urban food production. A relatively wet climate, large residential plot sizes and large open spaces within the city boundaries. A key feature of the Harare environment are vleis. Vleis are seasonally waterlogged drainage systems that occur on both clay and sandy soils (Mbiba , 2000). During the wet season (October to March), they become heavily waterlogged, resulting in surface marshes along all drainage systems. The vlei "soils" get wet with the first rains and then retain moisture long into the next wet season. Traditionally, communities have taken advantage of vlei properties to plant an early crop and a late crop thereby enabling them to produce two harvests a year from the same piece of land. The proximity of vlei soils to streams makes them favoured areas for gardening (ibid.). The topography of the city is hilly in rocky areas, flatter in the south and undulating in the north.

It is observed that fifty percent of Harare's urban farmers initiated production activities in the early 1990s when maize became the main crop (FAO, 2001). Now, since access to land was inadequate, these urban farmers began using public land. Therefore, approximately 75% of the open spaces of public land were utilised for maize cultivation and 25% used for sweet potato. Today, 94% of farming households in Harare grow maize and 25% grow sweet potato. In 25% of poor Harare households, urban crop production contributes 60% of food consumption. However, 80% of urban agriculture occurs on public land with no official recognition. Recently, though, farmers have lobbied for community participation in local governance and urban agriculture has gained legitimacy as a significant source of food security. In 1990, gardens covered 8% of land in the city; by 1994, 16% of land and by 2001, urban agriculture pervaded 25% of Harare's area. Throughout the developing world, municipal policymakers are waking up to the fact that properly managed agriculture can make a major contribution to a city's food security. It also has potential to provide employment, improve the environment and make productive use of vacant spaces within the city (Mougeot 2006).

It is highlighted that there are three types of urban agriculture in Harare; on-plot agriculture, off-plot agriculture and peri-urban agriculture (Mbiba, 1995). These types of urban agriculture in Harare are explained as follows:

(i) On-plot agriculture: This type of urban agriculture is dome on plots around houses. On-plot agriculture involves the production of crops such as maize and vegetables (Kanji 1995).

(ii) Off-plot agriculture: This form of urban agriculture is practiced on public open spaces and agricultural allotments (Mbiba 1995, Mudimu 1996, Boywer-Bower and Drakakis-Smith 1996). The production is mainly for home consumption, although a slightly higher percentage is sold as compared to on-plot production.

(iii) Peri-urban agriculture: This third type of urban farming involves the production of crops on the urban fringe. Because of the availability of land and existing rural agricultural support networks, this sector offers immediate and viable options for enhanced food production to meet the employment and nutritional needs of Harare.

In Harare, open space and backyard gardening are prominent and maize and vegetables are common crops in the city. Urban agriculture contributes to about 60 % of households' food requirements (subsistence).

There are many driving factors for urban agriculture in Harare. Urban dwellers rely on the market for food but with the surge in food prices beyond the reach of most urban residents. The poor urbanites in Harare have resorted to intensifying urban agriculture as a coping strategy to meet their immediate food needs (Kutiwa *et al.* 2010).

Poverty in urban areas such as Harare is affected by a particular combination of factors which produce a wide range of vulnerabilities. Most vulnerable urban populace are the urban poor dwellers who are more immersed in the cash economy but earning erratic, unreliable and small incomes . Also, most of the urban residents have no access to formal employment opportunities(ibid.). Therefore, urban agriculture becomes an option for livelihood and employment among the poor urban residents in Harare. The practice of urban agriculture is a response to economic crisis which is being experienced in the city of Harare (Kutiwa *et al.* 2010).

Some of observed innovations in the practice of urban agriculture in Harare relate to technical and institutional innovations as well as community level innovations. Farmers are using a combination of poultry manure, domestic sewage sludge, cattle manure and mineral fertilisers to boost their agricultural production and boost urban food security (Nyamasoka *et al.* 2012). A combined application of organic and inorganic nutrient sources, in adequate amounts, is a viable strategy to enable high productivity on the small pieces of land cultivated by most of the farmers. Farmers in Harare use at least one practice for managing soil water. The most common practices were preplant ridges and furrows. They are constructed to enable planting of maize on the ridge. The stover is then ploughed into the furrow after harvest and covered up to make a ridge thereby shifting the ridge's position in the following season. Ridges and furrows can result in increased yields by not only conserving soil moisture but also by reducing nutrient loss due to erosion and increasing plant rooting depth (Nyamasoka *et al.* 2012). In sandy soils, use of water management practices significantly improves maize yield. Maize yield is usually significantly higher where water management practices are used because rainwater collects in the furrows and can be available in times of low rainfall. A point of interest, Fambidzanayi Permaculture Centre, and the Government of Zimbabwe, were working on joint project on the production of organic fertilisers (Murungweni, 2013). Such an initiative would need to be publicised especially among Urban farmers, as this would help reduce the pollution of water resources from the use inorganic fertilisers. However, urban agriculture in Harare has flaws that create conflicts between farmers and the environmental Management

Agency (EMA). For example, urban farming in the Monavale Wetland has resulted in the depletion and degradation of this ecologically fragile ecosystem (Murungweni, 2013). Some farmers practising urban agriculture on wetlands do not adopt conservation measures leading to further deterioration and degradation of wetland biodiversity.

Discussion

Key debates and major lessons can be observed from the ongoing narratives on urban agriculture and food security in the two cities,. Both Harare and Havana have been subjected to serious economic instability, that affected most urban residents' ability to secure formal employment. This economic crisis is the major driver for urbanites to resort to urban agriculture as a livelihood alternative or survival strategy. Major differences and similarities can be isolated from theforegoing narratives on Harare and Havana. First, Havana is advanced in its approach to agriculture and food security. Many innovative measures have been put in place in Havana, while Harare still relies on conventional forms of urban agriculture such as farming on urban land. Havana use rooftop space in a bid to economise land. Urban Agriculture in Harare is not properly organised as there is no institutional framework within the City of Harare that address specifically issues of urban agriculture. This could be the reason productivity among urban farmers is often low. However, in Havana, there exists Urban Agriculture Department (UAD) and community associations meant to provide support services to urban farmers in the City. This arrangement seems effective on improving the output and productivity of farmers. As a result of such commitment from the Government, Havana produces food such as certified sugarcane for export to Europe, while farmers in Harare produce crops mainly for subsistence. In both cities, some innovativeness can be observed on the use of wastewater to boost urban agriculture productivity.

It has emerged from this study, urban residents in both cities are trying to be innovative to boost agricultural production and enhance urban food security. In Havana, we see indigenous knowledge systems being an important part of innovativeness in urban agriculture. In this case, indigenous knowledge systems are used as way to reduce environmental damage caused by poor agricultural practices. Under the section of innovations, the chapter has also indicated that decentralisation should be viewed as a significant innovative strategy in urban food security. However, in Harare, there is little or no reforms on decentralisation and urban and peri-urban agriculture. This is attributed to lack of realisation by City of Harare and the Central government on the significant contribution urban agriculture make to boosting food security in times of economic crisis . Havana shows a different picture altogether. In this city, decentralised structures such as communities have an active role in agricultural production. This is a reflection of serious commitment by the Cuban Government towards urban food security. The comparative aspects of the two cities is represented inTable 11.3.

Table 11.3 : Matrix of comparative aspects between Harare and Havana

Aspect	Harare	Havana
Climate Initiatives	Adoption and use of greenhouses to counteract extremely low temperatures and recycling of waste water to deal with water availability challenges.	Urban farmers are adopting waste water recycling so as to deal with problems of water availability
Land Management	The land management framework is not clear in terms of how to use land for urban farming	The government is trying to enhance land tenure security among the urban farmers. Use of land conservation techniques
Population	Harare has a population of about 2 098 199	Havana has a population of 2, 2 million
Farming Policy	There is no clear policy on farming in the city. Farmers just grow crops anywhere.	Decentralisation of state farm sector through new organisational forms
Transport Costs	Transport costs are generally low	Local authorities have located production near consumption to reduce the costs of transportation
Level of commercialisation	Harare urban farmers produce for subsistence purposes	Havana have taken steps to produce for export

Conclusion, Policy Options and Recommendations

In this chapter, the authors sought to advance the argument, the harsh economic conditions in cities can be a breeding ground for innovation towards food security among urban residents. To demonstrate this, we engaged in the cases of Havana, Cuba and Harare, Zimbabwe. The chapter has demonstrated that urban agriculture is indeed a key strategy in dealing with issues of food insecurity in the two cases. Major innovations have been put in place as a way of boosting urban food security in Havana and Harare. Such innovations include the recycling of wastewater to deal with water challenges, use of organic fertilizers and decentralization of state farm sector to create new organisational forms. From this chapter, key debates emerge. Firstly, urban agriculture in Havana, Cuba has surpassed the dimensions of what could be referred to as conventional vegetable gardening. Farmers are producing their crops for sale to other cities in the country. As a way of boosting food production, farmers in Havana have organised themselves into groups to facilitate the dissemination of technical knowledge and information. To date, Havana represents the best model of urban food production strategy. In the case of Harare, urban farming is not yet properly organised. Most the urban residents produce their crops mainly for household consumption purposes. From this evidence, we conclude that in Harare, urban agriculture is a matter of survival under a turbulent economic environment, whereas in Havana, urban farmers have gone beyond mere survival to growth through production for export.

In terms of policy, Zimbabwe needs to have a decentralised policy stance that promotes the adoption of urban agriculture. Urban agriculture should be recognised as a legitimate urban land use. Therefore, there is the need for it to be incorporated into statutory instruments and urban land use plans. Both central and local governments in Zimbabwe should create a good framework for easy access to vacant stands, municipal farms and planned sites not yet developed as it is in the case of Havana. There is also need for both governments to have strategies on the provision of infrastructure essential for efficacious urban agriculture. Local authorities should collaborate with donor communities and the private sector to finance infrastructure provision. Main emphasis should be given to water infrastructure such asboreholes and water harvesting tanks in order to promote all year cropping. Environmental management issues should be considered carefully when drafting policies on urban agriculture to avoid deforestation, land degradation and depletion of wetlands. Officials from the planning departments of the two cities might organise exchange programs so that best practices can be transplanted from one context to the other. Integration of urban agriculture into Havana and Harare's planning vision should be accompanied by policies that seek to expand the water supply infrastructure to accommodate urban agriculture. Given that the use of tap water for urban farming in the two cities raises vital ethical questions, efforts should focus on developing technologies that promote safe water recycling for urban agriculture use. Small-scale and low technologies, such as treadle pumps, can be important for smallholder urban farmers, who usually do not have sufficient resources to acquire more sophisticated irrigation systems. In addition, innovations in Havana are affordable and replicable for other urban farmers in cities with the similar context.

This chapter has demonstrated that indeed urban residents in Havana and Harare are trying to implement innovative strategies to boost urban food security regardless of the straining economic situations that they are facing. Urban food Security in these cities is heavily influenced by the innovative capacity of the urban populace. It also emerged from the debate that urban residents in Harare produce crops mainly for subsistence, while those in Havana have gone further to produce more for commercialisation. To improve on the current strategies, it is critical that the use of appropriate technologies that of low cost is also explored as another innovative measure. Urban agriculture is becoming increasingly significant in boosting urban household food security and improving livelihoods of urbanites. Therefore, it is critical for the City of Harare and Central Government set up proper and well organised institutional frameworks to support urban farmers. Such a measure will ensure urban agriculture in Harare is well-organised as in the case in Havana. This can also lead to improvement in innovations towards boosting urban food security in the city.

References

Alemayehu, M (2001). Ayeleck Fikre, an outstanding woman farmer in Amhara Region, Ethiopia. In Reij, C and Waters-Bayer, A (eds) (2001). Farmer innovation in Africa: A source of inspiration for agricultural development. Earthscan, London.

Barrett, C. B. (2002). Food Security and Food Assistance Programs. Elsevier Science, volume 2.

Cisneros, M, G (2012). Assessing the Potential of Small Scale Urban Agriculture in Havana. Masters Thesis in the Programme of International Development. University of Amsterdam.

Clay, E. (2002). Food Security: Concepts and Measurement. FAO Expert Consultation on Trade and Food Security.

Coyula, M and Hamberg, J (2012). The Case of Havana, Cuba.

Critchley, W.R.S. (2000). Inquiry, initiative and inventiveness; Farmer innovators in East Africa. Physics and Chemistry of the Earth: 25(3): 285-288.

FAO (2000). The State of Food Insecurity in the World 2000, FAO, Rome.

FAO. (2008). An Introduction to basic concepts of food security. FAO. Available on http//www.foodsec.org/docs/concepts_guide.pdf (Accessed 26/04/15).

Ignowski, E. A. (2012). Two Essays on Food Security in Zimbabwe. Urbana, Illinois: Submitted in partial fulfillment of the requirements for the degree of Master of Science in Agricultural and Applied Economics in the Graduate College of the University of Illinois at Urbana-Champaign .

Inocencio, A, Sally, A. and Merrey, D. J. (2003). Innovative Approaches to Agricultural Water Use for Improving Food Security in Sub-Saharan Africa. Sri Lanka : International Water Management (IWMI).

International Development Research Centre, Ottawa.

Kutiwa, S, Boon, E. and Devuyst, D. (2010). Urban Agriculture in Low Income Households of Harare: An Adaptive Response to Economic Crisis. Journal of Human Ecology , 32(2): 85-96.

Marumahoko, S and Fessha, Y, T (2011). Fiscal Autonomy of Urban Councils in Zimbabwe. A Critical Analysis. Law, Democracy and Development 15: 37-58

Mbiba , B. (2000). Urban Agriculture in Harare: Between Suspicion and Repression. In: Growing Cities, Growing Food. Urban Agriculture on the Policy Agenda. A Reader on urban Agriculture.

Mougeot, L.J.A. 2006 Growing better cities: Urban agriculture for sustainable development.

Moyo, S AND Yeros, P (2007). "The Radicalized State: Zimbabwe's Interrupted Revolution" Review of African Political Economy, 34(111): 103-121

Murisa, T (2010). Social Development in Zimbabwe. Discussion Paper prepared for the Development Foundation for Zimbabwe. Development Foundation for Zimbabwe.

Murphy, C. (2010). Cultivating Havana: Urban Agriculture and Food Security in the years of crisis . Oakland : Institute for Food and Development Policy .

Murungweni, F, M (2013). Effect of Land Use Change on Quality of Urban Wetlands: A Case of Monavale Wetland in Harare. A Scitechnol Journal; 1(15): 01-05

Nugent, R. (1999b). "Is urban agriculture sustainable in Hartford, Connecticut?" In: Furuseth O and Lapping M (eds), Contested countryside: the rural urban fringe in North America (London: Ashgate)

Nyamasoka, B, Nyamugafata, P, Madyiwa, S. and Nyamangara, J. (2012). Gender roles in soil fertility and water management for maize (Zea mays L.) production in urban agriculture: A case for Harare, Zimbabwe . Research Application Summary, 755-759.

Pangaribowo, E. N, Gerber, N and Torero, N. (2013). Food and Nutrition Security Indicators: A Review . Foodsecure working paper 05. Phiri, C (2008) "Urban Agriculture as a strategy for poverty alleviation: the case of Buffalo City, South Africa." Journal of Social Development in Africa 23: 111 -136

Scherr, S. J, Wallace, C. and Buck, L. (2010). Agricultural Innovation for Food Security and Poverty Reduction in the 21st Century: Issues for Africa and the World. Washingtion D.C: Issues Paper for State of the World 2011: Innovations that Nourish the Planet.

SRC (2007). What is resilience? Stockholm: Stockholm Resilience Centre.
http://www.stockholmresilience.org/21/research/what-is-resilience.html. Accessed 12/07/2017

UNISDR (2007). Resilience. Geneva: United Nations International Strategy for Disaster Reduction,
http://www.unisdr.org/we/inform/terminology#letter-r. Accessed 12/07/2017

Valent, P. (1998). Introduction to Survival Strategies . Melbourne : Paul Valent.

Printed in the United States
by Bookmasters

Printed in the United States
By Bookmasters